GREAT CHICKEN DISHES OF THE WORLD

GREAT CHICKEN DISHES OF THE WORLD

BY
TREVOR WILSON
AND
PATRICIA WILSON

McGRAW-HILL BOOK COMPANY

NEW YORK   ST. LOUIS   SAN FRANCISCO   TORONTO

First published 1978

Published in the United States of America by
McGraw-Hill Book Company
1221 Avenue of the Americas
New York, New York.

Copyright © T. Wilson Publishing Co. 1978

Library of Congress and ISBN 0-07 — 70754-5

Printed in Hong Kong

Contents and Illustrations
An asterisk indicates that the recipe is illustrated

Introduction
Carving the Chicken 1
Trussing the Chicken 1
Jointing the Chicken 2
Boning the Chicken 3

Recipes

Albania	Pule Medrop (Roast Stuffed Chicken)	4		
Algeria	Algerian Couscous	4		
Argentina	*Puchero de Pollo (Boiled Chicken Dinner)	5		
Austria	*Huehnerleberpastete (Chicken Liver Pâté)	6	*Wiener Backhendl (Viennese Fried Chicken)	6
Belgium	Waterzooï de Poulet (Chicken Soup)	8	Poulet à la Wallone *Brussels Chicken	8 9
Bolivia	*Pollo Rebozado (Fried Chicken in Corn Meal)	10		
Bulgaria	*Kokośka s Kesteni (Chicken with Chestnuts) Pile sâs Esik (Chicken with Tongue)	11 12	Drebolii ot Kokośka sâs Gâbi (Chicken Giblets with Mushrooms)	12
Burma	Panthay Khowse (Burmese Chicken and Noodles)	12		
Caribbean	*Chicken Creole *Carne de Aves (Marinated Chicken) Trinidad Pepperpot Devilled Chicken *Chicken Portello (Chicken in Coconuts)	13 14 14 14 16	*Pollo con Piña (Chicken with Pineapple) *Coconut Chicken *Creole Salad *Asopao (Chicken and Rice) Colombo Creole (Creole Chicken Curry)	17 18 19 20 20
Ceylon	Brinjal Smoore (Chicken and Egg-plant Casserole)	21		
Chile	*Escabeche de Gallina (Cold Pickled Chicken)	21		
China	*Introduction to Chinese Dishes *Lichee Gai (Lychee Chicken) Bor Lor Gai (Pineapple Chicken) Gai Chow Mein (Chicken Chow Mein) *Jeng Gai (Steamed Chicken) *Wart Gai Yee Chee Tong (Chicken and Shark's Fin Soup) Peking Stuffed Chicken	23 24 24 24 26 26 28	Chicken Shreds with Peppers and Cucumbers *Chicken and Bitter Melon *Crisp-skin Chicken *Chicken and Sweetcorn Soup Peking Chicken in Wine *Chicken with Sesame Sauce *Tse Bou Gai (Foil-wrapped Chicken) *Chicken with Bamboo Shoots and Seaweed *Chilled Spiced Chicken	28 29 30 30 32 32 33 34 35

	*Steamed Chicken in Wine	36	Hung Yun Gai (Chicken and Almonds)	38
	*Tangerine Peel Chicken	37		
	*Dar Bin Loo (Steamboat)	38		
Colombia	*Piquete (Colombian Chicken and Pork)	40	*Sancocho Valle Caucano (Chicken and Vegetable Soup)	42
	Ajiaco Bogotano (Creamed Chicken and Potato Soup)	40	Pollo al Cazador (Hunters' Chicken)	42
Egypt	Egyptian Lemon Chicken	42		
El Salvador	*Gallo en Chicha (Chicken in Cider)	44		
France	Poulet en Gelée (Chicken in Jelly)	45	*Chicken with Red Wine and Mushrooms	56
	Ballotine of Chicken with Prunes	45	Poulet à la Savoyarde (Chicken with Cheese Sauce)	56
	*Poulet Basquaise	46	*Poulet Sauté Vallée d'Auge (Chicken Calvados)	58
	*Pâté de Foie de Volaille	46		
	La Poule au Riz à la Crème (Chicken with Rice and Cream)	48	Poulet Rôti au Beurre (French Roast Chicken)	58
	Poulet Nivernais (Chicken in White Wine with Dumplings)	48	Poulet au Sel (Chicken in Salt)	60
			Chicken Mille Feuilles	60
	*Chicken Véronique (Chicken with Grapes)	49	*Suprêmes de Volaille Amandine (Chicken with Almonds)	61
	*Poulet aux Fruits de Mer (Chicken with Seafood)	50	*Bouchées à la Reine	62
	Chicken Provençale	50	Poulet à l'Estragon (Chicken with Tarragon)	62
	Poussins Dijonnaise	50	Poulet Sauté à la Crème (Chicken in Cream Sauce)	62
	*Coq au Vin	52		
	Chicken and Chicken Liver Omelettes	52	*Poulet en Pie	64
	*Poulet à l'Alsacienne	54	Poulet au Champagne (Chicken in Champagne)	64
	*Foies de Volaille au Riz (Chicken Livers with Rice)	55	*Mayonnaise de Volaille (Chicken Mayonnaise)	66
Germany	*Saueres Hühnchen (Sour Chicken)	67	*Backhahndel nach Suddeutscher Art (German Fried Chicken)	68
Great Britain	Roast Chicken with Bread Sauce	68	*Ragout of Chicken	72
	*Whisky Chicken	70	*Cock-a-Leekie	74
	*Potted Chicken	70	*Steamed Chicken with Oysters	74
	*Royal Hash	72		
Greece	*Kota Kapama (Chicken with Tomato and Cinnamon Sauce)	76	Kates Riganati (Oregano Chicken)	76
	Kotopolo alla Greca	76	*Soupa Avgolemono (Lemon Soup)	78
			*Piatella Athena	79
The Guianas	*Pom (Chicken and Potato Casserole)	80	*Chicken Pilau	80
Guinea	*Guinean Chicken Stew	82		
Hawaii	*Chicken with Macadamia Nuts and Pineapple	83	Moa Luau a me Wai Niu (Chicken and Coconut)	84
	*Hawaiian Salad	84		

Hungary	Ujházi Leves (Ujházi Chicken Soup with Liver Dumplings)	84	*Debreczeni Mazsolás Csirke (Debreczen Chicken with Raisins)	88
	*Paprikácsirke (Chicken Paprika)	86	*Chicken Budapest	89
	*Csirke máj Paprikával (Chicken Livers with Peppers)	87		
India	*Introduction to Indian and Indonesian Dishes	92	*Chicken Biryani	100
			Kundou Chicken	100
	*Mulligatawny (Curried Chicken Soup)	94	*Dhansak (Chicken with Lentils)	102
	*Chicken Curry	95	*Chicken Pidee (Chicken Curry with Dumplings)	104
	*Goa Moli (Goan Vinegar Curry)	96	Pilau	104
	Dum Murgi (Stuffed Chicken)	96	Lahore Chicken	104
			*Dahi Murgh (Chicken with Yoghurt)	106
	*Murgh Tikka (Spiced Chicken Kebabs)	98	*Shahjehan Kaleja (Spiced Chicken Livers)	107
	Tandoori Chicken	98		
Indonesia	*Goreng Ajam Balado (Fried Chicken with Chilli)	108	*Saté Ajam (Chicken Saté)	111
			*Ajam Santan (Chicken in Coconut Milk)	112
	Ajam Panggang Bumbu Saté (Roast Chicken with Saté)	108	Nasi Goreng	112
			Ajam Setan (Grilled Spiced Chicken)	112
	Semur Ajam (Chicken in Soy Sauce)	108	Ajam Masak Bali (Balinese Chicken)	114
	*Soto Ajam (Chicken and Ginger Soup)	110		
Iran	*Alo-Balo Polo (Chicken and Sour Cherries)	114	*Kababe Morgh (Skewered Chicken)	117
	*Chicken with Chick Peas	116		
Israel	*Tarnegolet Bemitz Hadarim (Chicken with Kumquats)	118	*Maafeh Awf Vematza Metubal Beshamir (Chicken, Matzoh and Dill)	118
Italy	Chicken in Vermouth	120	Pollo Tonnato	124
	*Pollo con Peperoni (Chicken with Peppers)	120	*Pollo Marsala	126
			*Pollo alla Cacciatora	126
	*Chicken Marengo	122	Pollo alla Napoletana	128
	*Pollo alla Crema (Chicken Baked in Cream)	124	*Pollo all'Aretina	128
			*Chicken with Egg-plant	129
	Pollo alla Parmigiana (Chicken with Cheese Sauce)	124	*Pollo alla Fontina	130
			*Pollo alla Diavola (Devilled Chicken)	130
Japan	*Yaki-Tori (Skewered Chicken and Chicken Livers)	132	*Chawan Mushi (Steamed Chicken and Egg)	132
Korea	*Toyaji-Kogi wa Tark-Kogi (Korean Chicken and Pork)	134	*Korean Chicken	135
Malaysia	*Spiced Malaysian Chicken	136		
Mexico	Pollo Pibil (Mexican Steamed Chicken)	136	*Pollo en Adobo (Chicken and Chillis)	140
	*Enchiladas de Pollo (Chicken-filled Tortillas)	139	*Pollo en Nogado (Chicken in Nut Sauce)	140

	Chicken Mole	142	*Mexican Chicken and Rice	142
Morocco	*Djeja M'Qalia (Chicken with Coriander and Mint)	144	Shoua (Moroccan Stuffed Chicken)	144
New Hebrides	Chicken Ginger Stew	144	*Chicken Casserole with Coconut Cream	146
Pakistan	*Murgh-I-Musallam (Spicy Baked Chicken)	147		
Peru	Ají de Gallina (Chicken in Nut Sauce)	148		
The Philippines	*Adobo (Chicken and Pork Casserole)	148		
Polynesia	*Mango Chicken	150		
Portugal	*Frango na Pucara (Chicken in the Pot)	151	*Portuguese Chicken Casserole	152
	Galuiha Rechiada (Stuffed Chicken)	152		
Rumania	*Pui cu Gutui (Chicken with Quinces)	154	*Wedding Soup	154
Russia	*Kotlety Po-Kyivskomu (Chicken Kiev)	156	Pechene Kuryata (Baked Chicken)	158
	Tabaka (Pressed Fried Chicken)	156	*Tushenaia Kuritsa pod Sousom iz Chernosliv (Chicken with Prunes)	160
	*Salat Olivier (Russian Chicken Salad)	158		
Scandinavia	Chicken with Mustard and Dill Sauce	160	Chicken with Horseradish Sauce	164
	*Danish Parsley Chicken	162	Norwegian Parsley Chicken	164
	*Kananmaksaa Omenien Kanssa (Chicken Livers with Apples and Onions)	162		
Spain	*Paella	164	*Arroz con Pollo (Chicken with Rice)	167
	*Chicken Majorca	166		
Switzerland	*Swiss Chicken	168		
Syria	Bamiyeh (Chicken and Okra Stew)	168	*Sambousiks (Curried Pastries)	170
Thailand	*Garlic Chicken	170	*Gaeng Phed Gai Gub Makhua-tes (Chicken, Tomatoes and Chilli)	172
	Gai P'Anaeng (Coconut Chicken)	172		
Turkey	*Cerkes Tavuğu (Cold Chicken with Walnut Sauce)	174	Turkish Chicken	174
U.S.A.	Chicken Kentucky Style	174	*Chicken à la King	177
	Barbecued Chicken	176	*Fried Chicken	178
	Scandia Chicken	176	*Chicken Gumbo	179
Uruguay	Pollo Guiso con Vegetales (Chicken and Vegetable Stew)	180		
Venezuela	*Cacerola de Gallina Rellena (Stuffed Chicken Casserole)	180	*Hallacas (Chicken and Corn Meal Pastries)	181
Yugoslavia	Pile u Kaimaku (Chicken in Cream Cheese)	182	*Pećena Kokoś sa Rakom Filana (Chicken with Lobster Stuffing)	183
	*Kokosja Supa (Chicken Soup with Red Peppers)	182		

Information and verification for these dishes has come from dozens of sources. The list is much too long for detailed acknowledgement but I would like everyone who helped in any way to accept my grateful thanks.

Trevor Wilson

Introduction

It would be impossible to guess how many millions of chickens are consumed each year throughout the world. The reasons for this popularity are obvious. Chicken meat is economical, it is a good source of protein, relatively low in fats, tasty and there is a range of national dishes as varied as the egg from which it emerged.

As a result there are literally thousands of ways of cooking poultry. So different in appearance and in taste are many of these dishes that you can eat chicken every day of the year without duplicating a dish. Its versatility makes it ideal for everything from haute cuisine to light lunches, picnic and snacks.

Throughout this book you will find reference to foods, spices and flavouring, some of which may be unfamiliar to you. One important criterion to justify the inclusion of a recipe in this book has been the availability of the authentic and original ingredients. We have not yielded to the temptation to suggest more easily obtainable substitutes. If you embark on the rewarding mission of adding authentic dishes to your culinary repertoire, recipes should guide you by listing the correct ingredients. Today these can usually be purchased in speciality or ethnic food shops. Many department stores now have well stocked food sections offering a wide range of exotic items ranging from Mexican tortillas to Eastern spices.

If a particular ingredient is not available, the resourceful and imaginative cook may be able to find a substitute which does not destroy the integrity of the dish, bearing in mind that there is never one single and absolute version of a national or regional recipe, since such dishes have invariably been shaped by the availability of local produce.

One minor concession has been made. It is recognized that most kitchens cannot always reproduce the original *method* of cooking. Hence, where a dish should be wrapped in banana leaves and buried over hot stones, we suggest practical alternatives; nor have we excluded Tandoori Chicken because the Tandoor oven is unobtainable.

There are separate introductions to Chinese (see page 23) and to Indian and Indonesian dishes (see page 92). These introductions deal specifically with ingredients and spices from these countries which may be unfamiliar to readers. The following information may also provide a useful general guide to the whole subject of cooking chicken recipes.

Size of Chicken

We specify chicken size simply by the terms 'large', 'medium', 'small', or 'very small'. A cooking recipe is not a scientific formula and cooks should be guided in choosing the exact size within the range specified by considerations of appetite and of the nature of the meal as a whole. The recipe should not be affected at all by such variations.

Storage

If you are buying chicken to store, you should buy already-frozen chicken. This will keep indefinitely under correct freezer conditions. It is best to thaw frozen chickens in the refrigerator. Whole chickens may need from twelve to sixteen hours (or even longer) to thaw. Chicken pieces will need from four to nine hours.

Sautéing or Browning

The cooking fats most characteristic of the country have been specified in most cases, and should be used. If alternatives are substituted for dietary or health reasons it should be understood that the flavour of the dish may be changed. The fat should be very hot to ensure that the chicken is sealed properly. Ingredients to be sautéed or browned should be thoroughly dry, otherwise a layer of steam may prevent proper sealing and browning. Never attempt to brown too many pieces at once; two or three pieces are sufficient to handle at one time. When browned, they can be kept warm while others are being cooked. This initial browning is often the most critical part of the cooking process, and care should be taken that the chicken is neither burned nor insufficiently sealed.

Basting

Take the roasting pan completely out of the oven in order to baste. Spoon the hot fat over the chicken with a basting spoon. Be careful not to break or pierce the skin while basting or turning the chicken or it may lose succulent juices and dry out.

Chicken Stock

Chicken stock may be made from the chicken carcass, trimmings and giblets, but not the liver which imparts a bitter flavour. The pieces should be lightly browned in two tablespoons of oil, together with a chopped onion. The pan should be removed from the heat, and five cups of water added, together with a teaspoon of salt, a few peppercorns and a bouquet garni*. Simmer for 1-2 hours and strain off the liquid. Stock cubes or powders provide a satisfactory alternative.

* Bouquet garni is a combination of parsley, thyme and bay leaf. If fresh, tie together with a string; if dried wrap in a piece of cheesecloth and tie.

Sauces

Sauce ingredients include quantities to ensure that the correct flavour and consistency is maintained. By all means increase the amount of sauce if you wish to, but make sure that the balance of ingredients is retained. Where egg yolks are specified for thickening be sure that the mixture does not boil. If it does your sauce will curdle, and you will have to start again.

Red Wine or White?
Many people are anxious about serving the correct wine. Dry white wines are always correct with chicken and may be served chilled with any such dish. These wines—Champagne, Riesling, dry Moselle, Hock, Chablis, White Burgundy—are especially suitable for cold dishes and for delicately-flavoured hot dishes such as Chicken Véronique or Poulet à l'Alsacienne. Chilled rosé wines are becoming very popular and can also be served with confidence with these dishes. With the more robust or highly-spiced creations, Coq au Vin or Chicken Cacciatora for instance, red wine should be served at room temperature.

Coconut Milk and Cream
Coconut milk and cream are dealt with in the Introduction to India and Indonesia. You will also find reference to Coconut Milk and Cream in the recipes of many other countries, especially those of South East Asia.

Chestnuts
Chestnuts may be peeled by nicking the skin, dropping the chestnuts into boiling water and boiling for five minutes. After cooling, both the outer and inner skins may easily be removed.

Cooking with Wine or Spirits
Some dishes specify wine or spirits as an ingredient. Non-drinkers may be re-assured by the fact that the heat of cooking always removes the alcohol entirely from the dish. Consequently the inclusion of alcoholic beverages should offend no-one.

Buying
Buy fresh rather than frozen chicken if you intend to cook the dish within a day or two. You will find the chicken is almost ready to cook when purchased. The chicken will have been eviscerated, cleaned inside and out, and will be free of pin-feathers. The head, feet and inedible organs are removed before grading and pricing. Giblets and neck are usually to be found in the body cavity.

CARVING THE CHICKEN

1. Place the chicken on a board or plate with the breast towards you, back uppermost. Holding the bird firmly with a carving fork through its back, slit the skin around the leg with a sharp knife. Place the knife between the leg and carcass and lever outward to expose the joint. Sever the joint, then slip the knife point under the back to release the oyster (choice meat on carcass bone) with the thigh bone.
2. Cut down parallel to one side of the wishbone for a good slice of breast with the wings on either side of the bird.
3. Remove the wishbone by carving behind it down the front of the carcass. Carve the remaining breast into good slices.
4. With a large chicken divide the leg into two for a good portion of thigh meat with the drumstick. Cut through the bone with chicken shears.

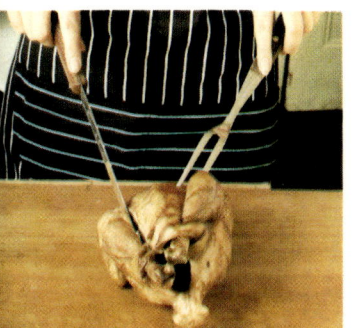  

TRUSSING THE CHICKEN

1. Turn the chicken on its back and cut a small hole for the tail to push through. This should close the vent.
2. Pull the skin over the neck and secure by folding the wing tips back over the skin. Run a skewer through the wings.
3. Run a piece of string around the skewer, cross it over the back, turn the chicken over and tie the legs together, keeping them close to the body.

JOINTING THE CHICKEN (A Simple Method)
1. Hold the chicken firmly on its back, breast towards you. With a heavy, sharp knife cut through the carcass from the vent to the neck. The breastbone is quite soft and severs easily.
2. Open up the carcass with both hands, pressing them down towards the bench. This should cause the chicken to break slightly along the backbone. Cut along the break until the chicken is in two pieces.
3. You will find that you can easily sever the wing portion from the leg portion. The backbone can be snapped about halfway along its length and the wing with most of the breast can be seen to overlap the leg portion. This is easily separated with a sharp knife.
4. Your chicken is now in four pieces. The backbone should be trimmed away (chicken shears are useful for this) and we prefer to completely remove the first two wing-joints, which makes for much neater pieces. Trim off untidy surplus skin and neck. The pieces may easily be cut up into smaller portions if the recipe calls for it.

BONING THE CHICKEN
1. Hold the chicken on its back with the breast towards you. As in the directions for Jointing, cut through the breastbone from vent to neck, and press the sides down towards the bench with both hands.
2. You will find it a simple matter to remove the rib cage and backbone, taking care not to break the skin. Sever the wing joint from inside.
3. Working from the inside, carefully cut away the flesh from each leg, pushing the leg in until the whole drumstick is clean and can be removed.
4. Sever the two outer wing-joints from the carcass. You may leave the inner piece of wing bone or remove it (if the recipe calls for it) by cutting the flesh away from inside the carcass until the bone is exposed.

Pule Medrop (Roast Stuffed Chicken)　　ALBANIA

SERVES SIX
1 large chicken
¼ cup seedless raisins
¼ cup currants
2 tablespoons chopped walnuts
2 tablespoons chopped hazelnuts
2 tablespoons chopped pistachio nuts
2 tablespoons chopped almonds
¼ cup sugar
2 cups breadcrumbs
¼ cup chicken stock
½ cup water (hot)
5 tablespoons butter
salt and pepper

Sauté the breadcrumbs for 5 minutes in 4 tablespoons of the butter. Then add the raisins, currants, walnuts, hazelnuts, pistachio nuts, almonds and sugar: add the chicken stock, and mix well. The mixture should be slightly moist.

Rub the inside of the chicken with salt and pepper, then stuff the chicken with the prepared mixture, and close the opening with thread or skewers. Cover the chicken with the remaining butter. Roast in the oven (180°C/350°F) for approximately 2½ hours, adding the hot water after 1 hour. Baste the chicken frequently.

Algerian Couscous　　ALGERIA

SERVES SIX
1 medium chicken, cut into serving pieces
500 g/1 lb lamb, diced
1 cup chick peas (canned)
1 cup zucchini (ridge cucumber) chopped
3 tomatoes, chopped
2 carrots, sliced
1 green pepper, sliced
2 onions, chopped
1 cup semolina
1 cup chicken stock
1 cup water
3 tablespoons olive oil
2 tablespoons butter
1 teaspoon ground cinnamon
¼ teaspoon cayenne pepper
salt and pepper

Brown the chicken pieces, the lamb and the onions in the olive oil in a large pan. Then add the tomatoes, carrots, green pepper, cinnamon, and salt and pepper to taste. Cover with water and cook over low heat for 45 minutes. Add the chick peas and zucchini, cover, and continue cooking until the chicken is tender (approximately 15 minutes).

Meanwhile, put the chicken stock and the water into a saucepan and bring to the boil. Stir in the semolina and 1 teaspoon salt. Reduce the heat and cook, stirring, until the mixture has thickened. Remove from the heat and stir in the butter. Put the cooked semolina in the centre of a serving platter and arrange the chicken, lamb and vegetables around it.

Puchero de Pollo (Boiled Chicken Dinner)

ARGENTINA

SERVES SIX

1 medium chicken, cut into 6 serving pieces
250 g/½ lb beef, sliced
250 g/½ lb salt pork, sliced
3 Spanish sausages, chopped
6 carrots, chopped
6 tomatoes, quartered
1 cup zucchini (ridge cucumber) chopped
½ cabbage, chopped
1 green pepper, seeded, chopped
6 leeks, chopped
6 potatoes, peeled, halved
2 ears sweetcorn, chopped
1 cup dried chick peas (soaked overnight and drained)
6 onions, chopped
5 1/8 pts water
6 cloves garlic, crushed

Bring the water to the boil in a large casserole, then add the chicken, beef, pork and chick peas and cook over moderate heat for 1½ hours. Add the sausages and carrots and cook for a further 30 minutes. Then add the tomatoes, zucchini, cabbage, green pepper, leeks, onions, potatoes, sweetcorn and garlic, and cook until the potato is soft (approximately 30 minutes). Arrange the meats and vegetables on a serving platter and serve the soup separately.

Huehnerleberpastete (Chicken Liver Pâté) — AUSTRIA

SERVES FOUR
500 g/1 lb chicken livers
1 tablespoon brandy
1 tablespoon madeira (or marsala)
6 tablespoons liquid aspic jelly
½ cup cream
2 tablespoons butter (creamed)
1 tablespoon butter (for frying)
½ teaspoon nutmeg
salt and pepper

Sauté the chicken livers gently in 1 tablespoon butter for a few minutes (do not overcook). Keep aside a few of the cooked pieces of liver and dice them. Take the remaining livers, while still warm, and push them through a sieve. Pour the brandy and madeira into the used fry-pan and, after mixing with any remaining juices, pour over the sieved livers. Then mix in the creamed butter, nutmeg and salt and pepper to taste. Stir in the cream and 4 tablespoons of the liquid aspic jelly. Lastly, fold in the diced chicken livers. Put the mixture into a terrine, level the top, and pour over the remaining 2 tablespoons of aspic jelly. Leave to set, and serve as a first course.

Wiener Backhendl (Viennese Fried Chicken) — AUSTRIA

SERVES FOUR
1 small chicken, cut into 4 serving pieces
1 egg, beaten
flour
breadcrumbs
½ tablespoon olive oil
2 tablespoons butter
lemon wedges (for garnish)

Dip the chicken pieces into the flour, and shake off any excess. Then dip the pieces into the beaten egg, and lastly into the breadcrumbs (again shaking off any excess). Fry the chicken in a mixture of the butter and the oil, adding the pieces when the oil is about to smoke and will cover the chicken with foam. Turn frequently and cook until golden-brown (approximately 20 minutes). Garnish with the lemon wedges and serve with a cucumber salad.

Poulet à la Wallone
BELGIUM

SERVES SIX TO EIGHT
1 large chicken
500 g/1 lb knuckle of veal
125 g/¼ lb veal, chopped
60 g/2 oz suet, chopped
1 veal sweetbread
250 g/½ lb mushrooms
4 carrots, halved
4 sticks celery, coarsely chopped
1 leek, coarsely chopped
1 onion
5 egg yolks
3 tablespoons flour
4 slices of bread, soaked in milk
⅓ cup madeira wine
1 cup thick cream
juice of 1 lemon
4 tablespoons butter
1 bay leaf
2 cloves
1 teaspoon mixed herbs
½ teaspoon nutmeg
salt and pepper

Put the knuckle of veal and a little salt and pepper into a pan of water. Boil, skim, then add the onion (stuck with the cloves), the carrot, celery, leek, bay leaf and mixed herbs. Cover and simmer for 1 hour. Strain the stock and return it to the pan.

Blanch the sweetbread by plunging it into boiling water. Then put the chicken and the sweetbread into the strained veal stock and simmer until the chicken is tender (approximately 1¼ hours). When the sweetbread becomes tender, remove it from the pan, chop it, and keep aside. When the chicken is cooked, place it on a serving platter and keep warm. Keep aside the stock.

Meanwhile, put into a blender the chopped veal and suet, the soaked bread, 3 egg yolks, ½ cup cream, the nutmeg, and salt and pepper to taste. Blend until a smooth mixture is formed. Shape the mixture into ovals with two tablespoons, then cook these quenelles in boiling water for 15 minutes. Drain and keep warm.

Melt 3 tablespoons of the butter in a saucepan, then remove from the heat and blend in the flour. Gradually add 2½ cups of the stock from the cooking of the chicken, return to the heat and cook, stirring, over low heat for 5 minutes. Sauté the mushrooms in 1 tablespoon butter, the lemon juice and 1 tablespoon water. Remove the mushrooms from their cooking juices and keep them aside. Then mix the cooking juices with the madeira, the remaining ½ cup of the cream, 2 egg yolks and a little of the hot sauce. Stir this mixture into the sauce in the pan and bring to the boil, stirring constantly.

Cover the chicken completely with the sauce, and garnish with the quenelles, chopped sweetbread and mushrooms.

Waterzooï de Poulet (Chicken Soup)
BELGIUM

SERVES FOUR TO SIX
1 medium chicken
chicken giblets
veal bones
2 parsley roots, chopped
2 sticks celery, chopped
3 sprigs of parsley
1 lemon, peeled, thinly sliced
2 egg yolks, beaten
2 cups dry white wine
6 cups water
4 tablespoons butter
bouquet garni
2 teaspoons salt
½ teaspoon pepper

Put the chicken giblets and the veal bones into a large pan. Add the water, parsley roots, parsley, celery, lemon slices, bouquet garni, salt and pepper. Bring to the boil, skim, then cover and cook over low heat for 2 hours.

Coat the chicken with the butter, and place it in another large pan. Strain the stock from the first pan, then pour it over the chicken. Add the white wine, cover, and cook over low heat until the chicken is tender (approximately 45 minutes). Remove the chicken, carve it into serving pieces, and keep warm. Beat a little of the soup with the egg yolks, then stir this mixture into the soup. Return the chicken pieces to the soup, and stir well. To serve, put the chicken pieces into individual bowls and pour the soup over them.

Brussels Chicken

BELGIUM

SERVES FOUR
4 chicken breasts
4 heads of chicory
2 tablespoons capers
½ cup grated gruyère cheese
1 tablespoon flour
½ cup breadcrumbs
⅓ cup lemon juice
½ cup water
8 tablespoons butter
2 tablespoons chopped parsley
¼ teaspoon celery seeds

Simmer the chicken in the water and 2 tablespoons of the butter until it is tender (approximately 45 minutes). Then remove the chicken and keep the stock aside. At the same time, simmer the chicory in the lemon juice and 2 tablespoons of the butter until it is tender (approximately 30 minutes), then drain.

Melt 1 tablespoon of the butter in a saucepan; remove from the heat, blend in the flour, then stir in ¾ cup of the stock. Bring the mixture to the boil, stirring constantly, and simmer until the sauce is thick; then add the cheese. Sauté the breadcrumbs in the remaining 3 tablespoons of the butter.

Heat the oven 180°C/350°F. Remove the bones from the chicken breasts and put the chicken into a buttered baking dish. Place one head of chicory on each piece of chicken, then sprinkle over the capers and celery seeds. Pour over the sauce, top with the breadcrumbs, and bake for 20 minutes. Sprinkle with the parsley, and serve.

Pollo Rebozado (Fried Chicken in Corn Meal)   BOLIVIA

SERVES FOUR
1 medium chicken, cut into serving pieces
6 tomatoes, peeled, seeded, chopped
1 onion, chopped
2 eggs, beaten
3 tablespoons yellow corn meal
6 tablespoons dry white wine
½ cup milk
6 tablespoons olive oil
bouquet garni
2 teaspoons salt
black pepper

Mix together the beaten eggs, the milk, corn meal, 1 teaspoon salt and ¼ teaspoon black pepper. Dip the chicken pieces into this batter, and brown them in a frying pan in 3 tablespoons of the oil.

Put the remaining oil into a large pan on moderate heat, add the onions and cook until they are transparent (4-5 minutes). Then add the tomatoes, wine, bouquet garni, 1 teaspoon salt and a little black pepper, and cook for 5 minutes. Add the chicken pieces, cover, and simmer over low heat until the chicken is tender (approximately 30-40 minutes). Remove the bouquet garni, and serve.

Kokośka s Kesteni (Chicken with Chestnuts)

BULGARIA

SERVES SIX

1 large chicken, cut into serving pieces
1 onion, finely chopped
500 g/1 lb chestnuts, peeled
1 tablespoon flour
1 tablespoon sugar
1 tablespoon tomato paste
2 cups water
½ cup butter
1 teaspoon paprika
¼ teaspoon cinnamon
1 teaspoon salt

Brown the chicken in the butter in a pan, then add the onion. Cover and cook over moderate heat until the onion is transparent. Add the paprika, salt and flour and mix well. Now add the chestnuts, the cinnamon and the water. Cover, and cook over low heat for 1¼ hours, stirring occasionally. Brown the sugar to a caramel, mix with the tomato paste, and add to the pan. Continue cooking until the chicken is tender (approximately 15 minutes).

Drebolii ot Kokośka sâs Gábi (Chicken Giblets with Mushrooms) BULGARIA

SERVES FOUR
Chicken giblets, wings, neck
250 g/½ lb mushrooms, sliced
2 tablespoons flour
5 cups water
5 tablespoons butter
salt and pepper

Boil the chicken giblets, wings and neck in the water, with a little salt, until they are tender (approximately 30 minutes). Remove the giblets, wings and neck from the stock; chop the giblets and remove the chicken meat from the wings and neck. Sauté the mushrooms in 2 tablespoons of the butter. Brown the flour lightly in 3 tablespoons of the butter, then blend in the stock, bring to the boil, and add the mushrooms, giblets, and the chicken meat from the wings and neck. Cook for 15 minutes, and season with pepper.

Pile sâs Esik (Chicken with Tongue) BULGARIA

SERVES SIX TO EIGHT
1 large chicken
1 calf's tongue (or 1 canned tongue)
2 egg yolks, beaten
½ cup long-grain rice
3 tablespoons flour
2½ cups chicken stock
3 tablespoons yoghurt
8 cups water (hot)
7 tablespoons butter
salt and pepper

Put the chicken and calf's tongue in the water with a little salt, and cook until tender (approximately 1 hour). (If using canned tongue, add this only after the chicken has been cooking for ¾ hour). Cut the chicken into serving pieces, peel and slice the tongue, and keep meats warm. Meanwhile, boil the rice for 15 minutes in 1½ cups of the chicken stock, then drain. Brown 4 tablespoons of the butter, pour it over the rice, and season with salt and pepper.

Melt 3 tablespoons of the butter in a saucepan, then remove from the heat and blend in the flour. Stir in 1 cup chicken stock, return to the heat, and cook until the sauce thickens. Beat together the egg yolks and the yoghurt, stir a little of the sauce into them, then pour this mixture into the sauce in the pan, and mix well.

Place the chicken pieces in the centre of a serving platter, make a ring of the rice around them, then place the slices of tongue against this. Pour the sauce over the top.

Panthay Khowse (Burmese Chicken and Noodles) BURMA

SERVES SIX
1 medium chicken, cut into serving pieces
250 g/½ lb pork, cut into strips
½ cabbage, shredded
4 onions, sliced
500 g/1 lb egg noodles, cooked, drained
1 cup water
1 cup peanut oil
6 cloves garlic, crushed
2 teaspoons ground ginger
½ teaspoon dried ground chilli peppers
2 teaspoons salt

Sauté the cabbage, onion and garlic in the peanut oil until the onion is transparent. Then add the chicken pieces and the pork and cook, stirring, for 10 minutes. Add the ground chillis, ginger and salt, then cover and cook over low heat until the chicken is tender (approximately 35 minutes). Uncover the pan and continue cooking until the liquids have evaporated. Remove the chicken pieces and keep warm. Add the cooked noodles to the pan and mix well with the pork and cabbage mixture. Put this mixture on to a serving platter, then arrange the chicken pieces on top. Serve with curry accompaniments.

Chicken Creole

CARIBBEAN

SERVES FOUR

1 medium chicken, cut into serving pieces
4 tomatoes, peeled, chopped
1 green pepper, cut into strips
2 sticks celery, diced
1 onion, sliced
¼ cup water
2 tablespoons olive oil
2 tablespoons chopped parsley
1 teaspoon dried tarragon
½ teaspoon paprika
1½ teaspoons salt

Sprinkle the chicken pieces with the paprika and ½ teaspoon salt, then brown the pieces in the oil in a large pan. Remove and keep warm. Put the green pepper, celery, onion and water into the pan, cover, and cook for 5 minutes. Return the chicken pieces to the pan, and add the tomatoes, tarragon and the remaining salt. Bring to the boil, then reduce the heat, cover, and simmer until the chicken is tender (approximately 40 minutes). Put into a serving dish and sprinkle with the parsley. Serve with rice.

Carne de Aves (Marinated Chicken)

CARIBBEAN (DOMINICAN REPUBLIC)

SERVES FOUR

1 medium chicken, cut into 12 serving pieces
2 green peppers, seeded, chopped
3 onions, chopped
1 cup stuffed green olives, sliced
4 tablespoons dark rum
4 tablespoons lime juice
½ cup olive oil
2 cloves garlic, crushed
1 teaspoon oregano
2 teaspoons salt
1 teaspoon pepper

Marinate the chicken pieces in the lime juice and rum for at least 2 hours, turning the pieces occasionally. Remove the chicken, and keep aside the marinade. Brown the chicken in the olive oil in a large pan. Then add the marinade, the green peppers, onions, olives, garlic, oregano, salt and pepper, and cook over low heat until the chicken is tender (approximately 30 minutes).

Trinidad Pepperpot

CARIBBEAN (TRINIDAD)

SERVES SIX

1 large chicken, cut into serving pieces
500 g/1 lb pork, diced
500 g/1 lb beef, diced
3 onions, sliced
2 tablespoons brown sugar
2 cups water
1 clove garlic, crushed
4 whole cloves
1 teaspoon ground cinnamon
1 teaspoon thyme
½ teaspoon dried ground chilli peppers
½ teaspoon pepper

Put the chicken pieces, the diced pork and beef, and the water into a large pan. Cover, and cook over moderate heat for 1 hour. Add the onions, garlic, sugar, cloves, cinnamon, thyme, ground chillis and pepper, and mix well. Cover, and cook over low heat for 30 minutes. Remove the cloves; then serve.

Devilled Chicken

CARIBBEAN

SERVES FOUR

1 medium chicken, cut into 8 serving pieces
3 tomatoes, peeled, chopped
2 spring onions, chopped
4 bananas, peeled
½ tablespoon flour
breadcrumbs
3 tablespoons rum
3 tablespoons chicken stock
3 tablespoons vinegar
6 tablespoons butter
2 cloves garlic
1 bay leaf
1 teaspoon paprika
¼ teaspoon cayenne pepper
¼ teaspoon salt
½ teaspoon pepper

Brown the chicken pieces in 4 tablespoons of the butter. When the pieces are brown, remove, coat them with breadcrumbs, then return them to the pan and cook until the chicken is tender and the breadcrumbs are crisp (approximately 20 minutes). Meanwhile, coat the bananas in breadcrumbs and fry them for a few minutes in 1½ tablespoons of the butter. Remove and keep warm.

When the chicken is cooked, remove the pieces from the pan, put them on a serving platter, and keep warm. Into the butter remaining in the pan, put the vinegar, garlic, bay leaf, paprika, cayenne pepper, salt and pepper, and reduce the liquids by half over moderate heat. Now add the spring onions, tomatoes, rum, and chicken stock. Then mix in a roux made from ½ tablespoon of the butter and the ½ tablespoon flour, and stir until a smooth sauce is formed. Remove the bay leaf and the garlic. Pour this sauce over the chicken pieces, and arrange the fried bananas around them.

Chicken Portello (Chicken in Coconuts)

CARIBBEAN (VIRGIN ISLANDS)

SERVES SIX

1 medium chicken, cooked, and meat diced
6 rashers of bacon, cut up
6 coconuts
3 ears sweetcorn, chopped
6 tomatoes, peeled, chopped
2 green peppers, seeded, chopped
3 onions, sliced
1 clove garlic, crushed
1 teaspoon salt
¼ teaspoon pepper

Puncture 3 holes in one end of each of the coconuts and pour out the liquid. At the punctured end, saw off approximately 4 cm/1½" of the coconut to make a 'lid'. With a sharp knife, remove the coconut meat from these 'lids' and then grate it.

Sauté the bacon in its own fat in a large pan, then add the sweetcorn, ¼ cup of the grated coconut, the onions, green pepper, garlic, salt and pepper, and cook until tender. Add the diced chicken and the tomatoes, and cook for a further 5 minutes.

Heat the oven to 180°C/350°F. Spoon the chicken mixture into the coconut shells and top with the 'lids'. Wrap each coconut completely in foil and place them in 2½ cm/1" of water in a roasting pan, and bake for 1¼ hours. Serve in the shells, topped with the remainder of the grated coconut.

Pollo con Piña (Chicken with Pineapple)

CARIBBEAN (CUBA)

SERVES FOUR
1 medium chicken, cut into serving pieces
3 tomatoes, peeled, seeded, chopped
1 onion, finely chopped
1 pineapple, diced
2 tablespoons seedless raisins
breadcrumbs
3 tablespoons dark rum
4 tablespoons lime juice
4 tablespoons olive oil
2 tablespoons butter
½ teaspoon oregano
salt and pepper

Marinate the chicken pieces in the lime juice for at least 1 hour. Dry the chicken pieces, fry them quickly in the oil until brown, then reduce the heat and cook for another 10 minutes. Add the onion and cook until transparent, then add the tomatoes, raisins, rum, oregano, and salt and pepper to taste, and stir. Cover, and cook over low heat until the chicken is tender (approximately 15-20 minutes). Meanwhile coat the pineapple pieces with breadcrumbs and fry lightly in the butter.

Arrange the chicken pieces on a serving platter or in pineapple shells, cover with the sauce, and top with the fried pineapple pieces.

Coconut Chicken

CARIBBEAN

SERVES FOUR
1 small chicken, cooked, and meat diced
2 coconuts
1 papaya (or melon), seeded balled or diced
4 tablespoons flour
3 tablespoons rum
4 tablespoons cream
3 tablespoons butter
2 teaspoons thyme
$\frac{1}{4}$ teaspoon ground ginger
$\frac{1}{4}$ teaspoon paprika
1 teaspoon salt
$\frac{1}{2}$ teaspoon pepper
Sauce

Sauce
1 tablespoon flour
1 tablespoon butter
$\frac{2}{3}$ cup chicken stock
salt and pepper

Puncture 3 holes in one end of each of the coconuts, pour out the liquid and keep it aside. Put the coconuts on to a hard surface, with the punctured end underneath, and tap them with a hammer. This will split them in half. Scrape out the coconut meat, grate it, then grill it until golden. Prepare the Sauce.

Season the flour with the thyme, ginger, paprika, salt and pepper, and dip the chicken pieces into this. Then fry the floured chicken in the butter for 3 minutes. Add the Sauce, the rum, the cream and $\frac{2}{3}$ cup of the liquid from the coconuts. Cook over low heat for 10 minutes, stirring frequently. Fill the coconut shell halves with the chicken mixture and top with the papaya (or melon) cut into balls or diced. Sprinkle some of the grilled coconut over the top. Serve the remaining coconut separately.

Melt the butter, then remove from the heat and blend in the flour. Add the chicken stock and season with salt and pepper. Return to the heat, bring to the boil, stirring continuously, and boil for 2 minutes.

Creole Salad

CARIBBEAN

SERVES FOUR

1 medium chicken, cooked, and meat diced
2 tomatoes, chopped
1 green pepper, seeded, sliced
½ cucumber, chopped
1 onion, chopped
1 lettuce
2 grapefruits, peeled, cut into segments
⅔ cup French dressing
⅔ cup mayonnaise
2 teaspoons chopped parsley
1 teaspoon chives
½ teaspoon curry powder

Pour the French dressing over the chicken, grapefruit, tomatoes, green pepper and cucumber, then chill in the refrigerator for 30 minutes. Mix the onion, chives, parsley and curry powder into the mayonnaise.

Line a salad bowl (or individual bowls) with the lettuce leaves. Drain the chicken mixture, blend with the mayonnaise mixture, and put into the prepared bowl(s).

Asopao (Chicken and Rice)

CARIBBEAN (PUERTO RICO)

SERVES FOUR TO SIX
1 medium chicken, cut into serving pieces
125 g/¼ lb cooked ham, cut up
5 rashers of bacon, cut up
2 tomatoes, chopped
1 green pepper, seeded, chopped
1 red pepper, seeded, cut into strips
1 onion, chopped
1 cup green peas
12 stuffed green olives
1 tablespoon capers
1 cup medium-grain rice, uncooked
1 tablespoon lime juice
1 tablespoon juice from capers
2½ cups water
2 tablespoons olive oil
2 cloves garlic, crushed
1 teaspoon oregano
3 teaspoons salt
¼ teaspoon pepper

Coat the chicken pieces with a mixture of the lime juice, oregano, 2 teaspoons salt and the pepper, and set aside for at least 30 minutes.

Fry the bacon in a large pan, then add the oil and brown the chicken in it. Next add the ham, onion, green and red peppers and garlic, and sauté until the onion is transparent. Then add the tomatoes, olives, capers, capers juice, rice, and 1 teaspoon salt. Cook for a few minutes, turning frequently. Add the water, cover, and cook until the chicken is tender (approximately 40 minutes). Add the peas 5 minutes before the end of the cooking time.

Colombo Creole (Creole Chicken Curry)

CARIBBEAN (GUADELOUPE)

SERVES SIX
1 medium chicken, cut into serving pieces
750 g/1½ lb pork, diced
1 egg-plant (aubergine) chopped
6 carrots, sliced
6 potatoes, peeled, diced
2 tomatoes, chopped
2 onions, chopped
2 cups water
½ cup olive oil
2 cloves garlic, crushed
1 teaspoon ground ginger
1 teaspoon ground turmeric
1 teaspoon ground cumin
1 teaspoon ground cardamom
½ teaspoon thyme
¼ teaspoon dried ground chilli peppers
2 teaspoons salt
½ teaspoon pepper

Sauté the onions in the oil in a large pan for 10 minutes, then remove and keep them aside. Brown the chicken and the pork in the pan, then return the onions. Cover and cook over low heat for 25 minutes, stirring occasionally. Add the egg-plant, carrots, potatoes, tomatoes, onions, garlic, chilli peppers, turmeric, ginger, cumin, cardamom, thyme, salt, pepper, and the water. Mix well, then cover and cook over low heat until the chicken is tender (approximately 45 minutes).

Brinjal Smoore (Chicken and Egg-plant Casserole) — CEYLON

SERVES SIX

1 large chicken, cut into serving pieces
1 egg-plant
2 tomatoes, sliced
1 green pepper, cut into strips
4 onions, peeled, chopped
2 tablespoons slivered almonds
2 tablespoons sugar
1 small can tomato paste
3 tablespoons lemon juice
2 tablespoons vinegar
water
peanut oil
$\frac{1}{3}$ cup butter
2 cloves garlic, crushed
10 cloves
5 cardamoms, peeled
1 stick cinnamon
$2\frac{1}{2}$ teaspoons turmeric
$\frac{1}{2}$ teaspoon paprika
5 teaspoons salt

Put the chicken pieces in a roasting pan and dot with the butter. Bake them for 30 minutes in the oven (220°C/425°F), basting occasionally. Mix together in a pan, the tomato paste, garlic, sugar, vinegar, cloves, cardamoms, cinnamon, paprika, $\frac{1}{2}$ teaspoon turmeric, 1 teaspoon salt, and $1\frac{1}{4}$ cups water. Bring to the boil and simmer for 5 minutes. Pour 1 cup of this sauce over the chicken pieces, reduce the oven temperature to 180°C/350°F, then continue baking until the chicken is tender (approximately 20 minutes). Meanwhile, simmer the green pepper and the onions in the remaining sauce for 10 minutes.

Cut the egg-plant into strips (do not peel). Sprinkle with the lemon juice, cover with water, then leave to stand for 5 minutes. Drain the egg-plant well and sprinkle it with a mixture of 2 teaspoons turmeric and 4 teaspoons salt. Fry the strips in hot peanut oil (190°C/375°F) for about 2 minutes; then drain.

Put the egg-plant, green pepper, onions and sauce over the chicken pieces in the roasting pan. Top with the tomato slices and sprinkle with the almonds. Return to the oven and bake for another 15 minutes.

Escabeche de Gallina (Cold Pickled Chicken) — CHILE

SERVES FOUR

1 medium chicken, cut into serving pieces
3 carrots, sliced
1 leek, sliced
2 onions, chopped
1 cup dry white wine
1 cup white vinegar
1 cup water
4 tablespoons olive oil
bouquet garni
2 teaspoons salt
lemon slices (for garnish)

Brown the chicken in the oil in a large pan. Then add the carrots, leek, onions, wine, vinegar, water, bouquet garni and salt, and bring to the boil over high heat. Reduce the heat and simmer until the chicken is tender (approximately 30 minutes). Remove the bouquet garni.

Put the chicken pieces into a serving dish. Pour the vegetables and liquid over them, and garnish with the lemon slices. Refrigerate until the liquid has jellied (approximately 6 hours).

Introduction to Chinese Dishes

Chinese ingredients

1. *Chinese cabbage*
2. *Oyster sauce*
3. *Sesame oil*
4. *Sesame sauce*
5. *Lotus root*
6. *Bean sprouts*
7. *Dried seaweed*
8. *Lychees*
9. *Red dates*
10. *Dried mushrooms*
11. *Bitter melon*
12. *Shark fins*
13. *Egg noodles*
14. *Black soy beans*
15. *Water chestnuts*
16. *Bamboo shoots*
17. *Hot pepper (chilli) oil*
18. *Soy sauce*
19. *Root ginger*
20. *Pine kernels*
21. *Transparent noodles*
22. *Sesame seeds*

No exotic cuisine is more familiar than that of the Chinese. There are long-established Chinese communities throughout the country and a Sunday meal at a Chinese restaurant is a way of life for many people. Most Chinese recipes are not difficult to prepare provided that you have the correct ingredients and do not attempt to substitute alternatives which are alien to the Chinese style.

Chinese dishes usually contain ingredients designed to provide a textural contrast with one another, bamboo shoots for crispness, abalone for its resilience. In most dishes vegetables are undercooked by Western standards but that is according to Chinese taste. Some vegetables can be bought fresh in season, bitter melon and the several varieties of Chinese cabbage for instance. These (and other authentic ingredients) are not difficult to buy in the 'Chinatown' areas of the cities and you will find Chinese merchants very helpful if they see that you are interested. Many ingredients are becoming increasingly available in supermarkets. Dried tangerine peel, however, is one which cannot be easily bought. (See recipe page 37). Make your own, by cutting fresh tangerine (mandarin) peel into strips, threading it onto a piece of fine string and hanging it for two to three days.

Sometimes Western palates reject prized Chinese delicacies but, viewed without prejudice and as a part of the way of life of another country, many of these foods may become much more acceptable.

You may wish to cook your dishes by the correct Chinese method. To do this you must use the wok, the Chinese frypan. Woks can be bought very cheaply from Chinese merchants and from the kitchen section of department stores. They are used both for frying and steaming and you will find that their use will greatly help you to develop a feeling for the Chinese approach to cooking.

Lichee Gai (Lychee Chicken)   CHINA

1 medium chicken, the meat finely chopped
1 onion, finely chopped
12 water chestnuts, finely chopped
1 large can lychees
¾ cup lychee juice
1 egg white, beaten
3 tablespoons cornflour
1 tablespoon Chinese rice wine
2 tablespoons chicken stock
peanut oil
3 tablespoons soy sauce
salt

Make a sauce by mixing together the lychee juice, chicken stock, 1 tablespoon soy sauce and 1 tablespoon cornflour. Cook over high heat, stirring constantly, until the sauce comes to the boil. Keep warm.

Mix together the finely chopped chicken, water chestnuts and onion. Add the egg white, the rice wine, 2 tablespoons cornflour, 2 tablespoons soy sauce, and salt to taste, then mix well. Form this mixture into small balls (using extra cornflour to aid adhesion, if necessary). Heat peanut oil in a wok, then fry the balls of chicken mixture in this until they are brown. Remove the balls, drain, then arrange them on a serving platter. Garnish with the lychees and serve with the sauce.

Bor Lor Gai (Pineapple Chicken)   CHINA

1 medium chicken
½ pineapple, diced
4 tablespoons pineapple juice
2 teaspoons sugar
1 tablespoon Chinese rice wine
¾ cup water
3 tablespoons peanut oil
½ cup soy sauce
1 clove garlic, finely chopped
2 teaspoons ground ginger
salt

Mix together the rice wine, soy sauce, sugar, ginger and a little salt. Rub this mixture all over the chicken, then leave to stand for 20 minutes. Heat the peanut oil in a large pan, add the garlic, then brown the chicken on all sides. Add the remaining soy sauce mixture, the pineapple juice and the water, and simmer until the chicken is tender (approximately $1\frac{1}{4}$ hours). Carve the chicken into serving pieces and place them on a serving platter with the pineapple pieces. Pour the sauce over and serve.

Gai Chow Mein (Chicken Chow Mein)   CHINA

1 small chicken, cooked, and meat shredded
½ cup lean pork, shredded
4 dried mushrooms, soaked for 20 minutes in warm water, sliced
½ cup bamboo shoots, thinly sliced
1 cup Chinese cabbage, shredded
250 g/½ lb egg noodles
1 tablespoon cornflour
1 teaspoon sugar
1 tablespoon Chinese rice wine
1 cup chicken stock
water
peanut oil
1 tablespoon soy sauce
1 teaspoon oyster sauce
salt

Deep-fry the noodles in peanut oil until they are golden-brown and crisp. Drain; then arrange on a serving platter and keep warm. Meanwhile, make a sauce by blending the cornflour with a little warm water, then mixing it with the chicken stock. Bring to the boil, then add the rice wine, soy sauce, oyster sauce and salt to taste. Simmer for a few minutes.

Heat a little peanut oil in a wok, and in it sauté the mushrooms with the sugar and a little salt. Mix in the chicken, ham, bamboo shoots, and Chinese cabbage, stirring constantly. Lastly mix in the sauce. Put this chicken mixture on top of the fried noodles; and serve.

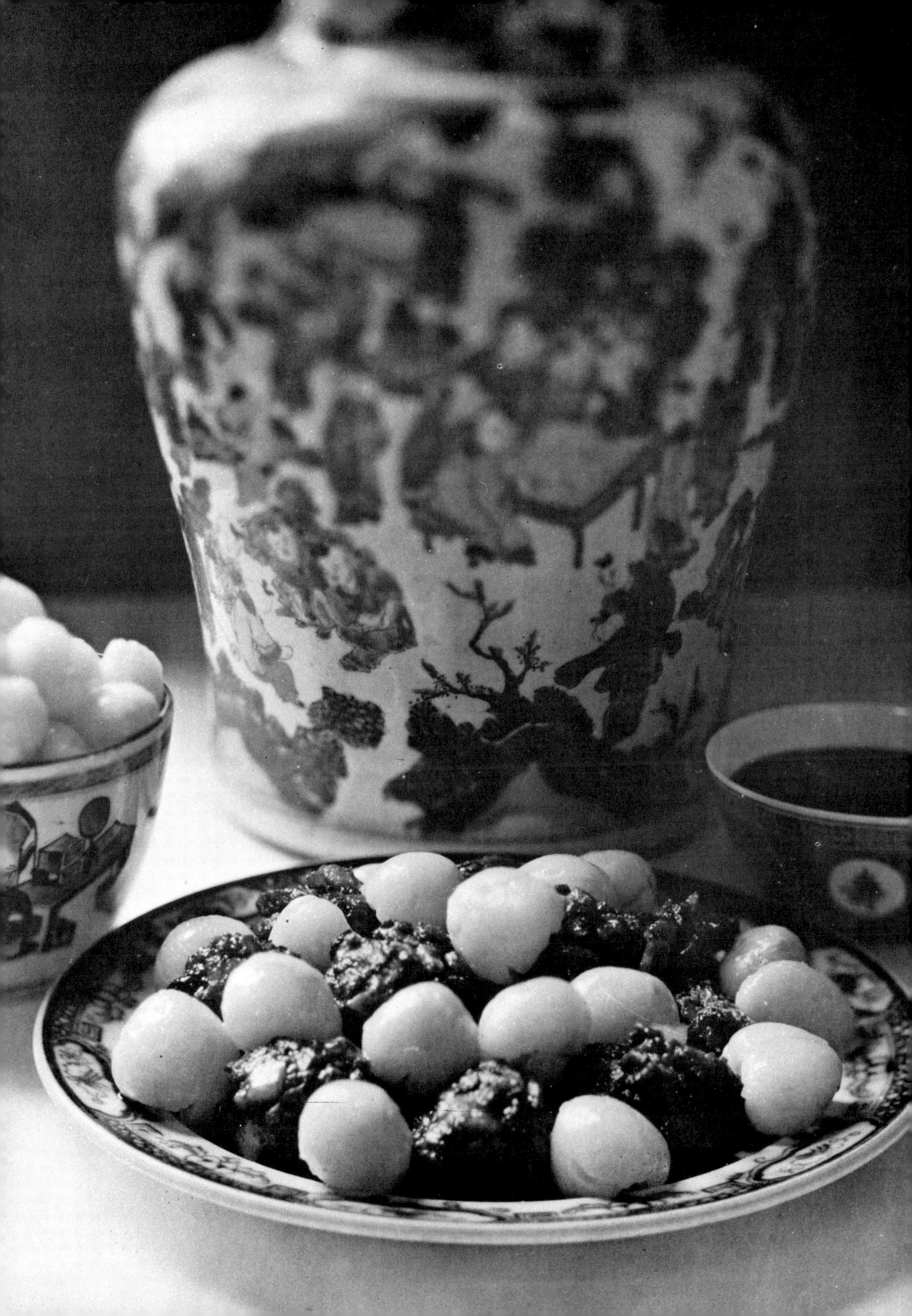

Jeng Gai (Steamed Chicken)   CHINA

1 medium chicken
6 spring onions, chopped
8 dried mushrooms, soaked for 20 minutes in hot water, sliced
5 red dates, soaked with the mushrooms, seeded, chopped
1 cup lotus roots, sliced
1 tablespoon sugar
1 tablespoon Chinese rice wine
3 tablespoons chicken stock
1 tablespoon peanut oil
2 teaspoons sesame oil
2 tablespoons soy sauce
2½ cm/1" green ginger, shredded
salt and pepper

Chop the chicken (including the bones) into bite-size pieces. Mix together the rice wine, soy sauce, sugar, ginger, and a little salt and pepper. Let the chicken pieces marinate in this mixture for 30 minutes. Put the lotus roots into a deep pan. Next add the chicken pieces and the marinade, the mushrooms, and the red dates. Pour the peanut oil, sesame oil and chicken stock over, and simmer for 20 minutes. Sprinkle with the spring onions, and serve.

Wart Gai Yee Chee Tong (Chicken and Shark's Fin Soup)   CHINA

1 small chicken
250 g/½ lb shark's fins
2 egg whites, beaten
cornflour
10 cups water

Put the chicken in the water in a large pan, and simmer for 2 hours. Cut the shark's fins into 5 cm/2" pieces, and add them to the pan. Continue to simmer until the fins become jelly-like (approximately 1 hour). Then remove the chicken from the pan, take off the breast meat and cut it into thin shreds. Bring the soup to the boil, return the shredded chicken meat to the pan, and cook over high heat for 5 minutes. Then stir the beaten egg whites well into the soup. Thicken with cornflour if necessary.

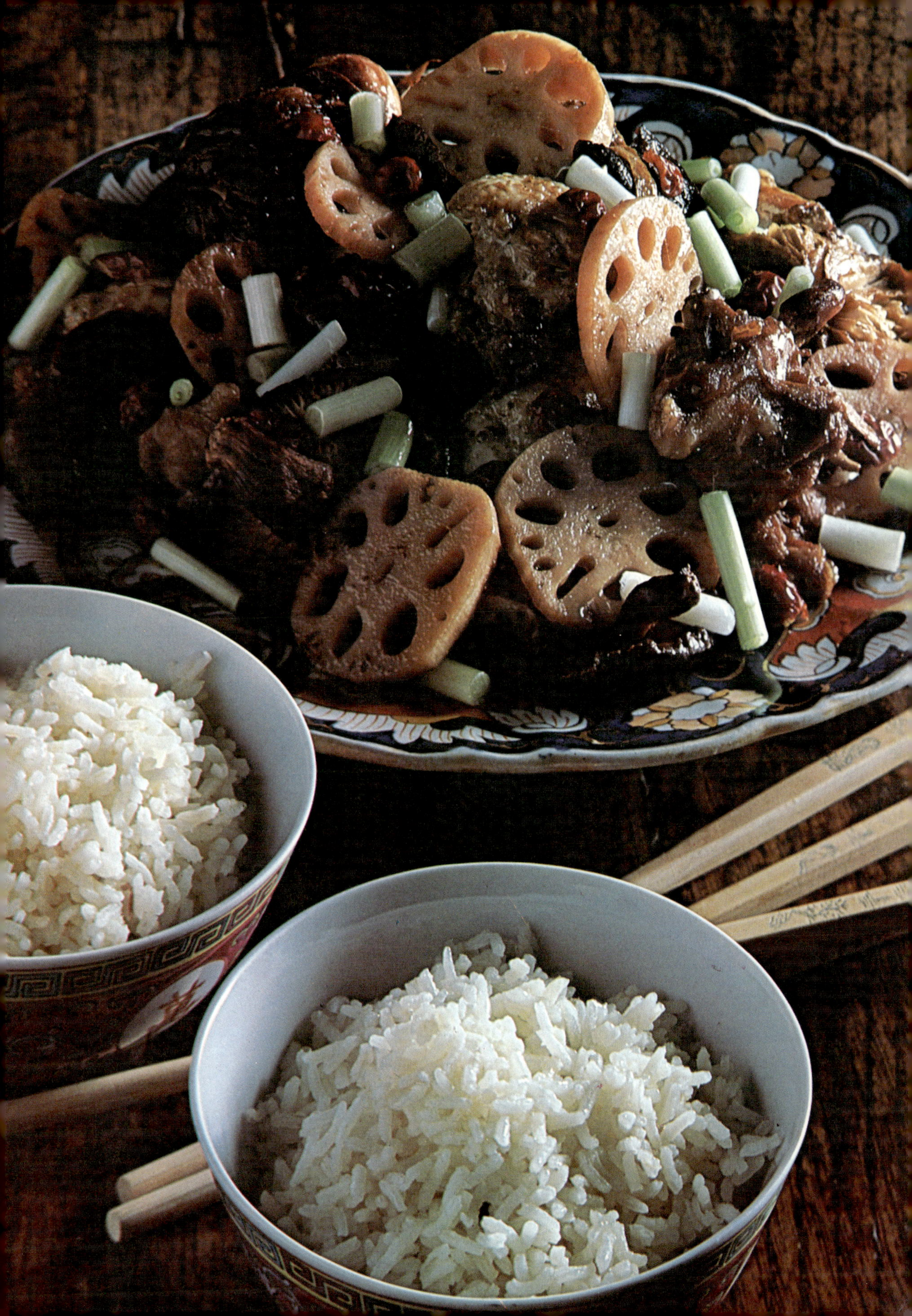

Peking Stuffed Chicken

CHINA

1 medium chicken
chicken kidneys and liver, diced
60 g/2 oz cooked ham, diced
250 g/8 oz dried mushrooms, soaked in warm water for 20 minutes, diced
½ cup bamboo shoots, soaked with the mushrooms, diced
3 tablespoons green peas
2 onions, sliced
3 tablespoons medium-grain rice, soaked in water for 10 minutes, drained
3 teaspoons cornflour
1 teaspoon sugar
2 tablespoons Chinese rice wine
6 tablespoons chicken stock
1 tablespoon lard
3 tablespoons soy sauce
1 teaspoon shrimp sauce
2 slices root ginger
4 tablespoons cooked lotus seeds, soaked in water for 10 minutes, drained
4 tablespoons pine kernels
2 tablespoons dried scallops
1 teaspoon salt

Soak the chicken kidneys and liver, the ham and the scallops in boiling water for 3 minutes; then drain. Prepare a stuffing by mixing together the chicken kidneys and liver, the ham, 2 tablespoons of the dried mushrooms, ¼ cup of the bamboo shoots, the rice, green peas, rice wine, lotus seeds, pine kernels, scallops and salt. Stuff the chicken with this mixture and close the opening with thread or skewers. Put the chicken into a casserole, and add to it the remainder of the mushrooms and bamboo shoots, the onions, ginger and 2 tablespoons soy sauce. Cover with water, bring to the boil, and simmer until the chicken is tender (approximately 1½ hours). Remove the chicken, put on to a serving platter, and keep warm.

Remove the mushrooms, bamboo shoots and onions from the casserole, and put them into a small pan. Add the sugar, 1 tablespoon soy sauce, the shrimp sauce, the cornflour (blended with 2 tablespoons water), the lard and the chicken stock. Cook all these ingredients together for 2 minutes, then pour the sauce over the chicken, and serve.

Chicken Shreds with Peppers and Cucumbers

CHINA

1 small chicken, the meat shredded
1 red sweet pepper, seeded, cut into strips
1 red chilli pepper, seeded, cut into strips
1 cucumber, cut into strips
1 egg white, beaten
½ cup transparent noodles (Tsi Phoon)
1 tablespoon cornflour
1 teaspoon sugar
2 tablespoons Chinese rice wine
2 tablespoons chicken stock
1 tablespoon vinegar
peanut oil
2 tablespoons sesame oil
2½ tablespoons soy sauce
¾ teaspoon salt

Mix the beaten egg white with the cornflour and ½ teaspoon salt, then add the shredded chicken and coat it well with this mixture. Cook the noodles for 3 minutes in boiling water, then drain. Place them in a serving dish and keep warm. Meanwhile, make a dressing by mixing together the sesame oil, vinegar, chicken stock, 1 tablespoon rice wine, 1½ tablespoons soy sauce and ¼ teaspoon salt.

Heat peanut oil in a wok, then add the shredded chicken and cook for 2 minutes; remove and drain. Put the sweet pepper and chilli pepper into the wok and cook over high heat for 1 minute, stirring constantly. Add the sugar, 1 tablespoon rice wine and 1 tablespoon soy sauce, and stir-fry for another minute; then remove and drain. Put the shredded chicken, the peppers and the cucumber on top of the noodles in the serving dish, then pour the dressing over them. Toss and mix all the ingredients together, then serve.

Chicken and Bitter Melon

CHINA

1 small chicken, the meat diced
500 g/1 lb bitter melons, halved, seeded, sliced
1 tablespoon Chinese rice wine
1½ cups water
1 tablespoon peanut oil
1 tablespoon soy sauce
1 tablespoon black soybeans, scalded, drained, crushed
2 cloves garlic, finely chopped

Mix together the rice wine and soy sauce, then mix the diced chicken with half of this mixture. Heat the oil in a wok, brown the garlic, then add the diced chicken meat. Stir well until the chicken is half-cooked. Then add the crushed black soybeans and cook for another 5 minutes, stirring constantly. Add the water and the remaining rice wine and soy sauce mixture, cover, and simmer for 15 minutes. Add the bitter melon, then continue to simmer for another 10 minutes. Serve immediately.

Crisp-skin Chicken
CHINA

1 small chicken
1 tablespoon Chinese rice wine
peanut oil (for deep-frying)
1 tablespoon soy sauce
1 clove garlic, crushed

Chop the chicken (including the bones) into bite-size pieces. Mix together the garlic, the rice wine and the soy sauce, then coat the chicken pieces with this mixture. Allow the mixture to dry, then repeat the procedure. Heat peanut oil in a wok. Deep-fry the chicken pieces in the oil over low heat at first and then brown them over high heat for the last few minutes of cooking time.

Chicken and Sweetcorn Soup
CHINA

1 small chicken
2 cups sweetcorn kernels
6 spring onions, chopped
1 egg, beaten
1 teaspoon Chinese rice wine
6 cups water
1 knob of ginger
4 peppercorns
salt

Put the chicken, the ginger, peppercorns, a little salt, and the water into a large pan. Bring to the boil, then simmer until the chicken is tender (approximately 30 minutes). Remove the chicken, take all the meat from the bones, then cut it into fine shreds. Strain the stock and return it to the pan.

Return the chicken shreds to the pan. Add the sweetcorn kernels and the rice wine, then cook for 10 minutes. Stir the beaten egg briskly into the soup. Thicken with cornflour if necessary. Serve the soup garnished with the chopped spring onions.

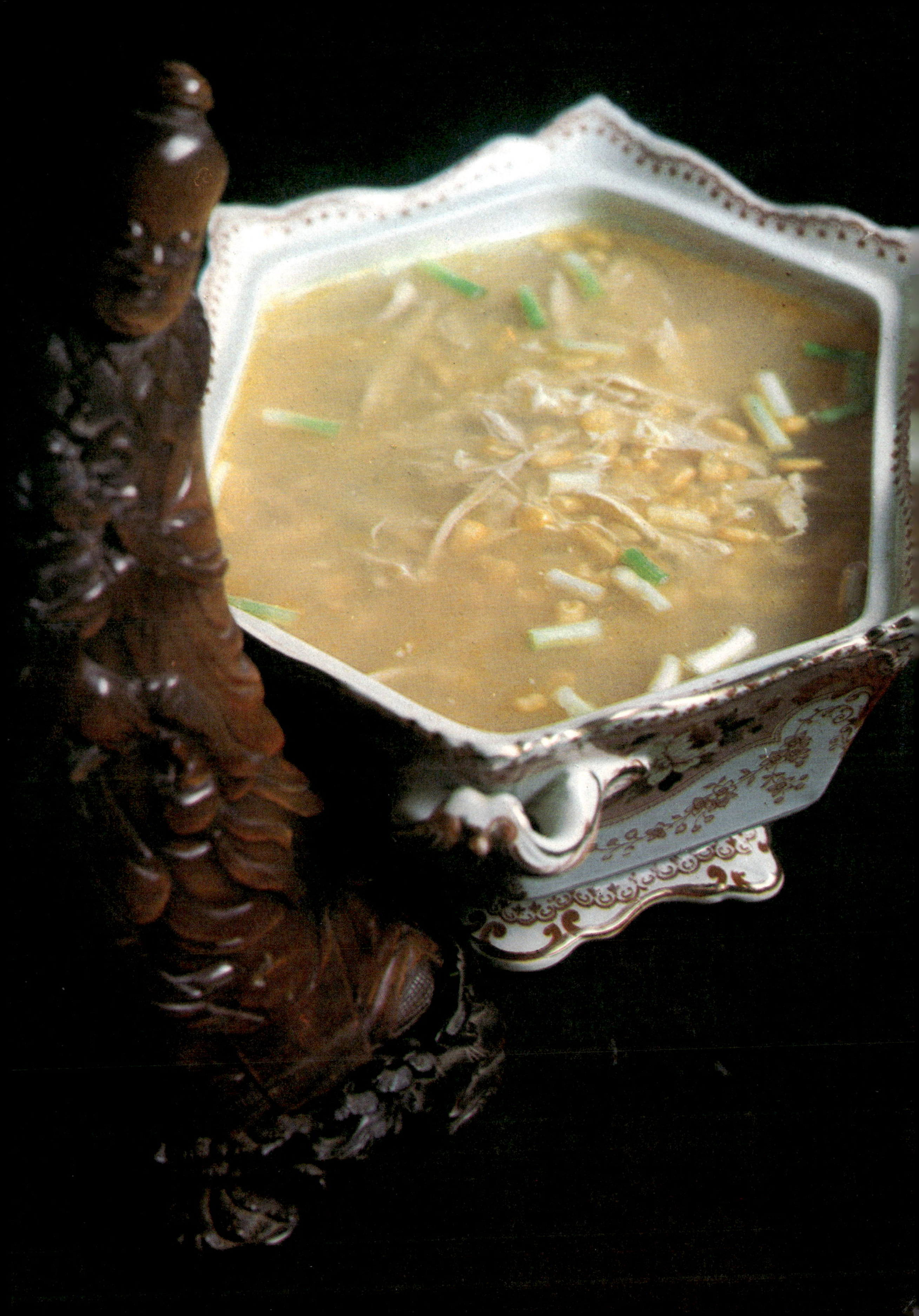

Peking Chicken in Wine

CHINA

1 medium chicken
2 onions, halved
5 tablespoons Chinese rice wine
1 cup Chinese red grape wine
6½ cups chicken stock
peanut oil
5 tablespoons soy sauce
1 clove garlic, crushed
1 teaspoon salt

Mix together 1 tablespoon of the rice wine and 2 tablespoons of the soy sauce. Coat the chicken inside and out with this mixture, then leave it to stand for 15 minutes. Coat the chicken again with the mixture, and leave to dry.

Heat peanut oil in a wok, and deep-fry the chicken and onions in it for 5 minutes (2½ minutes on each side of the chicken). Remove the chicken and put it into a casserole. Add the fried onion, the garlic, salt, chicken stock, the remaining 4 tablespoons of rice wine and the remaining 3 tablespoons soy sauce. Bring to the boil, then cover and cook over low heat for 1 hour (turning over the chicken after 30 minutes). Then turn the chicken over again, add the red grape wine, and continue cooking for another 30 minutes.

Chicken with Sesame Sauce

CHINA

1 small chicken, cooked, the meat shredded
2 slices of ham, shredded
1 cucumber, seeded, thinly sliced
1 cup bean sprouts, cooked in boiling water for 1 minute
2 spring onions, finely chopped
1 cup roasted peanuts
125 g/4 oz transparent noodles (Tsi Phoon), soaked in warm water for 15 minutes, coarsely chopped
1 tablespoon sugar
¼ cup vinegar
1 tablespoon sesame oil
1 tablespoon hot pepper oil
¼ cup soy sauce
4 teaspoons sesame paste
1 teaspoon mustard powder
pepper

Make a sauce by mixing together the spring onions, sugar, vinegar, sesame oil, hot pepper oil, soy sauce, sesame paste, mustard powder, and a little pepper. Put the shredded chicken, cucumber, bean sprouts, ham, peanuts and transparent noodles into a large bowl. Mix well, then stir in the sauce mixture. Put on to a serving platter, and serve cold.

Tse Bou Gai (Foil-Wrapped Chicken)　　　　CHINA

1 medium chicken, cut into 32 pieces
1 teaspoon sugar
1 tablespoon lemon juice
3 tablespoons peanut oil
3 tablespoons soy sauce
parsley sprigs
1 tablespoon sesame seeds
aluminium foil

Mix together the soy sauce, peanut oil, lemon juice, sesame seeds and sugar. Put the chicken pieces into this marinade and leave for 15 minutes. Then put each chicken piece in the centre of a 15 cm/6″-square piece of aluminium foil. Add a sprig of parsley, bring the 4 ends of the foil together, and twist to seal. Fry in hot deep oil (200°C/400°F) for 5 minutes. Serve immediately.

Chicken with Bamboo Shoots and Seaweed

CHINA

1 medium chicken, the meat diced
500 g/1 lb pork, diced
500 g/1 lb ham bones
500 g/1 lb bamboo shoots, cut into strips
125 g/$\frac{1}{4}$ lb dried seaweed, soaked in water for 1 hour
125 g/$\frac{1}{4}$ lb leeks, coarsely chopped
125 g/$\frac{1}{4}$ lb onions, thickly sliced
3 tablespoons sugar
$\frac{1}{2}$ cup Chinese rice wine
5 tablespoons vinegar
2 tablespoons sesame oil
5 tablespoons soy sauce
2 cloves garlic, crushed

In boiling water: cook the chicken for 2$\frac{1}{2}$ minutes, then drain; cook the pork for 5 minutes, then drain; simmer the bamboo shoots for 3 minutes, then drain; simmer the seaweed for 30 minutes, drain, then coarsely chop.

Put the ham bones in the bottom of a large pan. On top arrange the chicken, pork, seaweed, bamboo shoots, leeks and onions. Sprinkle with the garlic, sugar, rice wine, soy sauce, vinegar and sesame oil. Pour 10 cups of water over. Bring to the boil, then simmer over low heat for 3 hours.

Chilled Spiced Chicken

CHINA

1 medium chicken, chopped into 16 pieces
3 pairs pig's trotters
1 carrot, chopped
2 spring onions, coarsely chopped
2 onions, quartered
4 tablespoons Chinese rice wine
11 cups water
2 slices root ginger
2 teaspoons salt
pepper

Put the pig's trotters, onion and ginger in 7 cups of the water in a large pan. Bring to the boil, and simmer for 2 hours. By this time, the liquid should have reduced to half the original amount. Skim the stock, then strain, and return it to the pan.

Meanwhile, put the chicken pieces, the carrot and salt into the remaining 4 cups water in another pan, and simmer for 30 minutes. Skim, then put the chicken, carrot and half the cooking liquid into the strained stock. Add the spring onions, the rice wine and a little pepper, and simmer for 30 minutes. Now put the contents of the pan into a large dish, cool, then chill in the refrigerator for at least 2 hours. When it has set, turn the chicken and jelly out on to a serving platter. Garnish with vegetables (lettuce, tomato wedges) or even with flowers (chrysanthemums).

Steamed Chicken in Wine

CHINA

1 medium chicken
4 spring onions, coarsely chopped
2 teaspoons cornflour
2 cups Chinese rice wine
3 slices root ginger, halved

Mix together the spring onions and the ginger. Stuff the chicken with half of this mixture, then close the opening with thread or skewers. Put the stuffed chicken in the middle of a large piece of aluminium foil. Lift the sides of the foil, then pour the rice wine over the chicken and spread the remaining spring onions and ginger mixture over the top of it. Bring the edges of the foil up over the chicken and fold them together to seal in the chicken and the wine. Place this 'parcel' in a large pan, preferably lifted slightly away from the bottom (e.g. on a cake-stand). Then add water to the pan sufficient to come half-way up the chicken 'parcel'. Bring to the boil, cover the pan and simmer until the chicken is tender (approximately $1\frac{1}{2}$ hours).

Remove the 'parcel' from the pan and open it. Take out the chicken, put it into a serving dish and keep warm. Into a saucepan, put the juices which have accumulated in the foil. Blend the cornflour with 1 tablespoon water, then mix this into the juices. Heat this sauce, stirring, for 3 minutes, then pour it over the chicken.

Tangerine Peel Chicken

CHINA

1 small chicken
1 onion, finely sliced
2 tablespoons tangerine peel (dried)
2 teaspoons sugar
3 tablespoons Chinese rice wine
3 tablespoons chicken stock
1 tablespoon vinegar
peanut oil
2 tablespoons soy sauce
3 chilli peppers, seeded, quartered
2 slices root ginger
$\frac{1}{4}$ teaspoon black pepper

Chop the chicken (including the bones) into bite-size pieces. Heat peanut oil in a wok and deep-fry the chicken pieces in it until they are brown (approximately 5 minutes). Remove and drain.

Remove all but 2 tablespoons of the peanut oil from the wok, then into this put the tangerine peel, onion, chillis and ginger. Cook over high heat for 3 minutes, stirring constantly. Then add the rice wine, chicken stock, soy sauce, sugar and black pepper. Bring to the boil, then return the chicken pieces to the wok and coat well with the sauce. Cover, and cook for 6 minutes. Sprinkle with the vinegar, and serve.

Dar Bin Loo (Steamboat)

CHINA

1 small chicken
1 Chinese cabbage, coarsely chopped
6 eggs
bundle of transparent noodles (Tsi Phoon)
boiled rice
2 cups chicken stock
3 tablespoons peanut oil
1 tablespoon soy sauce
salt

Remove the chicken meat from the bones, then slice it thinly. Put the chicken carcass into a large pan, and add the soy sauce, chicken stock and water to cover. Add salt to taste, bring to the boil, and simmer for approximately 1 hour. Meanwhile, deep-fry half the noodles in the peanut oil in a wok. Soak the other half of the noodles in water for at least 30 minutes, then drain.

Put the chicken meat, the soaked noodles, the Chinese cabbage and the raw eggs on to serving plates, using a separate plate for each ingredient. Arrange these plates around the steamboat. Serve each person with a bowl of rice. Then put the hot stock into the steamboat, and let each person cook their own food by picking it from the plate and holding it in the stock with chopsticks. Break the eggs into the stock to poach them. As the food is cooked, it is eaten with the rice, the fried noodles, and a selection of dipping sauces (e.g. soy sauce and sesame oil, oyster sauce, hot chilli sauce, raw eggs).

Hung Yun Gai (Chicken and Almonds)

CHINA

1 small chicken, the meat diced
1 cup dried mushrooms, soaked in warm water for 20 minutes, diced
1 cup celery, diced
$\frac{3}{4}$ cup bamboo shoots, diced
1 onion, chopped
125 g/$\frac{1}{4}$ lb roasted almonds
$\frac{3}{4}$ cup water chestnuts, diced
1 egg white, beaten
$\frac{1}{2}$ bundle transparent noodles (Tsi Phoon)
2 tablespoons cornflour
1 tablespoon Chinese rice wine
1 cup chicken stock
peanut oil
1 teaspoon sesame oil
1 tablespoon soy sauce
2 teaspoons oyster sauce
pinch bicarbonate soda
salt

Mix together the egg white, 1 tablespoon cornflour, the rice wine, sesame oil, bicarbonate soda and a little salt. Add the diced chicken and coat well with this mixture. Mix together the soy sauce, chicken stock and 1 tablespoon of the cornflour; then keep this aside.

Heat peanut oil in a wok and deep-fry the diced chicken until slightly coloured. Remove the chicken, and drain. Take out all but 2 tablespoons of the peanut oil, then stir-fry the onion, mushrooms, bamboo shoots, celery and chestnuts in the wok. Return the chicken and mix well. Add the soy sauce mixture, the oyster sauce, and the almonds. Stir in well. Put on to a serving platter and surround with the cooked noodles.

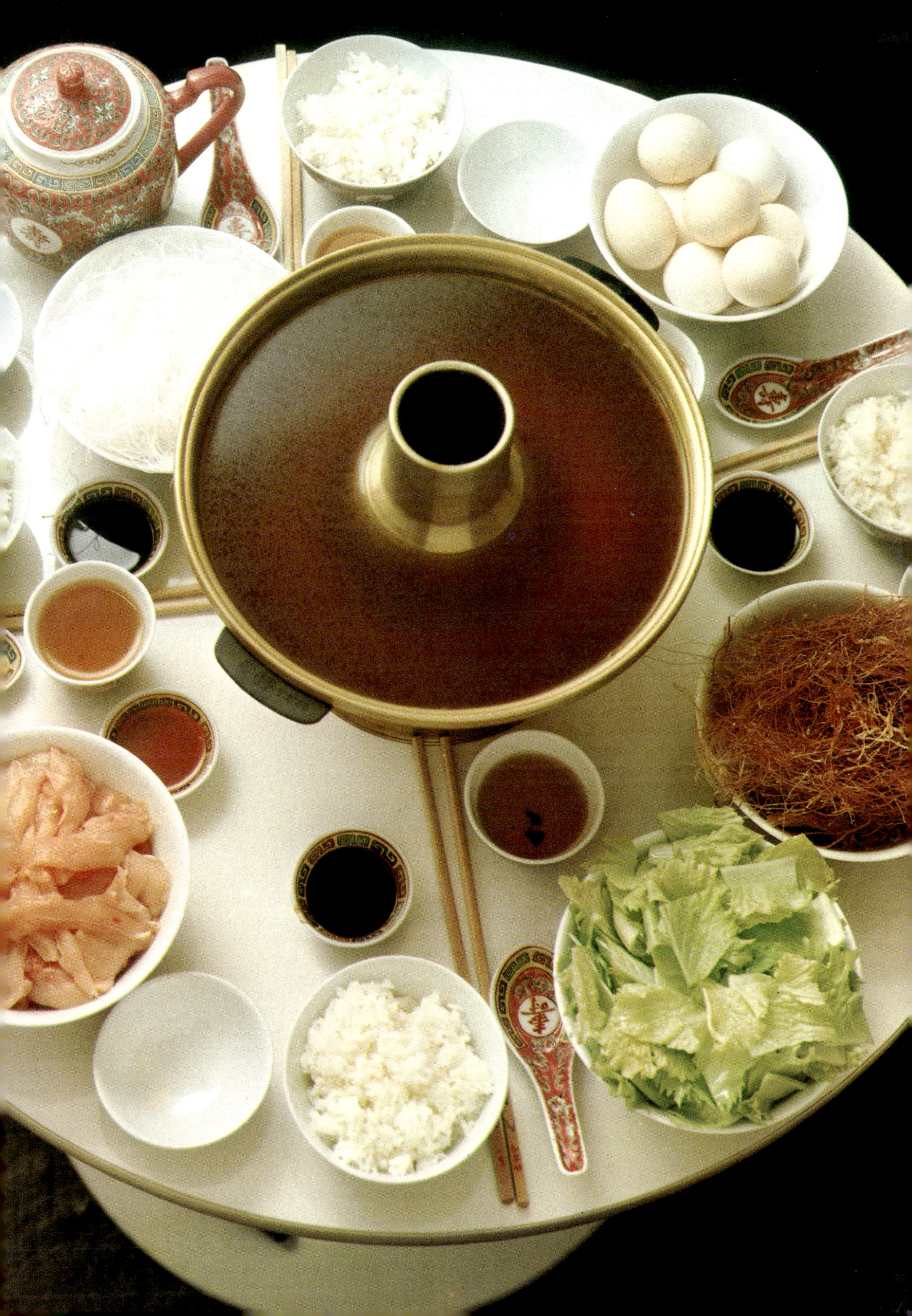

Piquete (Colombian Chicken and Pork)

COLOMBIA

SERVES SIX

1 medium chicken, cut into
6 serving pieces
6 pork chops
3 ears sweetcorn, halved
6 potatoes, unpeeled
3 sweet potatoes, peeled, halved
3 onions, finely chopped
10 cups water
2 cloves garlic, crushed
3 tablespoons chopped parsley
1 teaspoon ground cumin
½ teaspoon dried ground chilli peppers
2 teaspoons salt
Cheese and Tomato Sauce

Cheese and Tomato Sauce
2 tomatoes, chopped
2 onions, chopped
½ cup grated gruyère cheese
½ cup breadcrumbs
½ cup milk
2 tablespoons olive oil
1 teaspoon salt

Mix together in a blender the onions, garlic, parsley, chilli peppers, cumin and salt. Marinate the chicken pieces in this mixture overnight.

Put the chicken, the marinade and the water into a large pan. Bring to the boil, cover and cook over moderate heat until the chicken is tender (approximately 1 hour). Remove the chicken from the pan and put it into a greased baking dish. Then bake it in the oven (230°C/450°F) until it is brown (approximately 15 minutes). Meanwhile, boil the potatoes and the sweet potatoes in the stock from which the chicken has been removed, for 15 minutes. Then add the sweetcorn and continue cooking until the potatoes are soft. Fry the pork chops until they are tender.

Put the meats on one serving dish and the vegetables on another. Serve with the Cheese and Tomato Sauce.

Soak the breadcrumbs in the milk. Sauté the onions in the oil for 5 minutes, then add the tomatoes and cook over low heat for 10 minutes. Next add the breadcrumbs and milk and cook for another 2 minutes, stirring constantly. Add the cheese and the salt and cook, stirring, until the cheese has melted.

Ajiaco Bogotano (Creamed Chicken and Potato Soup)

COLOMBIA

SERVES SIX

1 medium chicken, cut into serving pieces
500 g/1 lb shin of beef, chopped
4 potatoes, peeled, sliced
3 ears sweetcorn, chopped
1 avocado, peeled, stoned, sliced
6 teaspoons capers
12 tablespoons thick cream
8 cups water
1 bay leaf
¼ teaspoon cumin
¼ teaspoon thyme
2½ teaspoons salt
¼ teaspoon pepper

Put the chicken, the beef and the water into a large pan; bring to the boil and skim. Add the onion, bay leaf, cumin, thyme, salt and pepper. Cover, and cook over moderate heat until the chicken is tender (approximately 30 minutes).

Remove the shin bones and the onion. Take out the chicken pieces, remove the skin, then take the chicken meat from the bones and cut it into strips. Strain the stock from the pan, then return it to the heat and bring to the boil. Put in the potatoes, cover, and cook until they are soft (approximately 30 minutes). Then mash the potatoes in the pan so that the soup becomes thick. Add the chicken and the sweetcorn and cook over low heat until the sweetcorn is tender (approximately 5-10 minutes).

Serve in individual soup bowls. Into each bowl put 2 tablespoons of the cream and 1 teaspoon of the capers, then pour the soup over. Top with the sliced avocado.

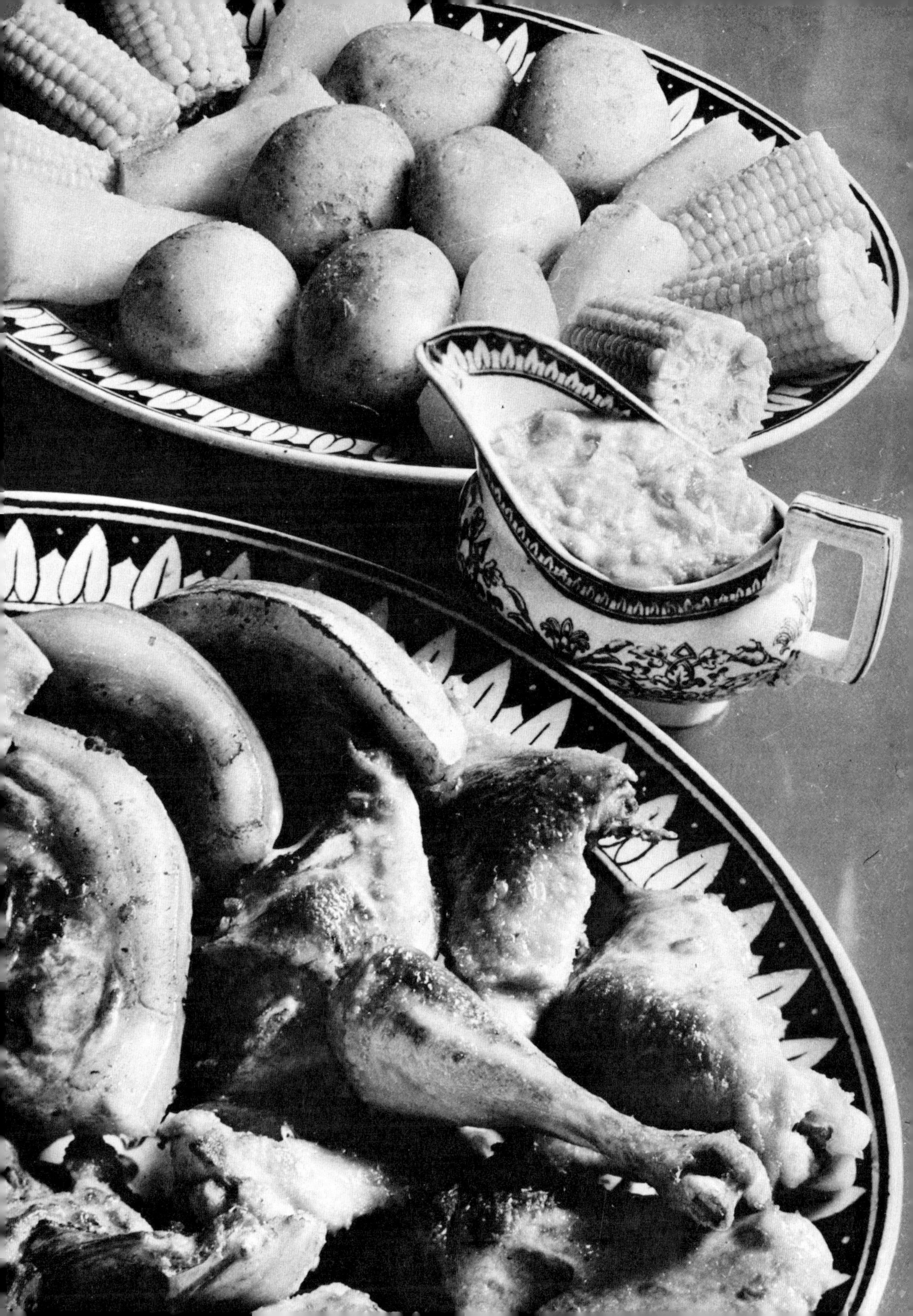

Sancocho Valle Caucano (Chicken and Vegetable Soup) COLOMBIA

SERVES FOUR TO SIX
1 medium chicken, cut into serving pieces
500 g/1 lb sweet potatoes, cut into strips
500 g/1 lb pumpkin, peeled, seeded, chopped
1 avocado, peeled, stoned, sliced
2 onions, chopped
2 green bananas, peeled, chopped
4 tablespoons white vinegar
$10\frac{1}{4}$ cups water
4 tablespoons olive oil
2 teaspoons coriander
1 teaspoon red chilli peppers, chopped
$\frac{1}{4}$ teaspoon turmeric
$1\frac{1}{2}$ teaspoons salt
$\frac{1}{4}$ teaspoon black pepper

Put the chicken, onions, black pepper, 1 teaspoon coriander, 1 teaspoon salt and 10 cups of the water into a large pan. Bring to the boil, skim, then cover and simmer until the chicken is tender (approximately 40 minutes). Remove the chicken and keep warm. Then put the bananas and sweet potatoes into the pan, cover, and cook over moderate heat for 20 minutes. Add the pumpkin and the turmeric and continue cooking for a further 20 minutes. Return the chicken pieces to the pan and cook for a few minutes to heat through.

Meanwhile, beat together the vinegar, olive oil, $\frac{1}{2}$ teaspoon salt and the remaining $\frac{1}{4}$ cup water. When the mixture is well blended, stir in the chilli peppers and 1 teaspoon coriander.

Put the chicken pieces into individual serving bowls, pour the soup over, and top with the avocado slices. Serve the sauce separately.

Pollo al Cazador (Hunters' Chicken) COLOMBIA

SERVES FOUR
1 medium chicken, cut into serving pieces
2 tomatoes, chopped
1 green pepper, seeded, sliced
1 cup mushrooms, sliced
2 onions, peeled, quartered
2 cups chick peas (canned)
2 tablespoons flour
1 cup red wine
3 tablespoons olive oil
1 bay leaf
$\frac{1}{4}$ teaspoon oregano
$\frac{1}{4}$ teaspoon dried ground chilli peppers
2 teaspoons salt
$\frac{1}{4}$ teaspoon pepper

Coat the chicken pieces with a mixture of the flour, the pepper, and 1 teaspoon of the salt. Brown the chicken in the olive oil in a large pan. Then add the tomatoes, green pepper, mushrooms, onions, wine, bay leaf, oregano, chilli peppers, and 1 teaspoon salt. Cover and simmer until the chicken is almost tender (approximately 40 minutes). Add the chick peas and continue cooking for another few minutes, until the chicken is tender.

Egyptian Lemon Chicken EGYPT

SERVES FOUR TO SIX
1 large chicken, cut into serving pieces
juice and grated rind of 1 lemon
4 tablespoons olive oil
5 tablespoons butter
1 clove garlic, finely chopped
2 tablespoons chopped parsley
$\frac{1}{4}$ teaspoon thyme
salt and black pepper

Marinate the chicken pieces for at least 2 hours in a mixture of the olive oil, lemon juice, lemon rind, garlic, thyme, salt and black pepper. Then butter a baking dish and put the chicken and the marinade into this. Dot the chicken with the butter and cook in a 180°C/350°F oven until the chicken is tender. Baste frequently. Remove the finished dish from the oven and sprinkle with the parsley.

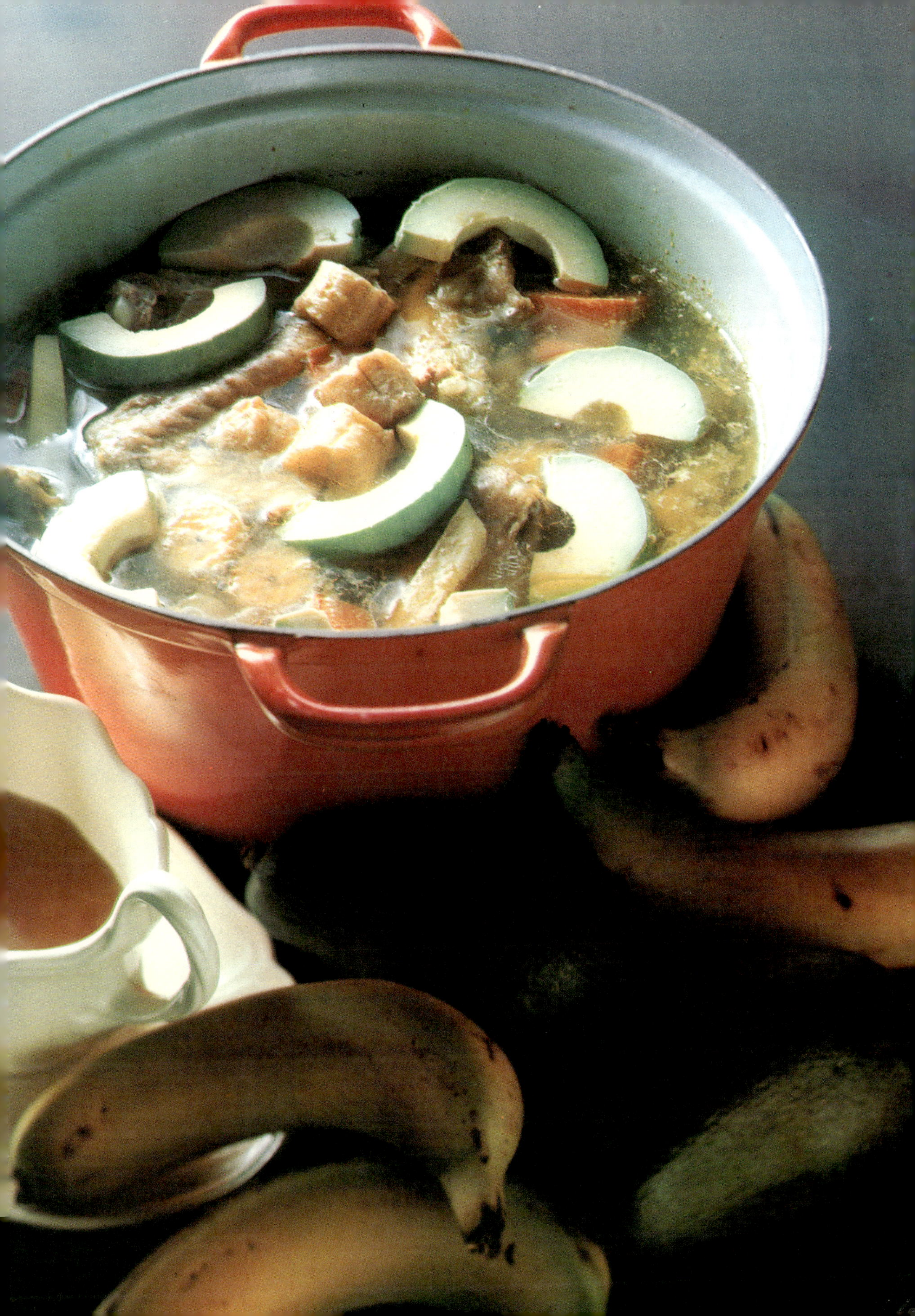

Gallo en Chicha (Chicken in Cider)

EL SALVADOR

SERVES SIX
1 large chicken, cut into 6 serving pieces
6 Spanish sausages, chopped
2 green peppers, finely sliced
4 potatoes, peeled, diced
3 onions, finely chopped
12 small white onions
12 stuffed olives
3 tablespoons capers
12 prunes, soaked, stoned
2 cups dry cider
3 tablespoons vinegar
4 tablespoons butter
2 cloves garlic, crushed
¼ teaspoon dried ground chilli peppers
salt and pepper

Sauté the finely chopped onions in the butter in a large pan. When brown, remove and keep aside. Now brown the chicken pieces in the same pan. Then return the onions, add the green peppers, garlic, ground chillis, cider and vinegar, and season with salt and pepper. Cover, and cook over low heat for 1 hour. Add the potatoes, prunes, olives, capers and the small onions, and cook for a further 10 minutes. Meanwhile, fry the sausages (in their own fat) in a separate pan for 5 minutes, then add these also to the chicken pan. Continue cooking until the chicken is tender (approximately 10 minutes).

Poulet en Gelée (Chicken in Jelly)   FRANCE

SERVES FOUR TO SIX
1 medium chicken
1 cup ham, diced
½ cup dry white wine
2 tablespoons brandy
2 tablespoons butter
2 tablespoons powdered gelatine
salt and pepper

Truss the chicken, then brown it on all sides in the butter in a large pan. Pour over the white wine and add the ham. Cover and cook over low heat for 40 minutes. Remove from the heat and leave to cool, then skin the chicken and cut it into serving pieces. Strain the cooking liquids into a saucepan and heat them. Dissolve the gelatine in a little of the hot liquid, then add to the pan. Pour in the brandy. Remove the saucepan from the heat and leave the liquids to cool; then skim. Re-heat a little of the jelly until it is soft, then brush it over the chicken pieces. Coat each piece twice, leaving an interval of 2 minutes between each coating. Chill the chicken and the remaining jelly until the following day.

Put the chicken pieces in the centre of a serving dish and re-glaze them with a little of the jelly (as before). Chop up the remaining jelly and arrange it around the chicken.

Ballotine of Chicken with Prunes   FRANCE

SERVES FOUR TO SIX
1 large chicken, boned
500 g/1 lb pork, minced
250 g/½ lb button mushrooms
250 g/½ lb small onions
1 large onion, finely chopped
500 g/1 lb prunes, soaked, drained
1 egg, beaten
1 tablespoon flour
1 teaspoon sugar
1 cup breadcrumbs
1 teaspoon tomato paste
1½ cups red wine or port
2 cups jellied chicken stock
6½ tablespoons butter
1 tablespoon chopped parsley
2 teaspoons dried sage
bouquet garni
salt and pepper

Cook the drained prunes in 1 cup of the wine. When cooked, keep the juice aside. Stone the prunes and leave to cool. Sauté the chopped onion in 1 tablespoon of the butter until transparent. Cool the onion, then mix it with the pork, breadcrumbs, parsley, sage, and salt and pepper to taste. Bind this mixture together with the beaten egg. Then spread the mixture over the boned chicken, put a line of prunes down the centre, and roll the chicken up. Sew it up with fine string and then tie. Brown this ballotine on all sides in 2 tablespoons butter, then pour over the remaining ½ cup wine. Cover and cook until tender (approximately 1½ hours).

Meanwhile, make a salpicon. Put the small onions into a saucepan with 1½ tablespoons butter and the sugar. Cover and cook until the onions are tender and are caramelised. Sauté the mushrooms in 1 tablespoon butter. Mix together the small onions, the mushrooms, and the remaining prunes. Keep aside.

Melt 1 tablespoon of the butter in a pan, blend in the flour, and cook until brown. Add the chicken stock, tomato paste and bouquet garni, and bring to the boil, stirring constantly. Season with salt and pepper, then simmer for 20 minutes. Remove the bouquet garni. Skim, then add the prune cooking juices and cook for another 10 minutes. Keep this sauce aside.

When cooked, slice the ballotine of chicken, pour over the sauce, and top with the salpicon of prunes, onions and mushrooms.

Note: See Introduction for boning chicken.

Poulet Basquaise

FRANCE

SERVES FOUR TO SIX

1 medium chicken, cut into serving pieces
4 tomatoes, peeled, seeded, chopped
2 green peppers, cut into strips
2 red peppers, cut into strips
6 onions, finely chopped
½ cup dry white wine
2 tablespoons olive oil
1 clove garlic, crushed
bouquet garni
salt and pepper

Brown the chicken pieces in the olive oil in a pan. Remove the pieces and put them into a casserole. Add the white wine, the bouquet garni, and salt and pepper to taste. Cover, and cook over moderate heat.

Meanwhile, sauté the onions in the oil until transparent. Then add the green peppers, red peppers and garlic and cook for 10 minutes. Add the tomatoes, and continue cooking until a thick sauce is formed. Transfer this mixture to the casserole. Cover and cook over low heat until the chicken is tender (total cooking time approximately 45 minutes). Remove the bouquet garni; then serve.

Pâté de Foie de Volaille

FRANCE

500 g/1 lb chicken livers
1 onion, finely chopped
strips of pork or bacon fat (to line terrine)
4 tablespoons brandy
¾ cup rendered chicken fat
1 tablespoon butter
¼ teaspoon anchovy paste
1½ teaspoons dry mustard
¼ teaspoon mace
2 teaspoons salt
½ teaspoon pepper

Wash the chicken livers and place in a pan with the onions and the butter. Sauté them very gently for approximately 5 minutes, taking care that the butter does not burn. Now put the livers into a blender with the chicken fat, anchovy paste, mustard, mace, salt, pepper, and the onions and butter from the pan. Add the brandy, and blend to the desired consistency.

Line a terrine or mould with strips of pork or bacon fat. Then fill the terrine with the mixture from the blender, pressing it down until it is quite firm. Cover the pâté with more strips of fat. Line the top with foil, place the cover on the terrine, and put it into a baking dish containing enough water to come half-way up the side of the terrine. Cook in the oven (180°C/350°F) for 1½ hours, then remove from the oven and cool. Serve the pâté from the terrine or turn it out on to a serving dish. The pâté will keep indefinitely in the terrine.

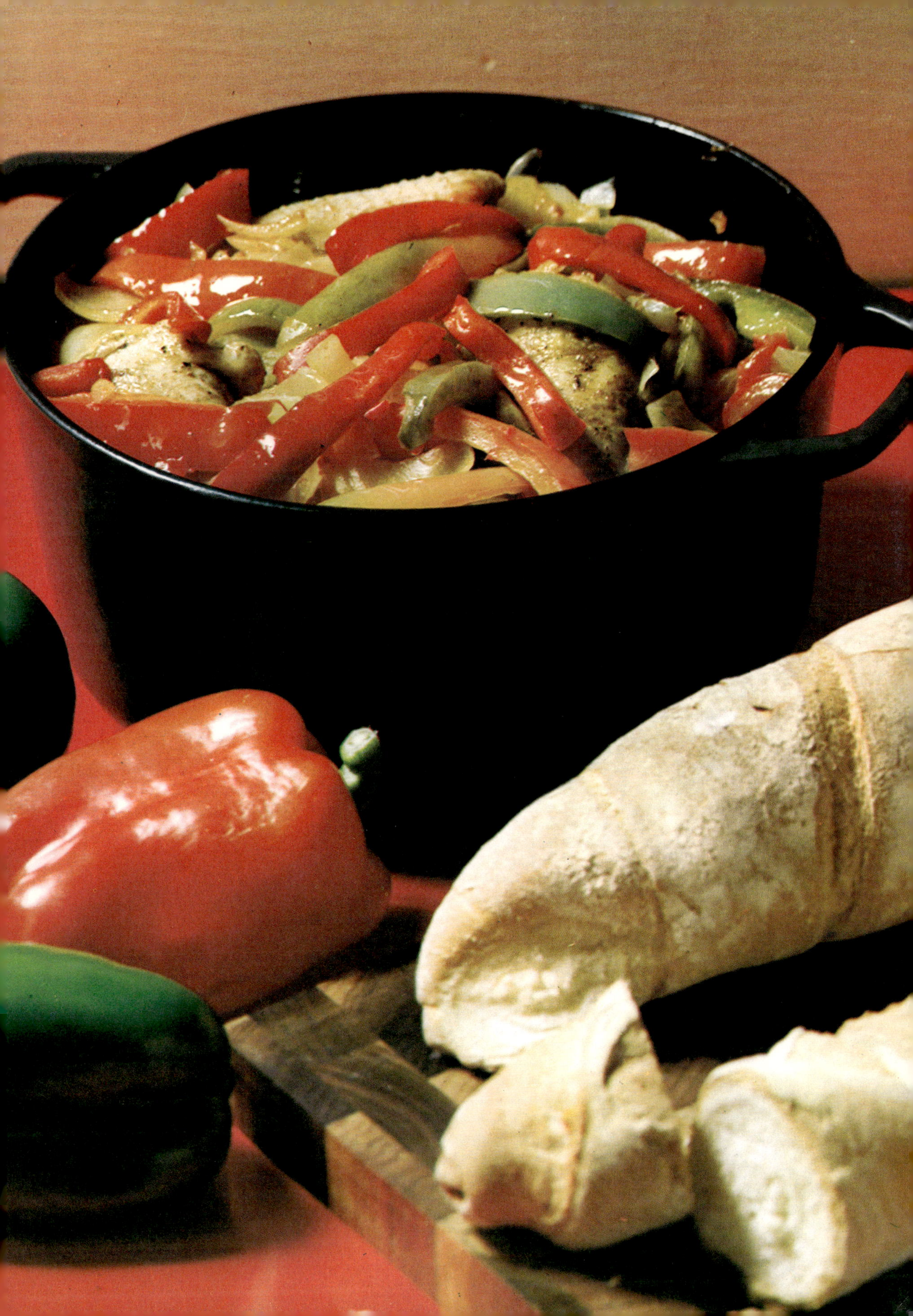

La Poule au Riz à la Crème (Chicken with Rice and Cream) — FRANCE

SERVES FOUR TO SIX
1 large chicken
125 g/4 oz bacon, cut into thin slices
4 carrots, sliced
2 onions, sliced
1 lemon
2 egg yolks
2 cups medium-grain rice
2 tablespoons flour
10 cups chicken stock
1 cup cream
butter
1 clove garlic, crushed
3 tablespoons chopped parsley
2 bay leaves
1 tablespoon tarragon
1 teaspoon thyme
salt and pepper

Put the bacon slices on to the bottom of a casserole. Rub the chicken with the lemon, then stuff it with a knob of butter mixed with a little salt and pepper. Place the chicken on top of the bacon and surround it with the onions and carrots. Cook over moderate heat for 15 minutes, then pour in the chicken stock, the garlic, bay leaves, thyme, 2 tablespoons parsley and $\frac{1}{2}$ teaspoon salt. Cover with buttered paper and the lid, and put the casserole into the oven (180°C/350°F). Cook until the chicken is tender (approximately 2 hours).

When the chicken has been cooking for $1\frac{1}{4}$ hours, turn it over and take out $5\frac{1}{4}$ cups of the stock. Boil the rice in salted water for approximately 7 minutes; then drain and rinse under cold water. Put the rice into a pan and pour 4 cups of the stock over it. Bring to the boil, then cover the pan and cook the rice in the oven for at least 25 minutes.

Meanwhile, melt 2 tablespoons butter in a pan, stir in the flour, then blend in $1\frac{1}{4}$ cups of the stock from the chicken pan. Add the cream and cook over low heat, stirring occasionally. Beat the egg yolks with a little lemon juice and then mix into the sauce. Add the tarragon and the remaining parsley. Carve the chicken into serving pieces, pour over the sauce, and arrange the rice around them.

Poulet Nivernais (Chicken in White Wine with Dumplings) — FRANCE

SERVES FOUR TO SIX
1 large chicken, cut into serving pieces
3 carrots, sliced
12 mushrooms
12 small white onions
2 eggs, beaten
$1\frac{1}{2}$ cups flour
$2\frac{1}{2}$ teaspoons baking powder
$1\frac{1}{4}$ cups dry white wine
$1\frac{1}{2}$ cups sour cream (scalded)
$\frac{1}{3}$ cup milk
2 tablespoons water (hot)
$\frac{1}{3}$ cup butter
1 clove garlic, crushed
4 tablespoons chopped parsley
1 bay leaf
2 cloves
$\frac{1}{2}$ teaspoon marjoram
$\frac{1}{2}$ teaspoon saffron
$\frac{1}{4}$ teaspoon thyme
salt and pepper

Brown the chicken in the butter in a casserole. Then add the carrots, mushrooms, onions (one of which should be stuck with the cloves), the wine, garlic, parsley, bay leaf, marjoram, thyme, and salt and pepper to taste. Cover and bake in a 190°C/375°F oven for 1 hour. Then remove the casserole from the oven and put on low heat. Dissolve the saffron in the hot water, then add this to the chicken. Next add the sour cream and stir lightly.

Mix together the flour, baking powder, eggs, milk and 1 teaspoon salt until a smooth mixture is formed. Bring the contents of the casserole to the boil, then drop teaspoons of this mixture around the edge of the casserole. Cover and cook over low heat for 15 minutes.

Chicken Véronique (Chicken with Grapes)

FRANCE

SERVES FOUR TO SIX

1 large chicken, cut into serving pieces
½ cup mushrooms, sliced
1 onion, finely chopped
1 cup white grapes, peeled, pipped
4 tablespoons flour
1 teaspoon sugar
2 cups chicken stock
½ cup thick cream
2 tablespoons lemon juice
½ cup butter
1 clove garlic, crushed

Brown the chicken in half the butter in a large pan; then remove and keep warm. Put the remaining butter into the pan, add the onion and garlic, and cook over low heat for 5 minutes. Add the mushrooms and cook over moderate heat for 2 minutes. Mix in the flour and sugar. Then add the chicken stock and the lemon juice and bring to the boil, stirring constantly. Return the chicken to the pan, cover, and simmer until the chicken is tender (approximately 25 minutes). Stir in the cream, then add the grapes and continue cooking for a few minutes. Arrange the chicken pieces on a serving platter and pour the sauce over them.

Poulet aux Fruits de Mer (Chicken with Seafood) FRANCE

SERVES SIX
1 medium chicken, cut into small serving pieces
2 cups scallops
1 cup oysters
1 cup mussels
6 large prawns, uncooked, shelled
2 spring onions, chopped
2 egg yolks, beaten
1 tablespoon cornflour
1 cup dry white wine
1 cup thick cream
1 teaspoon lemon juice
2 tablespoons butter
bouquet garni
salt and pepper

Sauté the chicken pieces in the butter in a large pan (do not brown). Remove and keep warm. Now sauté the spring onions until they are transparent. Return the chicken pieces to the pan, add the wine, bouquet garni, and salt and pepper to taste. Cook over low heat until the chicken is tender (approximately 30 minutes).

When the chicken is tender, remove the bouquet garni and skim the juices in the pan. Blend the cornflour with a little water, then stir into the pan with the cream. Bring to the boil, then add the scallops, oysters, mussels and prawns. Reduce the heat and simmer for 10 minutes. Remove the pan from the heat. Blend together the egg yolks, lemon juice and a little of the hot sauce. Then stir this mixture into the sauce in the pan.

Chicken Provençale FRANCE

SERVES FOUR TO SIX
1 medium chicken, cut into serving pieces
6 tomatoes, peeled, seeded, chopped
1 cup black olives, stoned
1 teaspoon tomato paste
$\frac{1}{2}$ cup dry white wine
3 tablespoons butter
4 cloves garlic
1 tablespoon chopped mixed herbs
salt and pepper

Put the chicken pieces (skin side down) and the garlic cloves into the butter in a large pan. Cook over low heat until the chicken is half cooked (approximately 15 minutes). Turn the chicken over, remove the garlic, and pour in the white wine. Let the wine reduce slightly. Add the tomatoes, tomato paste, black olives, and salt and pepper to taste. Continue cooking until the chicken is tender and the sauce reduced (approximately 15 minutes). Arrange the chicken pieces on a serving platter, pour the sauce over them, and sprinkle the mixed herbs over the top.

Poussins Dijonnaise FRANCE

SERVES FOUR
2 small chickens (half-chicken per person)
grated rind and juice of $\frac{1}{2}$ orange
$\frac{1}{2}$ tablespoon flour
$\frac{3}{4}$ cup chicken stock
1 tablespoon thick cream
4 tablespoons butter
2 teaspoons Dijon mustard
salt and pepper

Melt 2 tablespoons of the butter in a casserole and then put in the chickens and $\frac{1}{4}$ cup of the chicken stock, and season with salt and pepper. Cover, and cook over low heat until the chickens are tender (approximately 20-30 minutes). Remove the chickens and keep warm. Mix the flour into the juices remaining in the casserole, then add the remaining stock and stir until boiling. Strain and keep warm.

Split the chickens and trim away the backbones. Sprinkle them with the orange juice and a little salt and pepper. Melt the remaining butter, pour it over the chickens, and then grill them until they are golden-brown and crisp.

Add the Dijon mustard and the orange rind to the sauce, then stir in the cream. Arrange the chickens on a serving dish and pour the sauce over them.

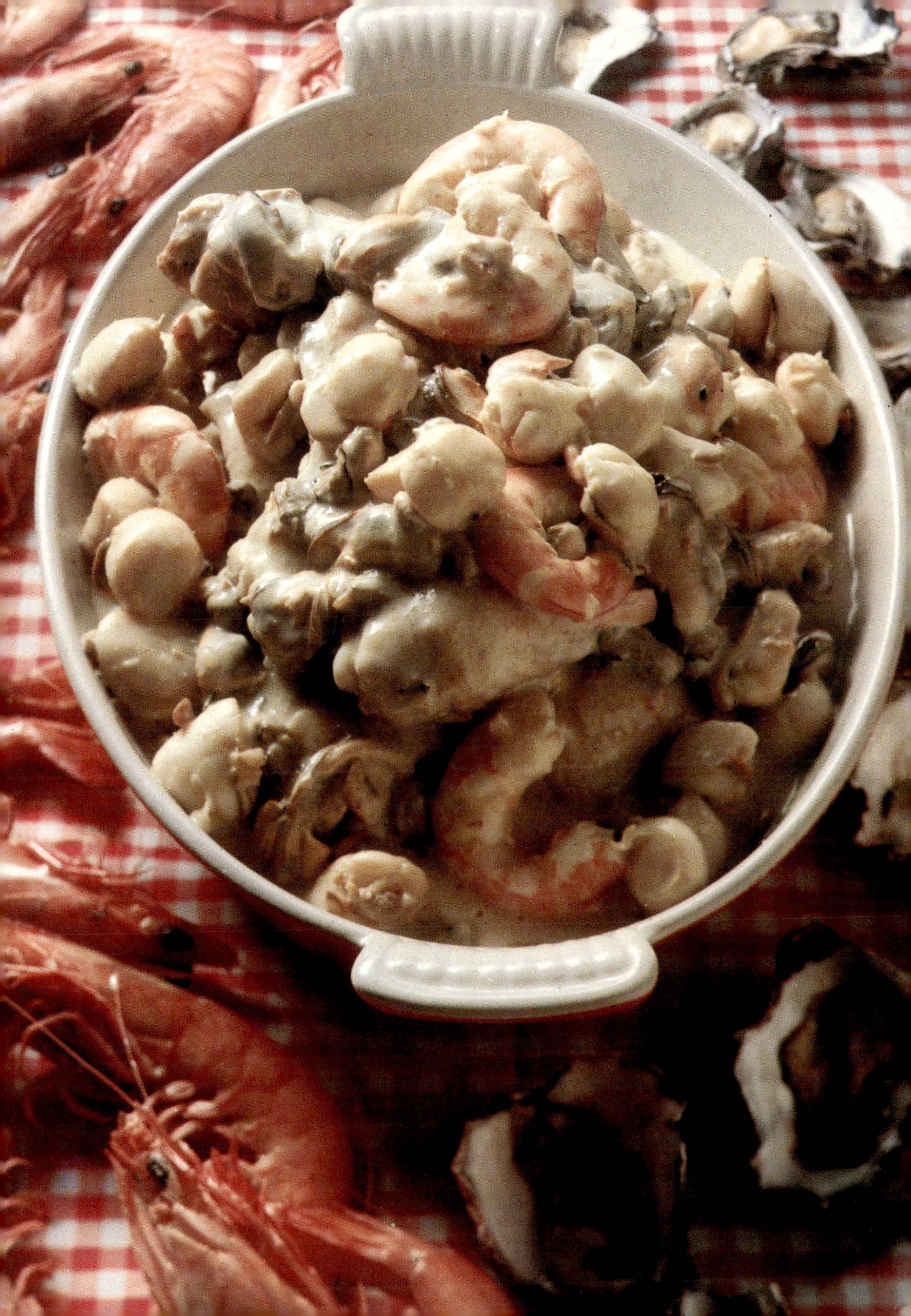

Coq au Vin

FRANCE

SERVES FOUR TO SIX
1 medium chicken, cut into serving pieces
125 g/¼ lb bacon, chopped
250 g/½ lb mushrooms
12 small onions
3 tablespoons flour
¾ bottle red wine
2 tablespoons olive oil
3 tablespoons butter
2 cloves garlic, finely chopped
1 tablespoon finely chopped parsley
2 bay leaves
2 teaspoons thyme
salt and black pepper

Sauté the bacon in a mixture of the olive oil and 2 tablespoons of the butter in a casserole. When the bacon becomes golden, add the onions and the mushrooms and cook over low heat until the onions become transparent. Remove the mixture from the casserole and keep warm.

Coat the chicken pieces with 2 tablespoons of the flour (seasoned with salt and black pepper) then brown them on all sides in the casserole. Return the bacon, onions and mushrooms to the casserole; add the garlic, parsley, bay leaves, thyme, and salt and black pepper to taste. Cover, and cook in the oven (180°C/350°F) until the chicken is tender (approximately 20 minutes). Then remove the chicken, bacon, onions and mushrooms and keep warm.

Skim the fat from the juices in the casserole, then put the casserole over high heat. Pour in the wine, bring to the boil, and continue cooking over high heat until the sauce has been reduced by half. Melt the remaining butter in a saucepan, remove from the heat and blend in 1 tablespoon flour until smooth. Stir this mixture into the casserole to thicken the sauce. Now strain the sauce and return it to the casserole. Also return the chicken pieces, bacon, onion and mushrooms. Cover and simmer in a low oven until heated through.

Note: This dish may be cooked in advance and heated through before serving.

Chicken and Chicken Liver Omelettes

FRANCE

SERVES ONE
3 eggs
1 tablespoon butter
salt and pepper
Chicken or Chicken Liver Filling

Heat the butter in an omelette pan until it is foaming. Meanwhile, beat the eggs lightly and add salt and pepper to taste. Pour the eggs into the omelette pan and cook quickly until the underside is golden, but the top is still very soft. Pour on the Chicken or Chicken Liver Filling. Fold over one side of the omelette, then fold over the other side. Turn out on to a serving plate; and serve.

Chicken Filling
½ cup diced chicken, cooked
1 mushroom, sliced
2 slices of tomato
½ tablespoon butter
1 tablespoon fines herbes

Sauté the mushroom in the butter, then add the chicken, tomato and fines herbes. Mix well, then pour over the omelette.

Chicken Liver Filling
1 chicken liver
1 mushroom, sliced
½ tablespoon butter
1 teaspoon fines herbes
garlic
salt

Sauté the mushroom in the butter, then add the chicken liver, fines herbes, and garlic and salt to taste. Mix well, then pour over the omelette.

Note: There are many varieties of Chicken or Chicken Liver Fillings for omelettes, e.g. with asparagus, artichokes, bacon, egg-plant, onions.

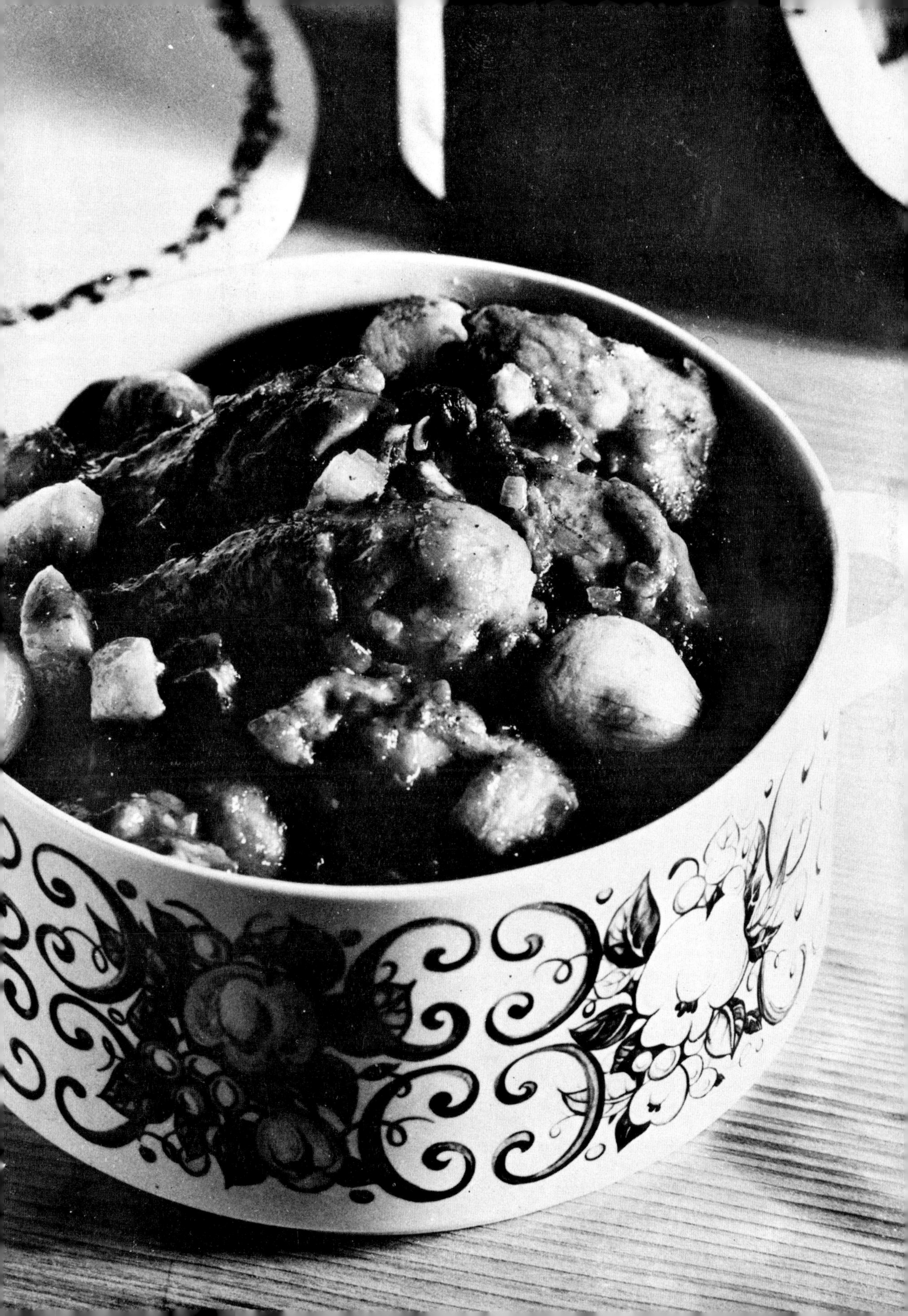

Poulet à l'Alsacienne

FRANCE

SERVES SIX
1 large chicken
5 chicken livers
185 g/6 oz pâté
90 g/3 oz ham
1 cup breadcrumbs (fried in butter)
2 teaspoons cornflour
1 cup Alsace white wine
¼ cup brandy
1 cup cream
1 tablespoon oil
salt and pepper

Finely chop the chicken livers, the ham and half the pâté. Then mix with the breadcrumbs, salt and pepper. Stuff the chicken with this mixture and close the opening with thread or skewers. Brown the stuffed chicken on all sides in the oil in a large pan. Then pour over half the Alsace wine, cover, and cook over low heat for 1¼ hours. Baste occasionally. Remove the chicken, place on a serving platter, and keep warm.

Skim the juices in the pan. Pour in the remaining ½ cup Alsace wine and cook over high heat until the liquids have reduced by half. Remove the pan from the heat and stir in the brandy, the remaining pâté, and the cornflour blended with the cream. Return to the heat and bring to the boil, stirring constantly. Cover the chicken completely with this sauce. Serve with buttered ribbon vermicelli sprinkled with crumbled vermicelli fried in butter.

Foies de Volaille au Riz (Chicken Livers with Rice)

FRANCE

SERVES FOUR

250 g/8 oz chicken livers, each cut into 2 or 3 pieces
90 g/3 oz cooked ham, chopped
1 cup long-grain rice
flour
3 tablespoons white wine or white vermouth or madeira
2¼ cups chicken stock
1 tablespoon butter
1 tablespoon chopped parsley
salt and pepper

Boil the rice in salted water for approximately 7 minutes; then drain and rinse under cold water. Put the rice into a pan and pour 2 cups of the chicken stock over it. Bring to the boil, then cover the pan and cook the rice in the oven (180°C/350°F) for 20 minutes.

Season the chicken livers and dust them with flour. Then sauté the chicken livers and the ham in the butter for a few minutes. Pour in the white wine and let it reduce slightly. Add the remaining stock and cook for another few minutes.

Put the rice on a serving platter, top with the chicken livers and ham, and sprinkle with the parsley. Serve as a first course.

Chicken with Red Wine and Mushrooms

FRANCE

SERVES FOUR TO SIX
1 medium chicken, cut into serving pieces
250 g/½ lb small mushrooms
5 spring onions, finely chopped
1 tablespoon flour
½ bottle red wine
1¼ cups chicken stock
3 tablespoons olive oil
1 tablespoon butter
bouquet garni
1 teaspoon thyme
1 teaspoon basil
black pepper

Mix together the mushrooms, spring onions, bouquet garni, thyme, basil, wine, 2 tablespoons olive oil, and black pepper to taste. Marinate the chicken pieces in this mixture for at least 1 hour, turning the pieces occasionally. Remove the chicken pieces, and keep aside the marinade.

Brush the chicken with the remaining 1 tablespoon olive oil, then cook it under the grill (skin side down) for 6 minutes. Turn the chicken over, brush with the olive oil again, and grill for another 6 minutes. Now remove the grilling rack and put the chicken pieces (skin side down) in the grilling pan (in which the cooking juices will have accumulated). Remove the bouquet garni, then pour the marinade over the chicken. Brush the chicken pieces once again with the olive oil, and grill for a further 5 minutes, basting occasionally. Turn the chicken over, reduce the heat, then cook, basting occasionally, for another 5 minutes. Remove the chicken and mushrooms, put them on to a serving platter, and keep warm.

Meanwhile, melt the butter in a saucepan, then remove it from the heat and blend in the flour. Stir in the chicken stock, blend well, then pour in the marinade. Return to the heat and bring quickly to the boil, stirring constantly. Pour this sauce over the chicken pieces; and serve.

Poulet à la Savoyarde (Chicken with Cheese Sauce)

FRANCE

SERVES FOUR
1 medium chicken
2 tablespoons grated gruyère cheese
2 tablespoons flour
breadcrumbs
4 tablespoons dry white wine
⅔ cup chicken stock
1¼ cups thick cream
2 tablespoons butter
butter (for roasting)
2 teaspoons French mustard
3 teaspoons tarragon
salt and pepper

Stuff the chicken with a knob of butter mixed with 2 teaspoons tarragon and a little salt and pepper. Put the chicken on its side in a baking tin and rub butter over the top. Cook for 20 minutes in the oven (200°C/400°F) and then turn the chicken over. Rub this side with butter then cook for a further 20 minutes. Turn the chicken over again and baste. Cook until the chicken is tender (approximately 20 minutes).

Meanwhile, melt the 2 tablespoons butter in a saucepan and stir in the flour until smooth. Mix in the chicken stock, then add the cream, a little at a time, and cook for 5 minutes. Add the mustard, the cheese, 1 teaspoon tarragon, and salt and pepper to taste. Cook over low heat, stirring occasionally, for 10 minutes.

When the chicken is cooked, carve it into serving pieces. Put a layer of the sauce on to a serving dish, put the chicken pieces on top, then pour the remaining sauce over. Sprinkle with breadcrumbs and pour over some of the butter from the chicken's baking tin. Put the dish under the grill for a few minutes until the top is golden.

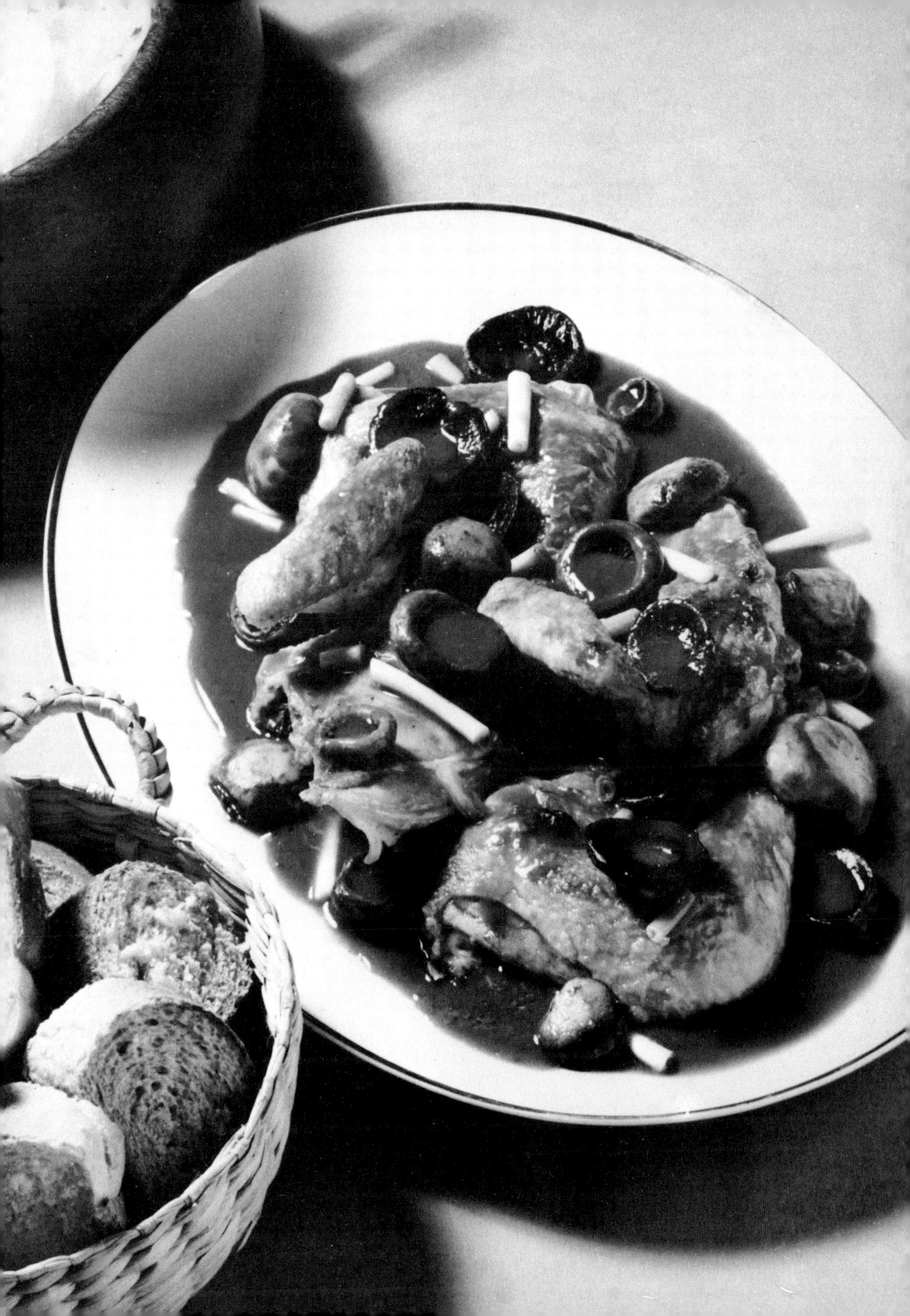

Poulet Sauté Vallée d'Auge (Chicken Calvados) — FRANCE

SERVES FOUR
1 medium chicken, cut into serving pieces
8 spring onions, finely chopped
1 stick celery, finely chopped
2 cooking apples, peeled, cored, chopped
2 egg yolks, beaten
½ cup Calvados
½ cup chicken stock
½ cup thick cream
2 tablespoons olive oil
3½ tablespoons butter
2 teaspoons thyme

Brown the chicken pieces in a mixture of the oil and 2 tablespoons of the butter in a large pan. Then remove from the heat. Warm the Calvados in a small pan, then light it with a match and pour it, still flaming, over the chicken. Now pour the chicken stock over the chicken. In a separate pan, melt the remaining 1½ tablespoons butter. In this cook the apples, spring onions, celery, and thyme until they are soft (approximately 10 minutes). Put these over the chicken pieces, return to high heat and bring the stock to the boil. Reduce the heat, cover, and simmer, basting occasionally, until the chicken is tender (approximately 30 minutes). Remove the chicken pieces, put them on to a serving platter, and keep warm.

Strain the juices from the chicken pan through a sieve into a saucepan, pressing down on the apples and vegetables to extract as much of their juice as possible. Skim off the surface fat, then boil over high heat, stirring, until the sauce has been reduced to ½ cup. Beat together the egg yolks and cream in a bowl, then add the sauce, a little at a time. Put this mixture back into the saucepan and cook over low heat for a few minutes, stirring constantly, until the sauce thickens. Do not boil. Pour this sauce over the chicken pieces; and serve.

Poulet Rôti au Beurre (French Roast Chicken) — FRANCE

SERVES FOUR
1 medium chicken
1 carrot, chopped
1 stick celery, chopped
1 onion, sliced
½ teaspoon lemon juice
6 tablespoons butter
½ teaspoon tarragon
salt and black pepper

Cream 2 tablespoons of the butter, then beat it until it becomes fluffy. Mix in the lemon juice, the tarragon, and a little salt and black pepper. Spread this seasoned butter inside the chicken, then close the opening with thread or skewers. Melt the remaining 4 tablespoons butter, then brush half of this over the chicken. Put the chicken on its side in a roasting pan and roast it in the oven (230°C/450°F) for 10 minutes. Then turn the chicken on its other side, brush again with the butter, and roast for another 10 minutes. Now reduce the oven temperature to 180°C/350°F. Put the chicken on to its back and brush with the remaining melted butter. Put the carrot, celery and onion into the roasting pan. Roast, basting occasionally, until the chicken is tender (1 hour altogether). Remove the chicken and put it on a carving board. Strain the juices and serve them separately.

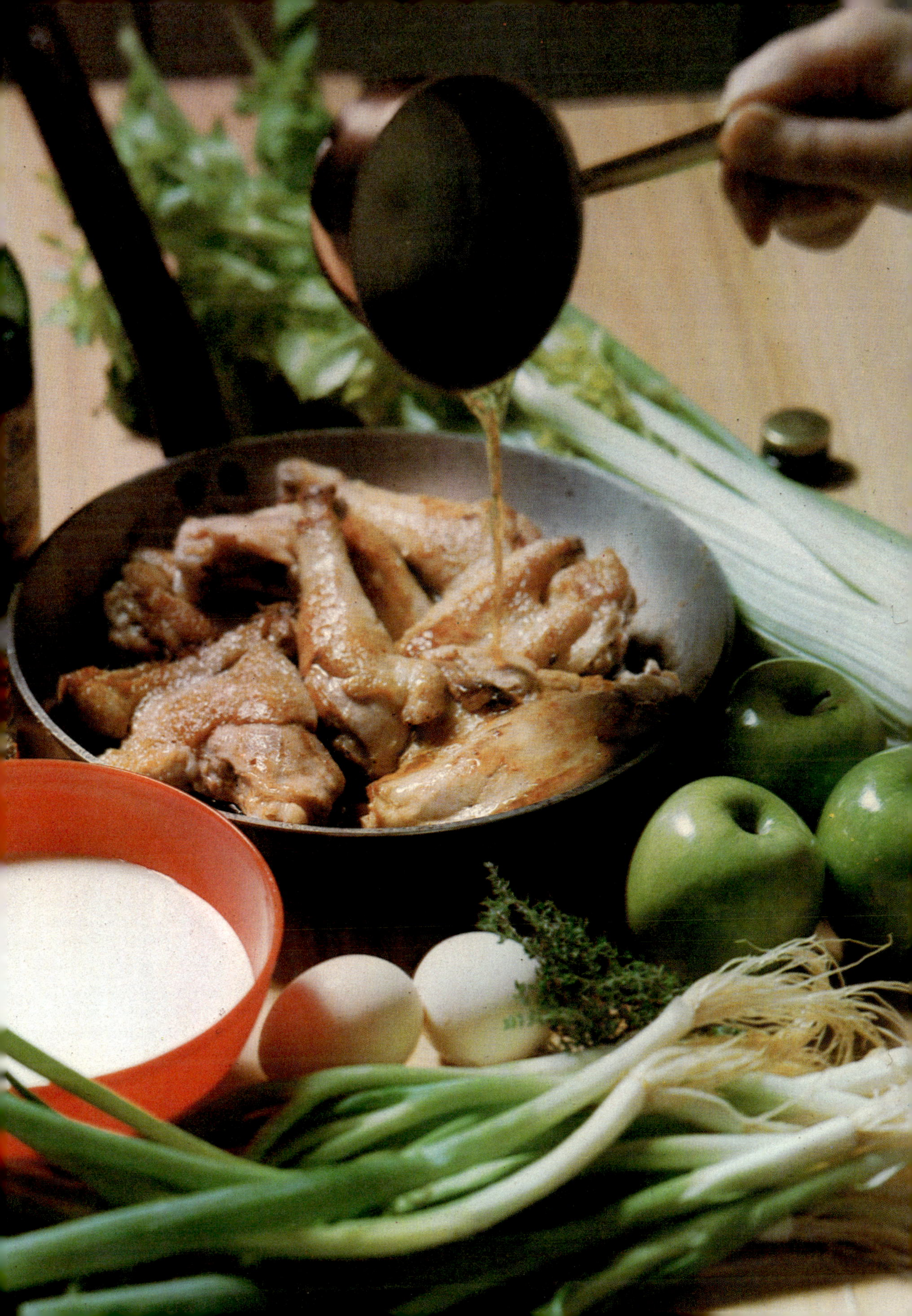

Poulet au Sel (Chicken in Salt) — FRANCE

SERVES FOUR
1 medium chicken
6 kg/12 lb coarse salt

Thickly cover the bottom of a large aluminium stew-pan with coarse salt. Truss the chicken, then place it (breast down) on the salt in the pan. Now fill the pan with the remaining salt, ensuring that the chicken is thickly covered. Cook over high heat, uncovered, for 1½ hours.

Turn the pan upside-down and remove the salt, which will have formed into a solid mass (you may need a hammer to break it open). The chicken should be cooked to perfection, golden-brown all over, and not at all salty.

Chicken Mille Feuilles — FRANCE

1 small chicken, cooked, meat finely minced
250 g/8 oz puff pastry
2 tablespoons thick cream, lightly whipped
2 tablespoons butter, creamed
salt and pepper
mushrooms (for garnish)
½ cup semi-liquid aspic jelly (for garnish)
Béchamel Sauce
Mayonnaise Collée

Roll out the pastry thinly and cut it into 3 strips approximately 10 cm/4″ wide and 25 cm/10″ long. Prick the pastry and put it on to a baking sheet which has been moistened with water. Bake in a 220°C/425°F oven until the pastry is golden-brown (approximately 20 minutes). Lift the pastry strips off the baking sheet and leave them to cool.

Mix the creamed butter into the minced chicken, adding a little at a time. Then add the Béchamel Sauce, season with salt and pepper to taste, and fold in the cream.

Trim the pastry strips. Spread half the chicken mixture on to one strip of pastry. Place a second strip on top and spread on this the other half of the chicken mixture. Top with the third pastry strip. Coat the top with the Mayonnaise Collée and decorate with the mushrooms. Coat with the semi-liquid aspic jelly and leave to set.

Place the mille feuilles on a serving platter and cut into slices to serve.

Béchamel Sauce
1 cup milk
1 tablespoon cream
2 tablespoons flour
2 tablespoons butter
1 slice of onion
1 bay leaf
1 blade of mace
6 peppercorns
salt and pepper

Warm the milk with the onion, bay leaf, mace and peppercorns in a covered pan over low heat for 5 minutes. Strain the milk and keep aside. Wipe out the pan, then melt the butter in it. Remove from the heat and mix in the flour until smooth. Gradually blend in the milk. Season with salt and pepper, then return to the heat and stir until boiling. Boil for 2 minutes only, then remove from the heat and stir in the cream.

Mayonnaise Collée
½ tablespoon gelatine
½ cup aspic jelly
1¼ cups mayonnaise

Dissolve the gelatine in the aspic jelly (do not boil). Whisk this mixture into the mayonnaise.

Suprêmes de Volaille Amandine (Chicken with Almonds)   FRANCE

SERVES SIX
6 chicken breasts, boned
1 onion, finely chopped
½ cup slivered almonds
1 tablespoon flour
1 teaspoon tomato paste
1¼ cups chicken stock
7 tablespoons butter
½ teaspoon dried tarragon

Brown the chicken breasts on all sides in 6 tablespoons of the butter in a large pan (approximately 25 minutes). Remove the chicken and keep warm. Now add the onion, almonds and the remaining butter to the pan, and cook over low heat until the almonds are brown. Blend in the tomato paste and the flour. Then gradually add the chicken stock, stirring constantly, until the mixture thickens and comes to the boil. Return the chicken breasts to the pan, and add the tarragon. Cover, and simmer for 20 minutes. Arrange the chicken breasts on a serving platter, and pour the sauce with the almonds over them.

Bouchées à la Reine

FRANCE

SERVES SIX

2 chicken breasts
1 veal sweetbread
125 g/4 oz mushrooms, sliced
1 carrot, halved
1 onion, halved
3 egg yolks, beaten
6 vol-au-vent cases
4 tablespoons flour
½ cup thick cream
juice of 1 lemon
6 cups water
3 tablespoons butter
bouquet garni
pinch of nutmeg
salt and pepper

Put the water, onion, carrot, bouquet garni, and a little salt and pepper into a pan. Bring to the boil and cook until the carrot is tender, then remove the bouquet garni. Add the chicken breasts and cook until they are tender (approximately 20 minutes). Remove the chicken from the pan, take off the skin and cut the meat away from the bones. Cut the chicken meat into small pieces and keep aside. Strain the stock and keep aside.

Melt the butter in a saucepan, remove from the heat and blend in the flour until smooth. Stir in 3 cups of the stock, return to the heat, and bring to the boil. Now add the chicken pieces, the chopped sweetbread, mushrooms, lemon juice and nutmeg. Reduce the heat, add the remaining stock, skim, then cook until the sauce has reduced and thickened. Remove the pan from the heat. Blend together the egg yolks and the cream, then stir into the chicken mixture in the pan. Return to the heat and cook gently for a few minutes.

Heat the vol-au-vent cases, fill them with the chicken mixture, and serve.

Poulet à l'Estragon (Chicken with Tarragon)

FRANCE

SERVES FOUR TO SIX

1 medium chicken, cut into serving pieces
4 tablespoons finely chopped spring onions
½ cup dry white wine
¾ cup water
4 tablespoons olive oil
4 tablespoons butter
2 tablespoons finely chopped tarragon
1 tablespoon finely chopped parsley
salt and black pepper

Brown the chicken pieces in the olive oil in a large pan. Then drain off any surplus oil, add the spring onions, stir well, and cook until the spring onions are transparent. Add the white wine, the water, and salt and black pepper to taste. Cover, and cook until the chicken is tender and the sauce has reduced to half the original amount (approximately 20 minutes). Remove the chicken pieces and put on to a serving dish.

Add the butter and the tarragon to the juices in the pan, stir well, and correct the seasoning. Pour the sauce over the chicken pieces, and sprinkle the parsley over the top.

Poulet Sauté à la Crème (Chicken in Cream Sauce)

FRANCE

SERVES FOUR TO SIX

1 medium chicken, cut into serving pieces
1 cup mushrooms, sliced
3 tablespoons dry white wine
¾ cup thick cream
2 tablespoons olive oil
3 tablespoons butter
1 tablespoon chopped parsley
salt and black pepper

Brown the chicken in a mixture of the oil and 2 tablespoons of the butter in a large pan. Then cover and cook over low heat, basting occasionally, until the chicken is tender (approximately 30 minutes). Remove the chicken pieces, put them on to a serving dish, and keep warm.

Pour off all but 1 tablespoon of the oil from the pan, put in the mushrooms, and sauté for 2 minutes. Then pour in the wine and cook over high heat until it has reduced to half the original amount. Stir in the cream and cook for a few minutes until it has thickened slightly. Season with salt and black pepper to taste. Remove from the heat and stir in the remaining butter and the parsley. Pour this sauce over the chicken pieces, and serve.

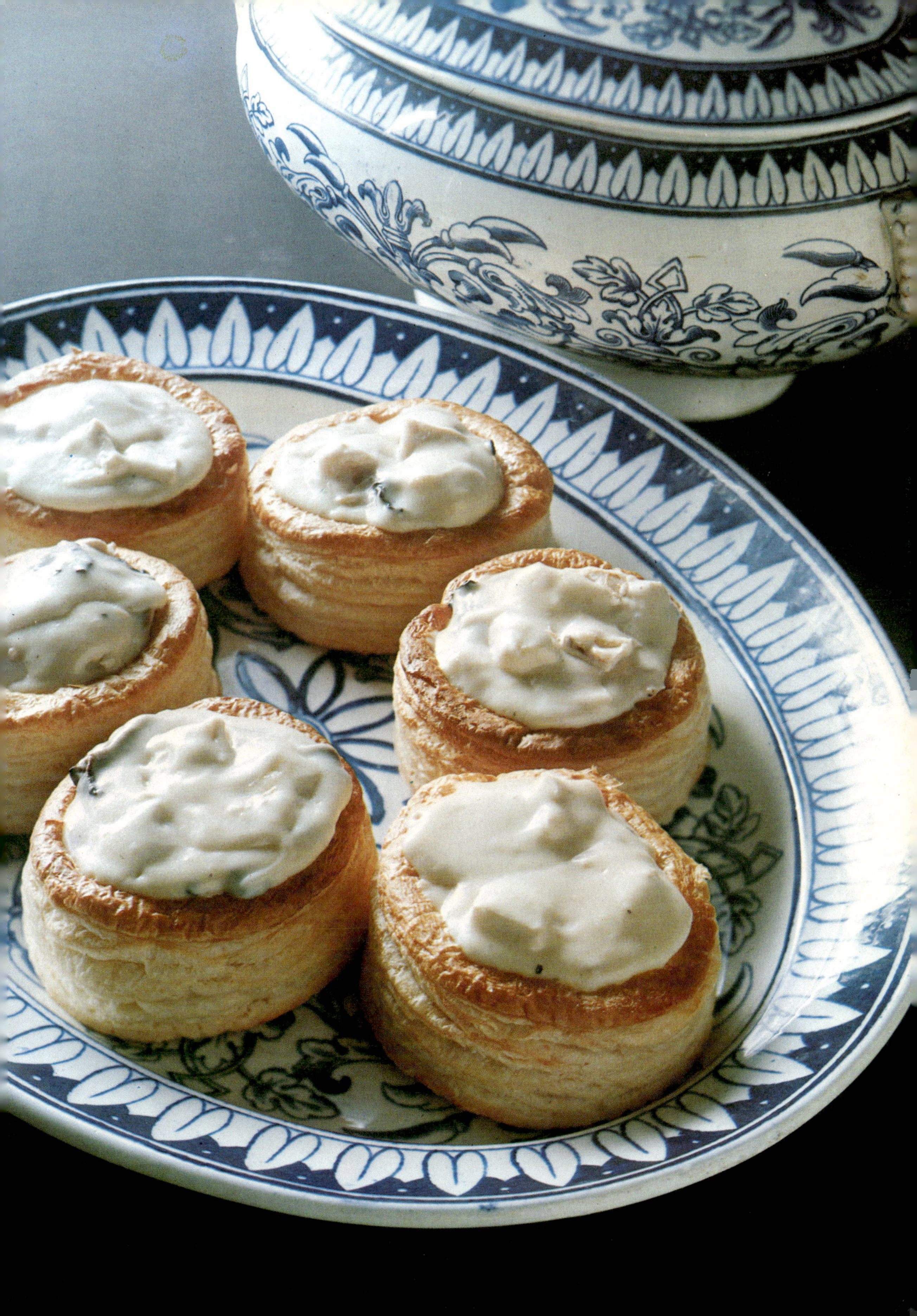

Poulet en Pie (Chicken Pie)   FRANCE

SERVES SIX
1 small chicken
4 chipolata sausages, halved
2 rashers of bacon, chopped
250 g/8 oz mushrooms, chopped
2 tomatoes, peeled, seeded, chopped
2 onions, chopped
2 spring onions, chopped
3 eggs, hard-boiled, halved length-wise
1 egg, beaten
1 egg white, beaten
250 g/8 oz puff pastry
2 tablespoons flour
1 cup chicken stock
2 tablespoons butter
1 tablespoon chopped parsley
1 sprig thyme, chopped
salt and pepper

Cut the chicken meat away from the bones, and then coat the chicken pieces with the flour. Make a layer of half the chicken pieces in the bottom of a pie dish. On this layer put half of the sausages, bacon, mushrooms, tomatoes, spring onions, onions, hard-boiled eggs, parsley and thyme. Sprinkle over a little salt and pepper. Now make a layer of the rest of the chicken and then add the remaining half of the other ingredients. Sprinkle a little salt and pepper over the mixture, and pour over the chicken stock (it should reach the same level as the chicken mixture). Dot the butter over the top.

Roll out the pastry and cut a strip sufficient to fit right around the rim of the dish. Moisten the strip with egg white, stick it down around the rim, and leave to dry. Cut out a piece of pastry to the shape of the dish but slightly larger all around. Moisten the pastry strip with the remaining egg white and apply the pastry pie top, sticking it down to the strip. Trim the pastry around the edge of the dish, then glaze the top with the beaten egg. Prick a few openings in the pastry top with the point of a knife. Cook in a hot oven (200°C/400°F) for 1½ hours.

Poulet au Champagne (Chicken in Champagne)   FRANCE

SERVES FOUR
1 medium chicken, cut into serving pieces
1 onion, finely chopped
3 egg yolks, beaten
1 tablespoon flour
½ bottle champagne
1½ cups thick cream
4 tablespoons butter
salt and black pepper

Put the chicken pieces, onion, and salt and black pepper to taste into the butter in a large pan. Cover and cook over low heat for 10 minutes. Sift the flour over the chicken pieces on both sides, turning and coating them well with the butter. Then pour over the champagne. Cover and simmer until the chicken is tender (approximately 25 minutes). Remove the chicken pieces, put them on to a serving platter, and keep warm.

Reduce the pan juices over high heat. Add 1¼ cups of the cream and cook, stirring occasionally, until the sauce is reduced by half. Beat together the egg yolks and the remaining ¼ cup cream, blend into them a little of the hot sauce, and then add this mixture to the sauce in the pan. Simmer over low heat until the sauce is thick and smooth. Do not boil. Pour the sauce over the chicken, and serve.

Poulet en Pie

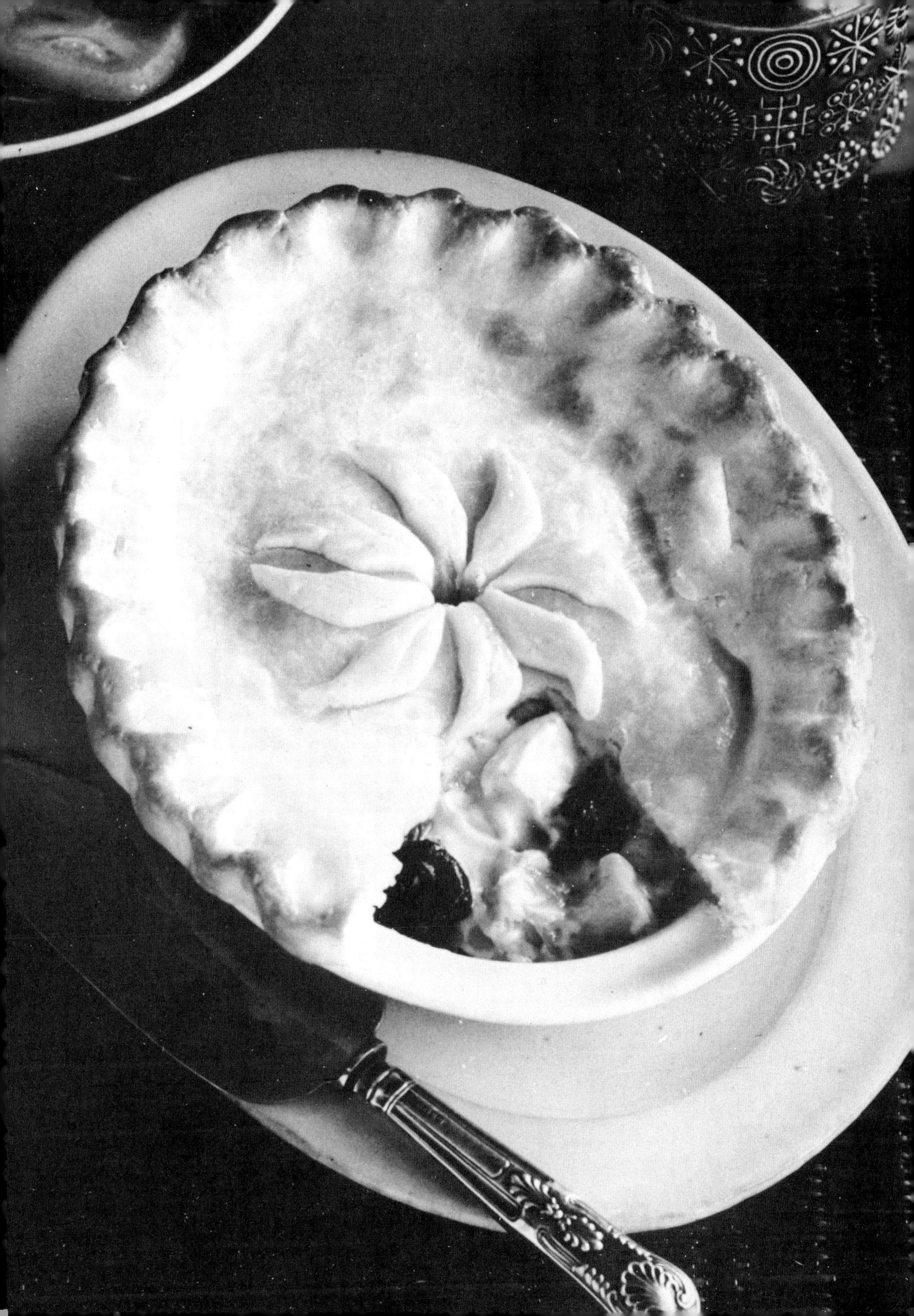

Mayonnaise de Volaille (Chicken Mayonnaise)

FRANCE

SERVES FOUR
1 medium chicken, cooked, and meat diced
1 cucumber, diced
1 red pepper, cut into strips
½ cup green olives, stoned
2 tablespoons finely chopped parsley
Mayonnaise

Mix the chicken meat with half the Mayonnaise, then put the mixture on to a serving platter, leaving a space all around. Cover the chicken mixture with the other half of the Mayonnaise. Arrange the cucumber, olives and red pepper around the edges. Sprinkle the parsley over the whole dish.

Mayonnaise
3 egg yolks
juice of ½ lemon
1¼ cups olive oil
½ teaspoon salt

Whisk the egg yolks in a bowl, then add the salt. Add the olive oil drop by drop at first, and stir in with a wooden spoon. As the olive oil begins to blend well with the yolks, more oil can be added at a time. Also add the lemon juice a little at a time.

Saueres Hühnchen (Sour Chicken)

GERMANY

SERVES FOUR

1 medium chicken, cut into serving pieces
1 onion, sliced
$\frac{2}{3}$ cup sour cream
$\frac{2}{3}$ cup vinegar
$\frac{2}{3}$ cup water
1 bay leaf
3 cloves
$\frac{1}{4}$ teaspoon nutmeg

Put the chicken pieces into a large pan and cover with the water and the vinegar. Add the onion, bay leaf, cloves and nutmeg. Cover and cook over low heat until the chicken is tender (approximately 30 minutes). Then stir in the sour cream and cook until it has blended in well and a creamy liquid is formed (approximately 10 minutes).

Backhahndel nach Süddeutscher Art (German Fried Chicken)   GERMANY

SERVES FOUR
1 medium chicken, cut into serving pieces
125 g/¼ lb mushrooms, finely chopped
3 egg yolks, beaten
3 tablespoons grated parmesan cheese
3 tablespoons breadcrumbs
1 tablespoon flour
4 tablespoons dry white wine
squeeze of lemon juice
dash of vinegar
3 tablespoons butter
salt and pepper
Béchamel Sauce

Béchamel Sauce
1 cup milk
1 tablespoon cream
2 tablespoons flour
2 tablespoons butter
1 slice of onion
1 bay leaf
1 blade of mace
6 peppercorns
salt and pepper

Dust the chicken pieces with the flour seasoned with salt and pepper. Then dip them into 1 of the beaten egg yolks and coat them with a mixture of the parmesan cheese and the breadcrumbs. Fry the chicken pieces in 2 tablespoons butter over moderate heat until the chicken is tender and the coating is golden (approximately 25 minutes).

Meanwhile, fry the mushrooms in 1 tablespoon of the butter, with the lemon juice and the vinegar. Mix in the Béchamel Sauce and then the white wine. Remove from the heat, blend in the remaining 2 beaten egg yolks and season with salt and pepper. Serve this sauce with the fried chicken pieces.

Warm the milk with the onion, bay leaf, mace and peppercorns in a covered pan over low heat for 5 minutes. Strain the milk and keep aside. Wipe out the pan, then melt the butter in it. Remove from the heat and mix in the flour until smooth. Gradually blend in the milk. Season with salt and pepper, then return to the heat and stir until boiling. Boil for 2 minutes only, then remove from the heat and stir in the cream.

Roast Chicken with Bread Sauce   GREAT BRITAIN

SERVES FOUR
1 medium chicken
4 rashers of bacon, rolled up
1¼ cups chicken stock
1 tablespoon butter
1 teaspoon mixed herbs
salt and pepper
Bread Sauce

Bread Sauce
1 onion
4 slices bread, crusts removed, crumbled
2 tablespoons cream
1¼ cups milk
1 tablespoon butter
2 cloves
pinch ground nutmeg
salt and pepper

Truss the chicken, rub the outside with butter, then season inside and out with the mixed herbs, salt and pepper. Put the chicken and the bacon into a roasting pan and cook in the oven (200°C/400°F) until the chicken is tender (approximately 1½ hours). When cooked, remove the chicken to a serving platter and keep it warm. Skim the excess fat from the juices in the roasting pan, then add the chicken stock and bring to the boil. Serve this gravy separately. Also serve the Bread Sauce.

Put the milk, with the onion (stuck with the cloves) and the nutmeg into a saucepan. Cover, and cook over very low heat for 5 minutes; then leave to cool. Now add the crumbled bread to the milk. Return to the heat, bring to the boil, then reduce the heat to very low and cook for 15 minutes. Remove the onion, then stir in the cream, the butter, and salt and pepper to taste. Heat through, but do not boil.

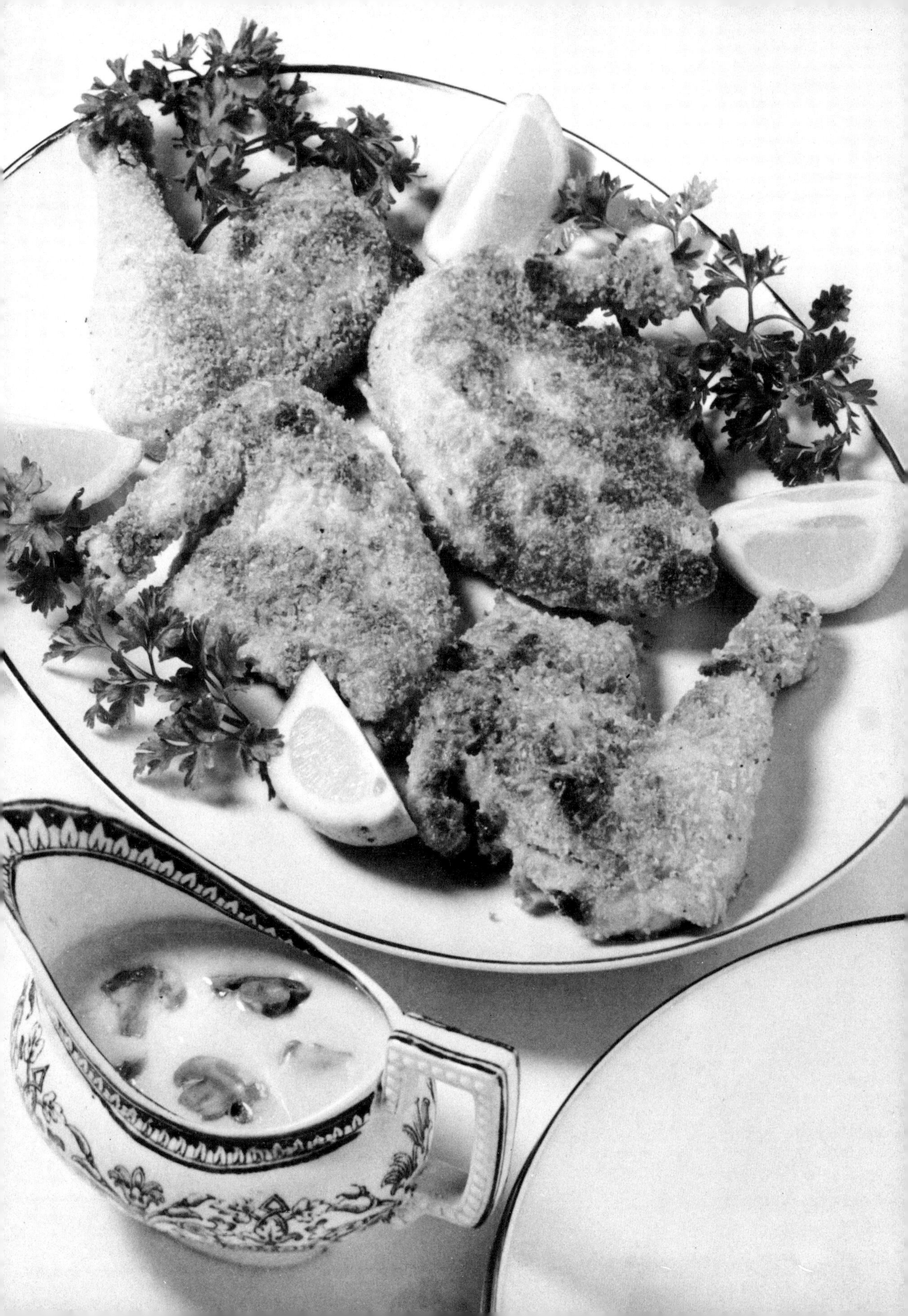

Whisky Chicken

GREAT BRITAIN

SERVES FOUR
1 medium chicken, cut into serving pieces
185 g/6 oz mushrooms, quartered
1 spring onion, chopped
2 teaspoons cornflour
1 cup Scotch whisky
½ cup thick cream
juice of 1 lemon
4 tablespoons butter
salt and pepper

Brown the chicken pieces in 2 tablespoons of the butter in a large pan. Add the whisky, then remove the pan from the heat and leave the chicken to marinate for at least 10 minutes, turning the pieces occasionally.

Meanwhile, squeeze half the lemon juice over the mushrooms and sauté them, together with the spring onion, in the remaining 2 tablespoons butter. Then add to the chicken pan. Also add half the cream, and salt and pepper to taste. Cover and cook over moderate heat until the chicken is tender (approximately 30 minutes). Remove the chicken pieces, place them on a serving platter, and keep warm.

Bring the sauce in the pan to the boil. Then add the cornflour, blended with the remaining cream, and remove the pan from the heat. Stir the sauce until it thickens, then stir in the remaining lemon juice. Pour the sauce over the chicken pieces; then serve.

Potted Chicken

GREAT BRITAIN

SERVES FOUR
1 small chicken, cooked, the meat chopped
2 slices ham, chopped
½ cup butter
clarified butter (melted)
1 teaspoon ground mace
½ teaspoon ground nutmeg
¼ teaspoon cayenne pepper
salt

Put the chopped chicken meat and ham, the butter, mace, nutmeg, cayenne and salt to taste into the blender. Blend until a smooth paste is formed. Put the mixture into a pot or pots and pour a ½ cm/¼"-layer of melted clarified butter over the top of it. Cool, then leave to firm in the refrigerator. Serve as a first course.

Potted Chicken

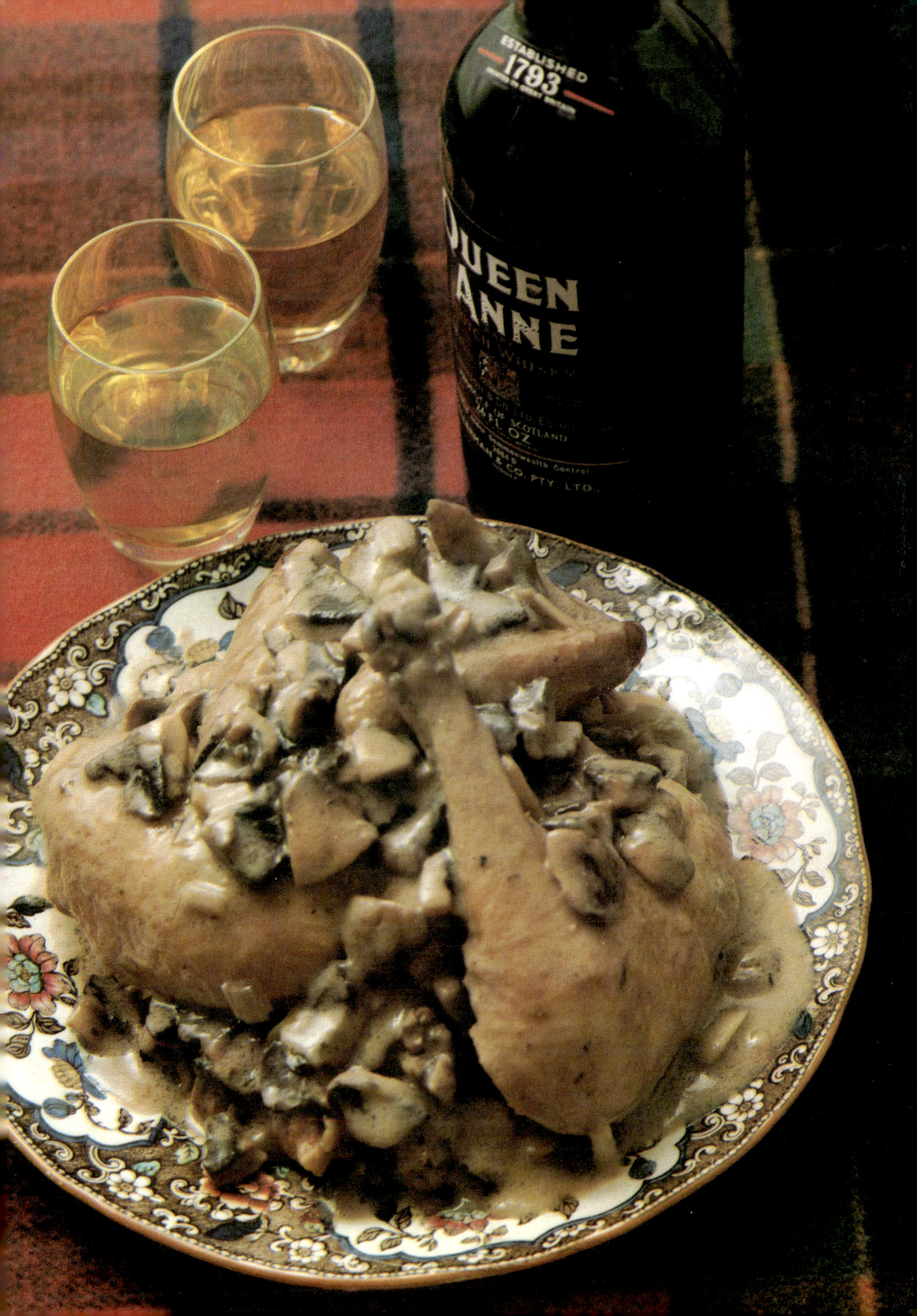
ESTABLISHED
1793
PTY. LTD.

Royal Hash

GREAT BRITAIN

SERVES FOUR TO SIX
1 large chicken, cooked, the meat diced
500 g/1 lb mushrooms
½ cup gruyère cheese, grated
½ cup parmesan cheese, grated
1 tablespoon flour
2 tablespoons sherry
1 cup cream
1 cup milk (hot)
4 tablespoons butter
salt and pepper

Melt 1 tablespoon of the butter in a saucepan, remove from the heat and stir in the flour until smooth. Then blend in the hot milk, return to the heat, and stir until boiling. Remove from the heat, cool slightly, and blend in the cream, sherry, and salt and pepper to taste.

Sauté the mushrooms in 2 tablespoons of the butter, then chop them finely. Mix the diced chicken and the mushrooms together, then pour the prepared sauce over them and stir well. Put this chicken mixture into a baking dish and heat through in the oven. Sprinkle with the gruyère and parmesan cheese and dot with the remaining tablespoon of butter. Put under the grill until the cheese becomes golden.

Ragout of Chicken

GREAT BRITAIN

SERVES FOUR
1 medium chicken, cooked, cut into small serving pieces
2 slices of ham, diced
2 spring onions
1 onion
2 teaspoons flour
½ teaspoon castor sugar
2½ cups chicken stock
1 tablespoon lemon juice
1 tablespoon butter
bouquet garni
2 blades of mace
salt and pepper

Put the chicken trimmings, the ham, spring onions, onion, mace and chicken stock into a pan. Bring to the boil, and simmer for 1 hour. Strain the stock and keep aside. Melt the butter in a pan, remove from the heat, and blend in the flour. Add the strained stock, blend in well, then return to the heat and bring to the boil. Boil for a few minutes, and strain again. Put the stock back into the pan, then add the chicken pieces, lemon juice, sugar, and salt and pepper to taste. Heat the chicken through, remove the pieces and put them on to a serving dish. Pour the sauce over the chicken pieces; garnish with croutons.

Ragout of Chicken

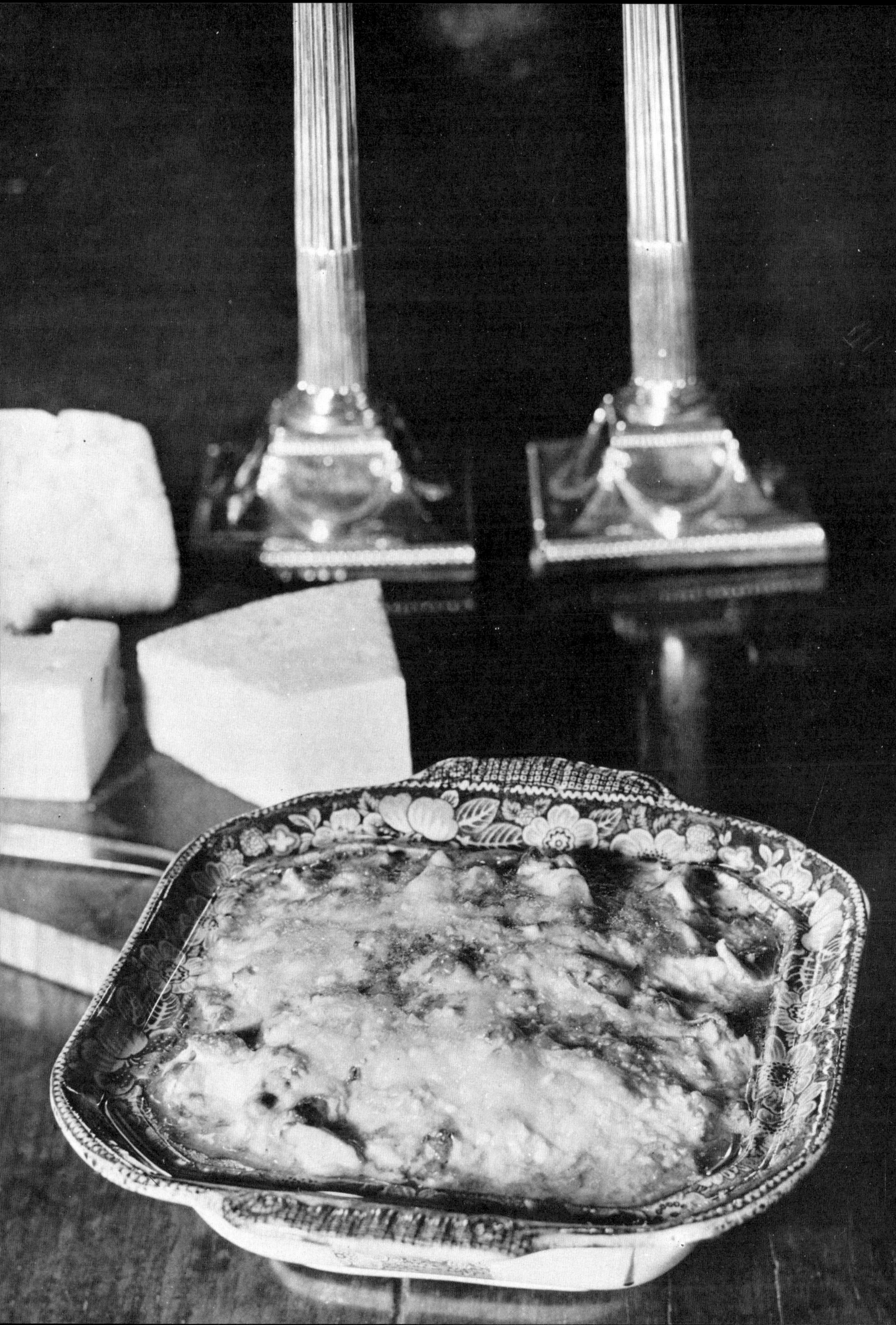

Cock-a-Leekie

GREAT BRITAIN

SERVES SIX TO EIGHT
1 large chicken
10 leeks, sliced
500 g/1 lb prunes, soaked overnight, stoned
½ cup pearl barley, soaked
2 tablespoons chopped parsley
salt and pepper

Put the chicken (breast down) into a large pan and cover it with water. Bring to the boil, then skim. Add the pearl barley and half the leeks, then cover the pan and simmer until the chicken is almost cooked (approximately 1 hour). Add the prunes, the remaining leeks, and salt and pepper to taste, and continue cooking over low heat for a further 30 minutes. Then stir in the parsley. Carve the chicken and put it into individual serving bowls, then pour over the soup (with the leeks and prunes).

Steamed Chicken with Oysters

GREAT BRITAIN

SERVES FOUR
1 medium chicken
3 dozen oysters
2 egg yolks, beaten
⅔ cup cream
1 teaspoon ground mace

Stuff the chicken with the oysters (keep a few aside) and close the opening with thread or skewers. Put the stuffed chicken in the centre of a large piece of aluminium foil, then bring the corners of the foil up over the chicken and fold the edges together to seal it in. Place this 'parcel' in a large pan, preferably slightly lifted away from the bottom (e.g. on a cake-stand). Then add water to the pan sufficient to come half-way up the chicken 'parcel'. Bring to the boil, cover the pan, and simmer until the chicken is tender (approximately 1½ hours).

Remove the chicken 'parcel' from the pan and open it. Take out the chicken, place it on a serving platter, and keep warm. Cooking juices from the chicken and the oysters will have accumulated inside the foil. Put these juices into a pan and stir in the cream, egg yolks, mace, and the remaining oysters. Cook gently for a few minutes, then pour some of this sauce over the chicken and serve the rest separately.

Steamed Chicken with Oysters

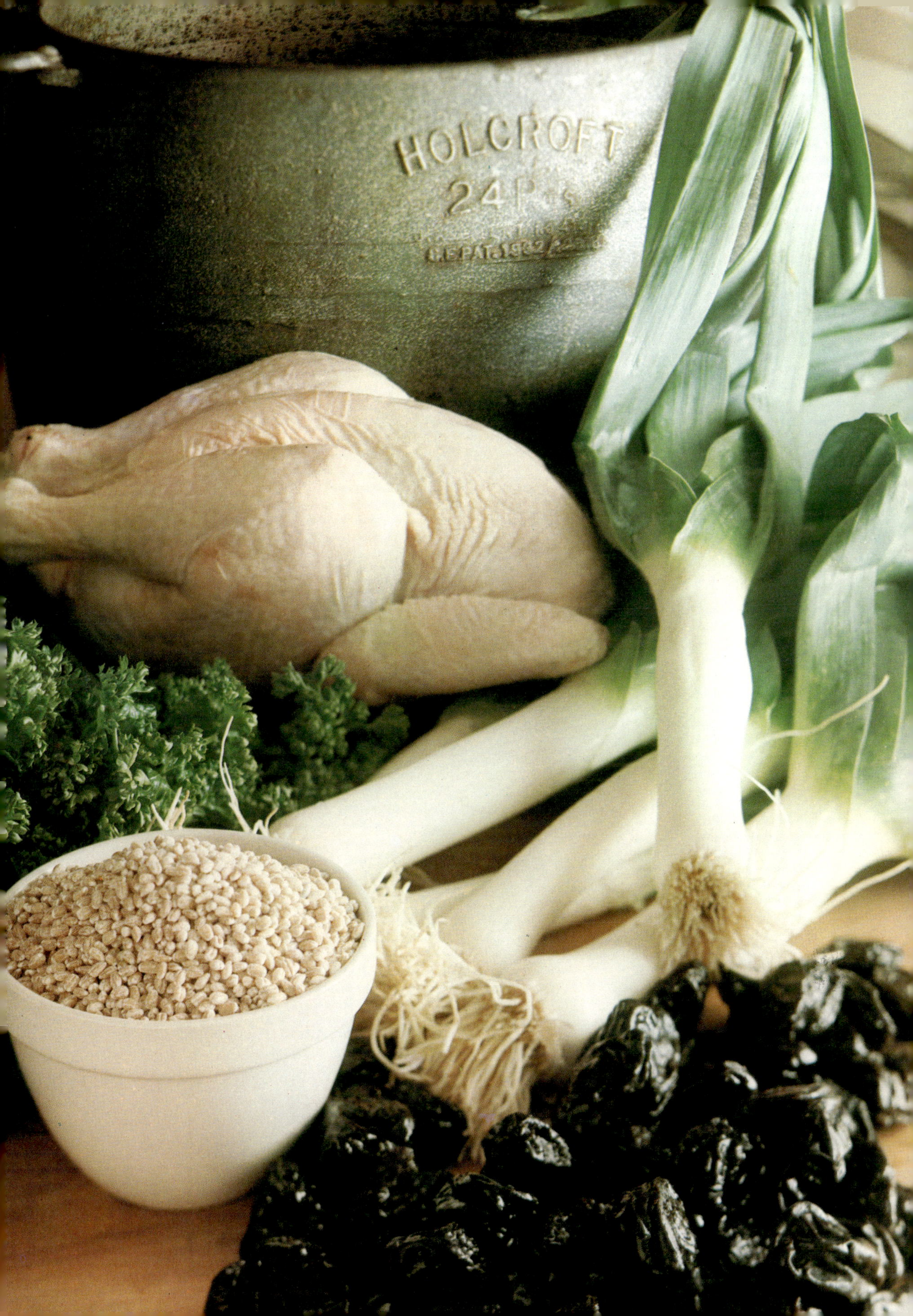
HOLCROFT

Kota Kapama (Chicken with Tomato and Cinnamon Sauce) — GREECE

SERVES FOUR
1 medium chicken, cut into serving pieces
6 tomatoes, peeled, seeded, chopped
3 onions, finely chopped
2 tablespoons grated kefalotiri or parmesan cheese
1½ tablespoons tomato paste
6 tablespoons chicken stock
3 tablespoons olive oil
2½ teaspoons finely chopped garlic
10 cm/4" stick of cinnamon
½ teaspoon salt
¼ teaspoon black pepper

Brown the chicken in the oil in a large pan; remove and keep warm. Pour off all but 1 tablespoon of the oil from the pan, add the onions and garlic to the pan and sauté until the onions are golden (approximately 8 minutes). Add the tomatoes, tomato paste, chicken stock, cinnamon, salt and pepper; stir well, then bring to the boil. Return the chicken to the pan and mix with the sauce. Cover and cook over low heat, basting occasionally, until the chicken is tender (approximately 30 minutes). Put the chicken pieces on to a serving platter, remove the cinnamon stick, and pour the sauce over them. Sprinkle the grated cheese over the top.

Kotopolo alla Greca — GREECE

SERVES FOUR
4 chicken breasts, boned
4 slices of ham
4 slices of feta cheese
1 egg, beaten
2 tablespoons flour
breadcrumbs
2 tablespoons tomato paste
½ cup dry white wine
3 tablespoons olive oil

Coat the chicken breasts with the flour, then tap off any excess. Beat the eggs with 1 tablespoon of the olive oil, then dip the chicken breasts into this mixture. Now coat them with breadcrumbs. Heat the remaining 2 tablespoons oil in a large pan and fry the chicken gently until it is tender and golden-brown (approximately 20 minutes). Remove the chicken breasts, place on each a slice of ham topped with a slice of feta cheese. Place under a hot grill until the cheese has melted (approximately 5 minutes).

Meanwhile, pour off the oil from the pan, add the tomato paste and heat gently. Pour in the white wine and stir. Serve one chicken breast to each person, and pour over the tomato and wine sauce.

Kates Riganati (Oregano Chicken) — GREECE

SERVES FOUR TO SIX
1 large chicken
4 tomatoes, peeled, coarsely chopped
4 tablespoons lemon juice
½ cup olive oil
½ cup butter
2 teaspoons oregano
3 teaspoons salt
1 teaspoon pepper

Mix together the olive oil, lemon juice and 2 teaspoons of the salt, then rub this mixture into the chicken inside and out. Put the chicken in a roasting pan and roast in the oven (190°C/375°F) for 1 hour.

Melt the butter in a saucepan. Add the tomatoes, oregano, pepper and 1 teaspoon salt. Cook over moderate heat for 5 minutes, stirring occasionally. Pour this mixture over the chicken, reduce the heat to 180°C/350°F and continue roasting until the chicken is tender (approximately 1 hour). Baste frequently.

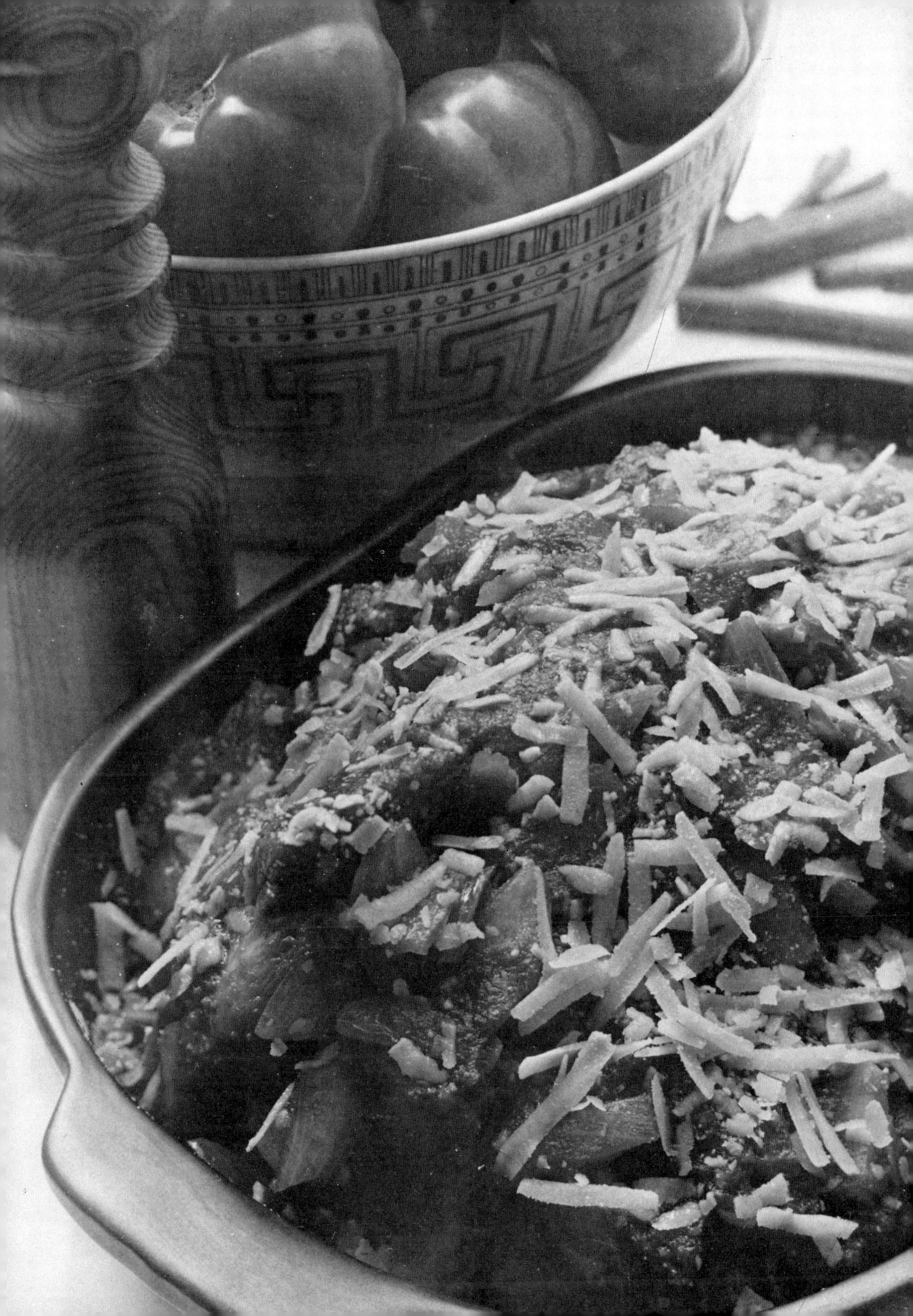

Soupa Avgolemono (Lemon Soup)

GREECE

SERVES SIX
500 g/1 lb chicken parts (necks, backs, feet)
1 carrot, coarsely chopped
1 stick celery, coarsely chopped
1 onion, quartered
2 egg yolks, beaten
½ cup medium-grain rice, soaked in warm water for 15 minutes, rinsed
2 tablespoons lemon juice
15 cups water
2 teaspoons salt
lemon slices (for garnish)

Wash the chicken parts, then put them in a pan with the carrot, celery, onion and water. Bring to the boil, skim, then cook over moderate heat for 2 hours. Strain the stock, then return it to the pan. Discard chicken parts. Add the rice to the stock and cook over low heat for 15 minutes. Beat together the egg yolks, lemon juice and salt. Gradually blend in the stock from the pan, beating constantly. Return the mixture to the pan and heat, stirring constantly (but do not boil). Serve garnished with lemon slices.

Piatella Athena

GREECE

SERVES FOUR

1 medium chicken, cut into serving pieces
1 cup ham, diced
1 cup prawns, shelled
1 cup small carrots
12 black olives, stoned
12 small onions
½ cup tomato paste
1 cup dry white wine
2 tablespoons olive oil
2 cloves garlic, crushed

Heat the oil in a fry-pan, then add the onions and garlic and sauté gently until the onions are golden. Remove the onions and place them in a casserole. Brown the chicken pieces in the oil and place them in the casserole together with the diced ham, carrots, black olives, white wine and tomato paste. Cover, and cook over low heat for 30 minutes. Stir in the prawns, cover, and continue cooking for a further 10 minutes.

Pom (Chicken and Potato Casserole) THE GUIANAS

SERVES SIX

1 large chicken, cut into pieces
4 tomatoes, peeled, coarsely chopped
3 sticks celery, chopped
6 potatoes, peeled, grated
3 onions, chopped
$\frac{1}{2}$ cup orange juice
1 cup butter
2 teaspoons nutmeg
1 tablespoon salt
2 teaspoons pepper

Brown the chicken in the butter in a large pan. Then add the onions and sauté for 5 minutes. Add the tomatoes, celery, nutmeg, salt and pepper. Cover and cook over low heat until the chicken is tender (approximately 1 hour). Remove the chicken and cut the meat from the bones.

Mix $\frac{3}{4}$ cup of the sauce from the pan with the grated potato and the orange juice. Butter a casserole and line it with $\frac{2}{3}$ of this mixture. Put the chicken mixture into the lined casserole and pour the rest of the sauce from the pan over it. Cover the top with the remaining potato mixture. Bake in the oven (180°C/350°F) for $1\frac{1}{4}$ hours; and serve.

Chicken Pilau THE GUIANAS

SERVES FOUR TO SIX

1 large chicken, halved
$1\frac{1}{2}$ cups seedless raisins
$1\frac{1}{2}$ cups medium-grain rice
1 cup cream
water
3 tablespoons butter
$\frac{1}{4}$ teaspoon nutmeg
1 tablespoon salt

Place the chicken halves in a large pan and almost cover with water. Cover the pan, and cook over moderate heat. Wash the rice, then put it in a saucepan of water. Bring to the boil, then remove from the heat and leave for 5 minutes. Drain the rice and add it, with the salt, to the chicken pan. Cover and cook over moderate heat for 45 minutes. Add the raisins and continue cooking until the chicken is tender.

Put the chicken on to a serving platter and keep warm. Remove the rice and the raisins and mix them with the cream, butter and nutmeg. Put the rice mixture into small moulds and turn them out on to the serving platter to surround the chicken.

Chicken Pilau

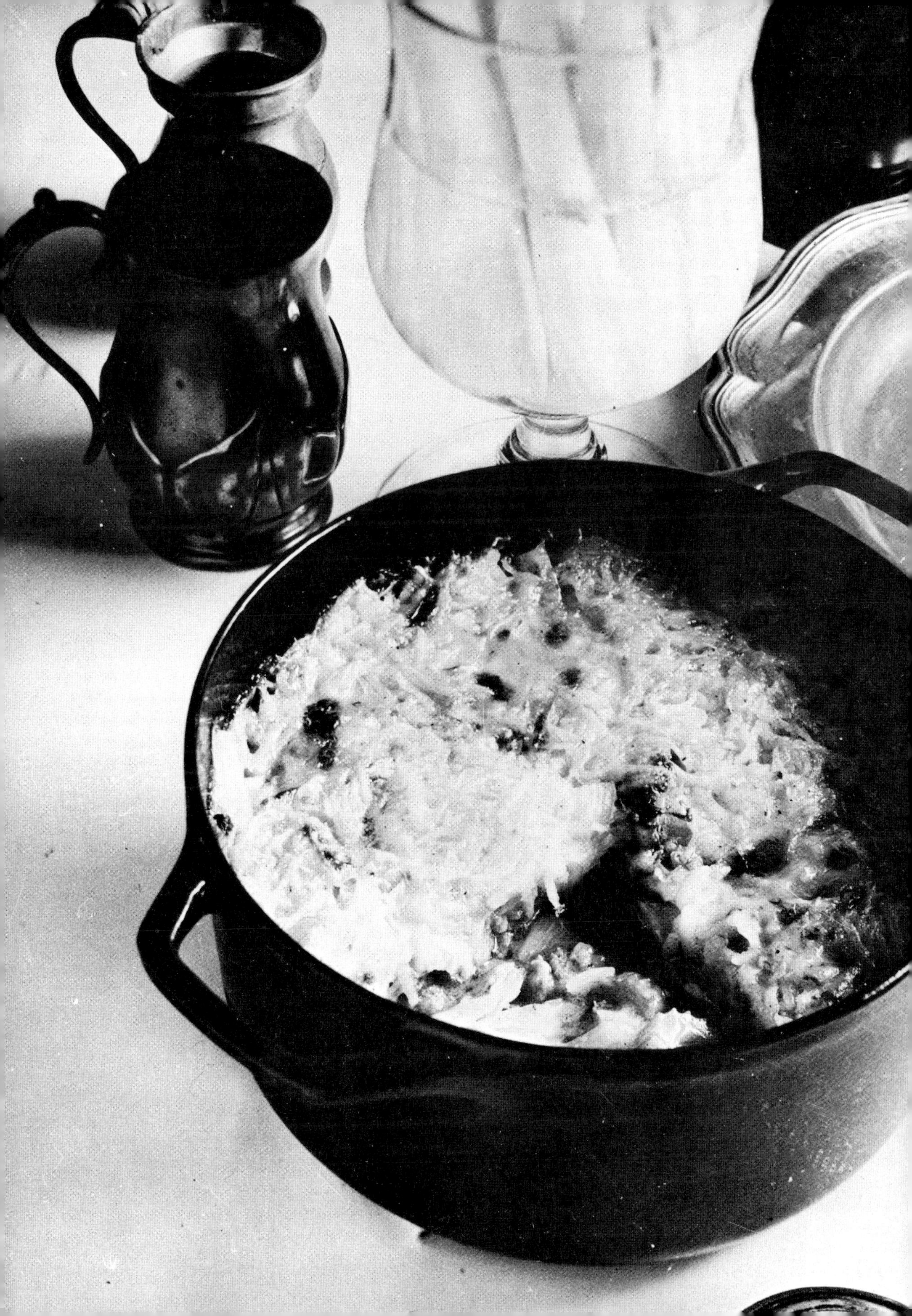

Guinean Chicken Stew

GUINEA

SERVES FOUR TO SIX

1 medium chicken, cut into serving pieces
2 tomatoes, chopped
375 g/¾ lb okra
2 onions, chopped
½ cup peanut butter
1 small can tomato paste
2 cups water
3 tablespoons peanut oil
2 cloves garlic, crushed
½ teaspoon dried ground chilli peppers
1 teaspoon salt

Brown the chicken pieces in the oil in a large pan, then remove and keep warm. Put the onions and garlic into the pan and sauté until the onions are golden. Add the tomatoes, tomato paste, ground chillis, salt, and 1½ cups of the water. Then return the chicken pieces to the pan. Bring to the boil, cover, and simmer for 40 minutes. Mix together the peanut butter and ½ cup water. Add this mixture and the okra to the pan, and stir well. Continue cooking until the chicken and okra are tender (approximately 10 minutes).

Chicken with Macadamia Nuts and Pineapple

HAWAII

SERVES FOUR TO SIX
1 medium chicken
1 cup Chinese cabbage, shredded
½ cup celery, diced
1 onion
½ pineapple, diced
1 cup macadamia nuts, chopped
½ teaspoon sugar
3 cups water
3 tablespoons oil
2 tablespoons soy sauce
2 teaspoons salt
pepper

Put the chicken into a large pan with the water, onion, salt and a little pepper. Bring to the boil, then cook over low heat until the chicken is tender (approximately 35 minutes). Remove the chicken and cut the meat from the bones. Strain the stock and keep it aside.

Sauté the chicken meat, the cabbage and the celery in the oil in a pan for 3 minutes. Add the macadamia nuts, soy sauce, sugar and 2 cups of the stock. Cover, and cook over moderate heat for 5 minutes. Add the pineapple pieces and cook for a further 3 minutes.

Hawaiian Salad

HAWAII

SERVES FOUR
4 breasts of chicken, cooked and diced
2 sticks celery, sliced
1 pineapple, sliced
½ cup roasted almonds, slivered
½ cup mayonnaise

Mix together the diced chicken, the celery and almonds. Put 2 slices of the pineapple on to each of 4 individual serving plates. Top the pineapple slices with the chicken mixture, then pour the mayonnaise over the top. Chill in the refrigerator before serving.

Moa Luau a me Wai Niu (Chicken and Coconut)

HAWAII

SERVES FOUR
1 medium chicken, the meat diced
1 cup grated coconut
1 kg/2 lb spinach, coarsely chopped
1 onion, finely chopped
flour
1 cup milk (hot)
1¼ cups water
½ cup butter
1½ teaspoons salt

Lightly dust the diced chicken with flour, then brown it in the butter in a large pan. Add 1 cup of the water and 1 teaspoon salt. Cover, and simmer until the chicken is tender.
   Meanwhile, pour the milk over the grated coconut and leave for 15 minutes. Then simmer for 10 minutes. Cook the spinach and onion in ¼ cup water and ½ teaspoon salt for 5 minutes. Drain, then add to the chicken pan. Also add the coconut and milk to the pan. Simmer for 3 minutes; and serve.

Ujházi Leves (Ujházi Chicken Soup with Liver Dumplings)

HUNGARY

SERVES FOUR TO SIX
1 small chicken, and giblets
250 g/½ lb beef bones
1 carrot, coarsely chopped
2 sticks celery, coarsely chopped
1 parsnip, coarsely chopped
6 mushrooms, sliced
1 onion, coarsely chopped
1 cup thin egg noodles
water
3 tablespoons chopped parsley
salt
Májgombóc (Chicken Liver Dumplings)

Place the chicken, chicken giblets, beef bones, carrot, celery, parsnip, onion and parsley into a large pan. Cover with cold water to which salt has been added. Bring to the boil, then simmer until the chicken is tender. When cooked, remove the chicken, the giblets and the beef bones from the pan. Take the chicken meat from the bones, chop it into small pieces, and return it to the pan. Add the mushrooms and the noodles and continue cooking until they are tender. Add the Májgombóc (Chicken Liver Dumplings) and cook for a further 10 minutes.

Májgombóc

125 g/¼ lb chicken livers, minced
1 onion, finely chopped
2 eggs, beaten
2 slices bread, soaked in milk
½ cup breadcrumbs
flour
1 teaspoon butter
1 teaspoon chopped parsley
salt and pepper

Sauté the onion in the butter until golden. Press the excess milk from the bread, then crumble it and mix it with the onion. Now mix in the chicken livers, eggs, breadcrumbs, parsley, and salt and pepper to taste. With floured hands, shape the mixture into approximately 12 small balls, then drop them into the soup.

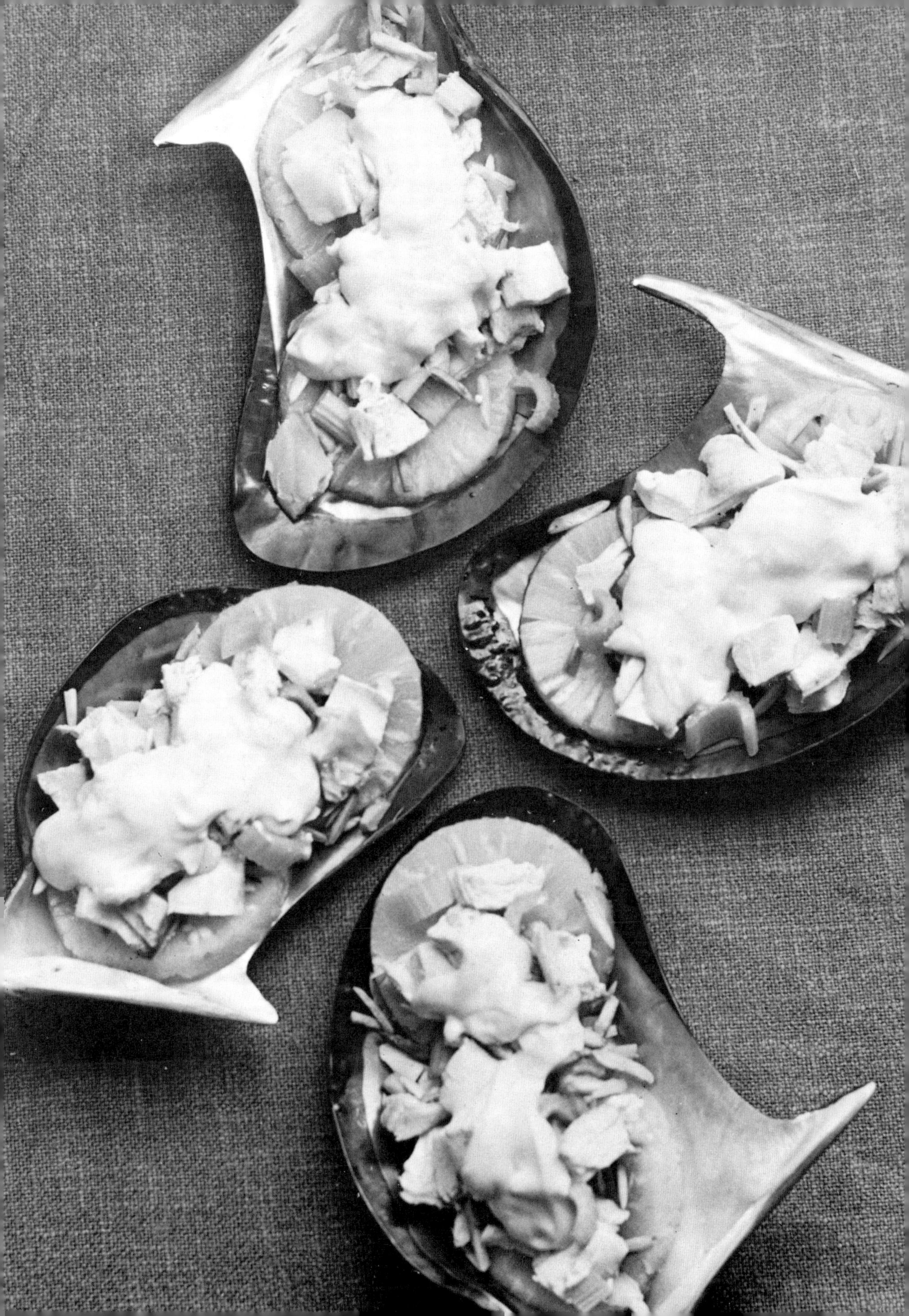

Paprikácsirke (Chicken Paprika) HUNGARY

SERVES FOUR
1 medium chicken, cut into serving pieces
2 onions, sliced
1 cup sour cream
juice of ½ lemon
4 tablespoons butter
1½ tablespoons Hungarian paprika
Nockerl

Nockerl
4 eggs
1¾ cups flour, sifted
5 tablespoons butter
½ teaspoon salt

In a large pan sauté the onions with the paprika in the butter. After 3 minutes add the chicken pieces, and brown them. Reduce the heat, cover the pan and cook for 30 minutes, stirring occasionally. Stir in the sour cream and lemon juice, and simmer for a further 15 minutes. Arrange the chicken pieces and the Nockerl on a serving platter, and pour the sauce over them.

Cream the butter until light and fluffy, then add the eggs one at a time, beating constantly. Add the salt to the flour, then mix this into the butter and egg mixture. Mix well, then shape into a long, thin roll and set aside for 15 minutes.

Break off very small pieces and drop them into boiling water (or soup). Remove the Nockerl as they rise to the top (approximately 3 minutes). Drain. If preferred, the Nockerl can be fried in butter.

Csirke Máj Paprikával (Chicken Livers with Peppers)

HUNGARY

SERVES FOUR TO SIX
375 g/¾ lb chicken livers
3 tomatoes, peeled, seeded, chopped
1 sweet green pepper, seeded, chopped
1 hot green chilli pepper, seeded, chopped
2 onions, chopped
1 tablespoon flour
3 tablespoons butter
salt

Sauté the onions in 2 tablespoons of the butter until golden. Add the chicken livers and simmer for 10 minutes. Sprinkle the flour over and simmer for a further 5 minutes. In another pan fry the peppers in the remaining 1 tablespoon butter. Then add the tomatoes, salt to taste, and cook over low heat for 20 minutes. Add the chicken liver mixture and continue cooking over low heat for a further 15 minutes. Serve as a first course.

Debreczeni Mazsolás Csirke (Debreczen Chicken with Raisins)   HUNGARY

SERVES FOUR TO SIX
1 medium chicken
½ cup seedless raisins
1 lemon, thinly sliced
2 teaspoons flour
½ cup sugar
1 cup dry white wine
½ cup vinegar
water
3 teaspoons butter
2 teaspoons salt

Put the chicken in a large pan and cover with boiling water to which the salt has been added. Cook over low heat until the chicken is tender (approximately 2 hours). Meanwhile, put the lemon slices, vinegar and ½ cup water into a saucepan and cook for 30 minutes. Drain, then keep the lemon slices aside. Also cook the raisins, sugar and wine together until the raisins are plump. Keep this mixture aside.

When the chicken is cooked, place it on a serving platter and keep warm. Now melt the butter over low heat, and blend in the flour. Add 1 cup of the stock from the cooking of the chicken, and stir in well until a thick, smooth sauce is formed. Stir in the lemon slices and the raisins in wine. Pour this sauce over the chicken; serve.

Chicken Budapest

HUNGARY

SERVES FOUR TO SIX

1 medium chicken, cut into serving pieces
500 g/1 lb lobster meat
3 tomatoes, peeled, seeded, chopped
1 onion, chopped
1¼ cups dry white wine
¼ cup cream
2 tablespoons butter
1 tablespoon paprika

Brown the chicken pieces and the onion in the butter in a large pan. Then add the tomatoes and white wine, and simmer for 10 minutes. Add the paprika and continue to cook over low heat for another 20 minutes. Now add the lobster and continue cooking for 10 minutes. Remove the chicken and the lobster and arrange on a serving platter. Stir the cream into the sauce remaining in the pan, and heat through. Strain the sauce, pour it over the chicken and lobster, and serve.

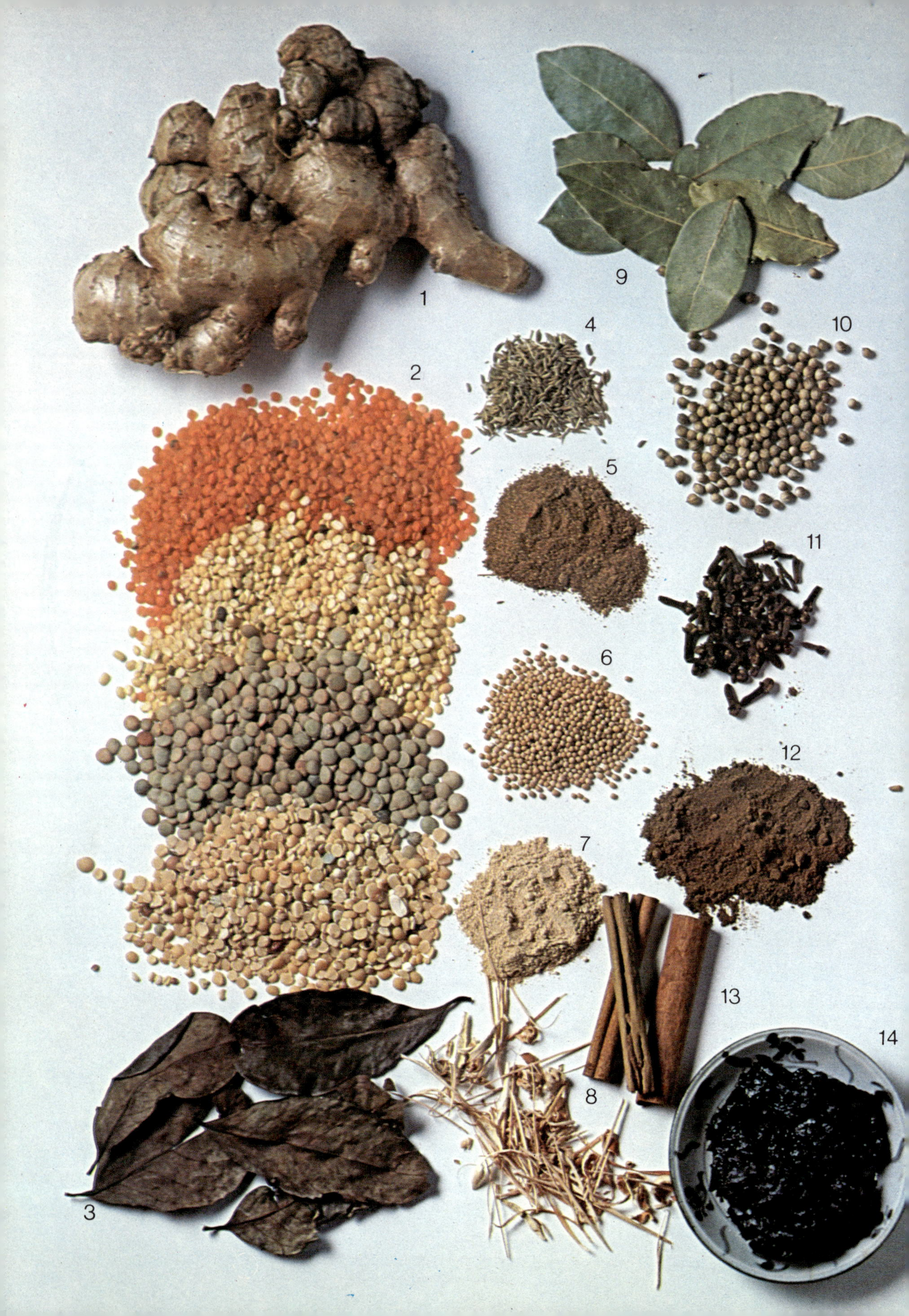
1
2
3
4
5
6
7
8
9
10
11
12
13
14

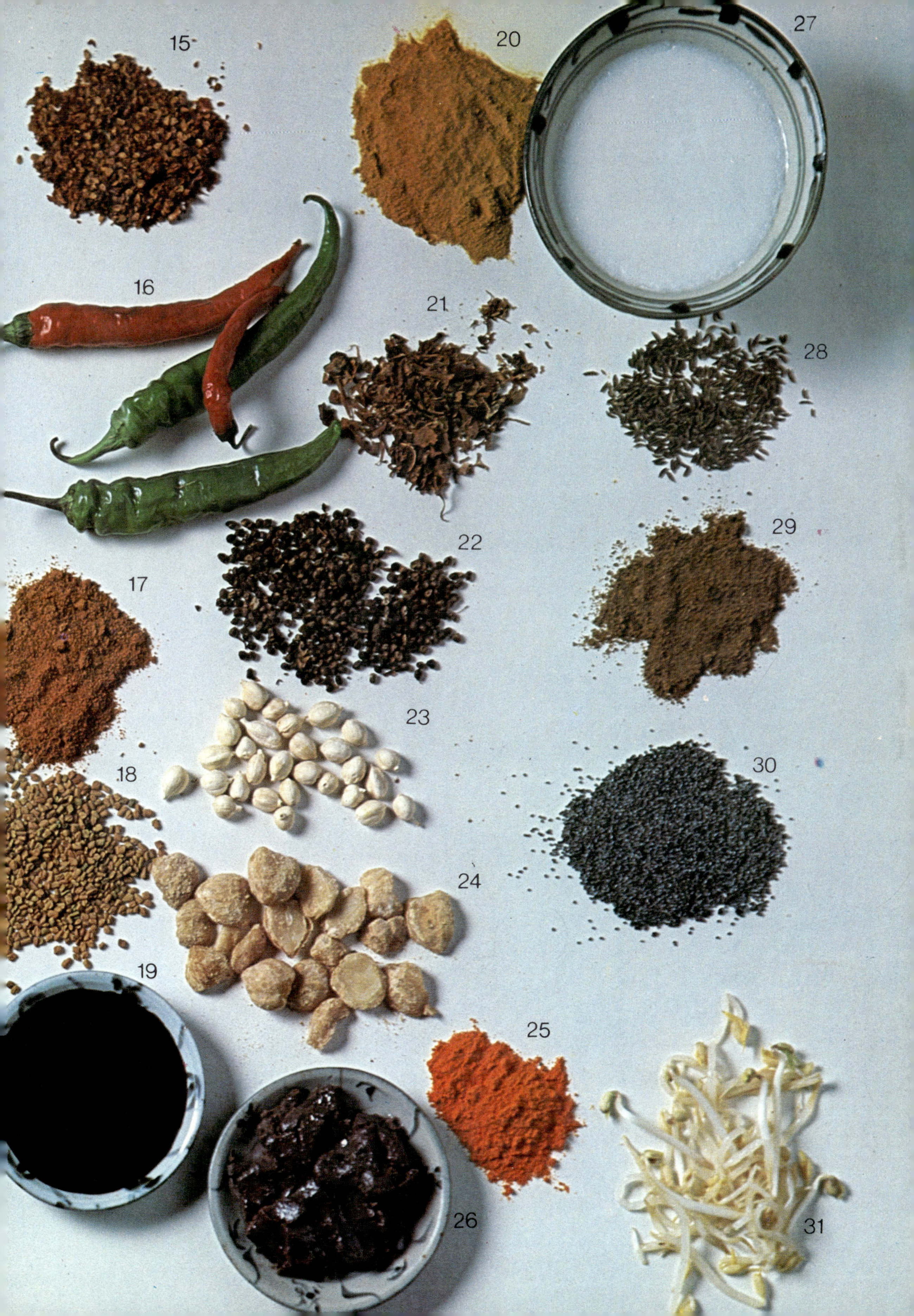
15
20
27
16
21
28
22
29
17
23
30
18
24
19
25
26
31

Introduction to Indian and Indonesian Dishes

Indian and Indonesian ingredients

1 *Root ginger*
2 *Dhal (lentils)*
3 *Daun salam*
4 *Cumin seed*
5 *Garam masala*
6 *Mustard seed*
7 *Laos*
8 *Lemon grass*
9 *Bay leaves*
10 *Coriander*
11 *Cloves*
12 *Allspice*
13 *Cinnamon sticks*
14 *Tamarind*
15 *Ground chilli peppers*
16 *Chilli peppers*
17 *Cayenne*
18 *Fenugreek*
19 *Soy sauce*
20 *Turmeric*
21 *Mace*
22 *Cardamom pods*
23 *Cardamom seeds*
24 *Candle nuts*
25 *Saffron*
26 *Shrimp paste*
27 *Coconut milk*
28 *Caraway seed*
29 *Nutmeg*
30 *Poppy seeds*
31 *Bean sprouts*

Only a very few years ago the average cook would be discouraged from attempting authentic Indian and Indonesian dishes because of the difficulty in purchasing the essential ingredients. Fortunately, that is not the case today. Indian, Indonesian and South Asian spices are readily obtainable from many speciality food departments in supermarkets and stores. Chinese merchants sometimes stock a wide range of Indian and South East Asian foods and spices in addition to their traditional Chinese foods.

If you wish to take the short cut to Indian curry, you can obviously use curry powder or paste. But we can assure you that the dish will not be as good. In addition you will also miss the opportunity of understanding the subtle changes in taste brought about by varying the quantities and range of spices. There is immense satisfaction in adding more of this or that ingredient to satisfy your own palate and to know that the resultant dish reflects a little of your own perceptions and preferences. However, if for reasons of geography you cannot purchase the ingredients listed, substitute the best curry powder or paste that you can find. The result should be very good. Simply use a quantity of curry powder or paste equivalent to the sum total of the curry ingredients.

If you find the curry too formidable or too mild after trial, it is perfectly acceptable to vary the quantities to suit your taste and no apology is needed. Remember, Indian cooking is regional and the hotness of curries varies with the district, from very hot in the South to quite mild in the North. If you are new to Indian cooking, advance with caution and beware of inflicting dishes on your friends that are too hot for them to handle. To do this might mar what is otherwise a wonderful new taste experience.

Many versions and varieties derived from Indian curry are to be found throughout Asian countries. Each country lends its own national character to the original dish.

Indonesian dishes reflect the long Dutch influence on these East Indian islands. They are a blend of Western and Eastern cooking. Many of the spices are identical with those used in Indian cooking and can produce equally hot results.

What to Drink?
India is a teetotal country. For this reason it is not regarded as correct to serve alcoholic beverages with the meal. Iced fruit drinks or yoghurt mixed with iced water and salted is a refreshing alternative. If you prefer to drink alcohol, light beer is best. Wine cannot compete with curry and is not recommended.

Indians often drink tea, iced or hot and without milk, at the end of a meal. It can be sweetened, spiced with cinnamon, or served with lemon. Indonesian tastes run to very hot, very sweet coffee at the end of a meal.

Curry Accompaniments
Curry should be served with accompaniments chosen for coolness or hotness, for texture, for colour and appearance, or simply to add variety to the dish. Two excellent accompaniments are Raita and Banana and Coconut Sambal (see recipes below). Also serve a selection from such items as sliced tomatoes, pineapple pieces, sliced fried bananas, cashews or peanuts, sultanas, and of course chutneys, ranging from mild, sweet or fruity, to very hot. Hot chutneys must be handled with extreme care until you are sure that you can cope with the hotter varieties.

Raita

1 cucumber
sugar
½ cup plain yoghurt
Salt and black pepper

Peel the cucumber, then grate it on to a plate. Sprinkle with salt, cover, and leave to stand in the refrigerator for 30 minutes. Then drain the cucumber, mix it with the yoghurt and add black pepper and a little sugar to taste.

Banana and Coconut Sambal

3 bananas
1 tablespoon desiccated coconut
sugar
1 tablespoon lemon juice
salt

Peel the bananas and cut them into ½ cm/¼" thick slices. Sprinkle with the lemon juice, and salt and sugar to taste. Then cover with the desiccated coconut.

Coconut Milk and Cream
You will find coconut milk or coconut cream listed as an ingredient in many dishes from India, Indonesia or other countries in South East Asia. Coconut milk in this context is *not* the liquid to be found in the fresh natural coconut, which liquid is not used in cooking. Below are instructions for making coconut milk or cream.

Method
Boil 250 g/½ lb desiccated coconut in 1½ cups of water for 15 minutes. Squeeze the mixture through muslin, extracting as much liquid as you can. This will yield *thick* coconut milk or cream. Repeat the process using the same desiccated coconut to yield thin coconut milk.

Mulligatawny (Curried Chicken Soup)

INDIA

SERVES FOUR TO SIX

1 medium chicken, cut into pieces
1 onion, sliced
1 cup ground almonds
1 tablespoon gram flour
2 tablespoons coconut cream
10 cups water
1½ tablespoons ghee
1 clove garlic, crushed
chilli powder
½ teaspoon garam masala
2½ cm/1" stick of cinnamon
salt
½ teaspoon black pepper

Put the chicken pieces, the coconut cream, the cinnamon, the water, and salt to taste into a large pan. Cover, and simmer until the chicken is tender (approximately 30 minutes). Remove the chicken pieces and take the meat from the bones. Then dice the chicken meat and keep aside. Return the chicken bones to the pan and cook until the liquid has reduced to about 4 cups. Add the almonds, garlic, garam masala, black pepper, and ½ teaspoon ground chillis. Stir well, and bring to the boil. Strain this stock and keep aside.

Sauté the onions in the ghee until golden, then add the gram flour and blend. Pour in the stock, stir well, and cook until a thick soup is formed. Add the diced chicken to the pan and cook for another 2 minutes. Serve the soup in individual dishes and sprinkle with ground chillis.

Chicken Curry

INDIA

SERVES FOUR

1 medium chicken, cut into 8 serving pieces
3 tomatoes, peeled, seeded, chopped
2 onions, chopped
1½ cups yoghurt
1 tablespoon coconut cream
2 tablespoons ghee
2 cloves garlic, finely chopped
2 teaspoons tamarind (soaked in 1 cup water)
1 tablespoon ground coriander
1 teaspoon dried ground chilli peppers
1 teaspoon ground turmeric
½ teaspoon ground ginger
½ teaspoon ground cinnamon
½ teaspoon ground cardamom

Brown the chicken pieces in the ghee in a large pan; then remove and keep warm. Add the onions to the pan and sauté them until golden. Then add the garlic, ground chillis, coriander, turmeric, ginger, cinnamon and cardamom, and cook for 2 minutes. Stir in the coconut cream and the tamarind and water, then bring to the boil. Add the yoghurt and stir. Return the chicken pieces to the pan, then cover and simmer for 20 minutes. Add the tomatoes and continue cooking until the chicken is tender (approximately 15 minutes). This dish should be served with white or saffron rice, and curry accompaniments.

Goa Moli (Goan Vinegar Curry) — INDIA

SERVES FOUR

1 medium chicken, cut into serving pieces
6 onions, sliced
2 cups vinegar
3 tablespoons ghee
3 cloves garlic, crushed
3 green chilli peppers, chopped
2 tablespoons ground coriander
2 teaspoons ground ginger
2 teaspoons ground cumin
1 teaspoon dried ground chilli peppers
1 teaspoon ground cloves
1 teaspoon ground turmeric
½ teaspoon ground cardamom
½ teaspoon ground cinnamon
salt

Brown the chicken pieces in the ghee in a large pan; then remove and keep warm. Add the onions, garlic, chilli peppers and ginger to the pan and cook over low heat for 5 minutes. Mix together in the blender the ground chillis, coriander, cumin, cloves, cardamom, cinnamon, turmeric and 1 tablespoon of the vinegar. Blend until a smooth paste is formed, then add this to the pan and fry for 10 minutes. Return the chicken pieces to the pan and coat them well with the spice mixture. Add the remaining vinegar and salt to taste. Cook over low heat until the chicken is tender (approximately 30 minutes).

Dum Murgi (Stuffed Chicken) — INDIA

SERVES FOUR TO SIX

1 medium chicken
125 g/4 oz chick peas, cooked
5 onions, finely chopped
60 g/2 oz seedless raisins, chopped
60 g/2 oz blanched almonds
3 eggs, hard-boiled, chopped
2 tablespoons desiccated coconut
1 tablespoon yoghurt
1 tablespoon milk
1¼ cups water
4 tablespoons ghee
2 cloves garlic, crushed
2 green chilli peppers, finely chopped
1 teaspoon dried ground chilli peppers
1 teaspoon ground ginger
½ teaspoon ground cinnamon
½ teaspoon ground turmeric
½ teaspoon ground cloves
½ teaspoon ground nutmeg
½ teaspoon ground cardamom
¼ teaspoon ground saffron
¼ teaspoon ground coriander
salt
1 teaspoon black pepper

Mix together the milk, saffron, nutmeg and ¼ teaspoon of the cardamom. Spread this mixture inside the chicken. Sauté 3 of the onions in 1 tablespoon of the ghee until they are golden. Remove the onions from the pan and mix them with the cooked chick peas, the raisins, almonds, chopped chilli peppers, ginger, and salt to taste. Next add the hard-boiled eggs and mix well. Stuff the chicken with this mixture and close the opening with thread or skewers.

Brown the stuffed chicken on all sides in the remaining 3 tablespoons ghee in a large pan. Remove and keep warm. Pour off all but 1 tablespoon of the ghee from the pan. Add to this the remaining 2 onions and the garlic. Cook over low heat for a few minutes, then add the ground chillis, cinnamon, coriander, turmeric, cloves, black pepper, and the remaining ¼ teaspoon cardamom. Stir well, and continue cooking over low heat for 5 minutes. Add the yoghurt and cook, stirring constantly, for another 10 minutes. Return the chicken to the pan, placing it on top of this masala mixture. Add the water, cover, and simmer until the chicken is tender (approximately 1 hour). Garnish with the desiccated coconut.

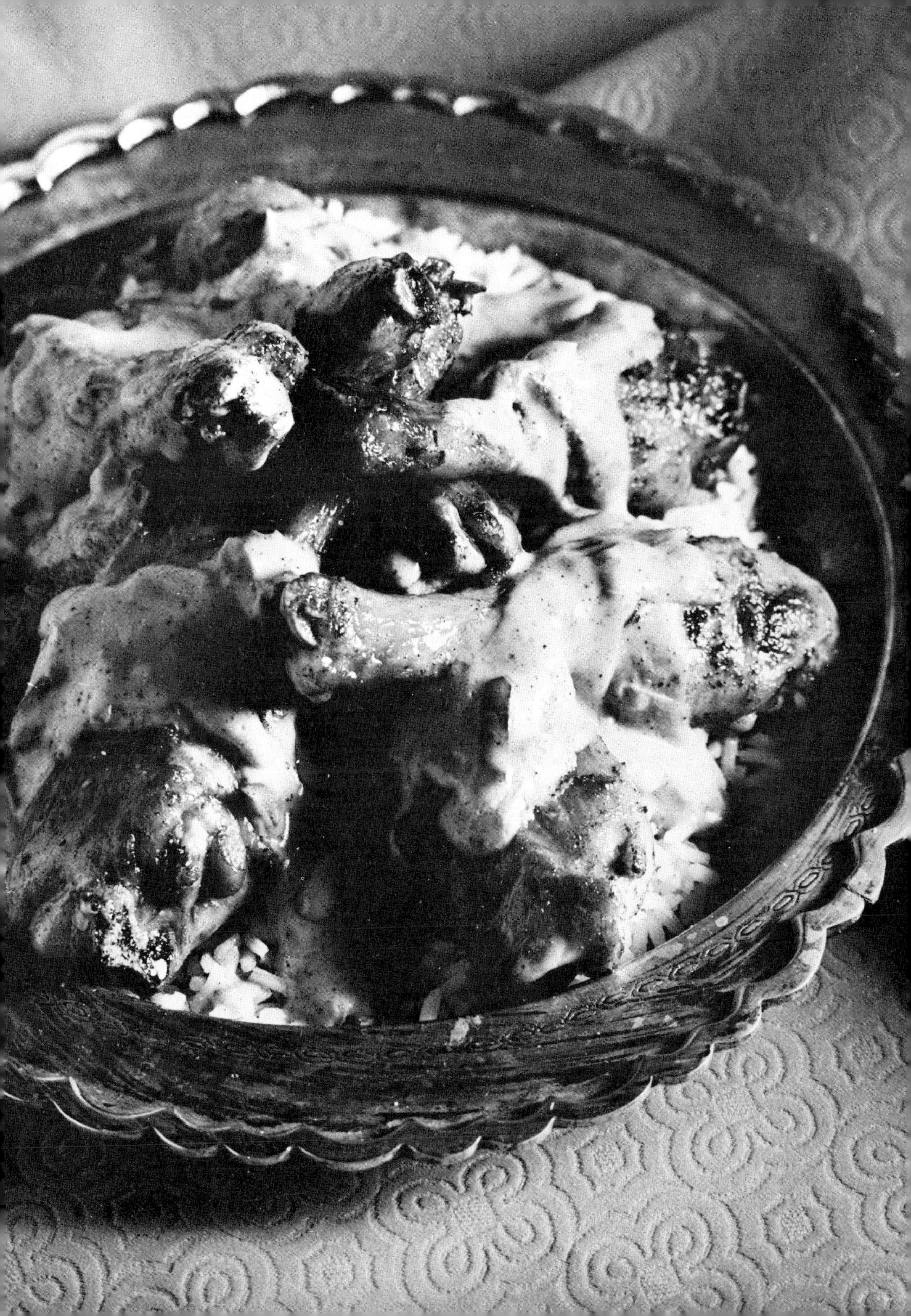

Murgh Tikka (Spiced Chicken Kebabs) — INDIA

SERVES FOUR TO SIX
1 large chicken, the meat cut into skewer-size pieces
2 onions, grated
1 cup yoghurt
juice of 1 lemon
2 cloves garlic, crushed
1 teaspoon ground ginger
1 teaspoon ground coriander
1 teaspoon dried ground chilli peppers
1 teaspoon garam masala
salt
few drops of red colouring

Mix together the onions, garlic, ground chillis, ginger, coriander, garam masala, yoghurt, lemon juice, and salt to taste. Add a few drops of red colouring. Stir the chicken pieces well into this mixture and leave to marinate for at least 2 hours.

Put the chicken pieces on to skewers and coat them again with the marinade. Cook over a barbecue or under a grill until the chicken is tender (approximately 10 minutes). Serve with lemon wedges and chappatis.

Tandoori Chicken — INDIA

SERVES FOUR TO SIX
1 medium chicken
1 onion, finely chopped
$\frac{2}{3}$ cup yoghurt
3 cloves garlic, finely chopped
$1\frac{1}{2}$ teaspoons ground coriander
1 teaspoon ground ginger
1 teaspoon ground cumin
$\frac{1}{2}$ teaspoon dried ground chilli peppers
$\frac{1}{4}$ teaspoon cayenne pepper
$\frac{1}{2}$ teaspoon salt
black pepper
few drops of red colouring

Put all the ingredients except the chicken into a blender, and blend until a smooth mixture is formed. Remove the skin from the chicken and slash the flesh in a few places with a sharp knife. Marinate the chicken in the yoghurt and spice mixture for at least 1 hour (preferably longer).

Grill the chicken under high heat for approximately 20 minutes, turning frequently. It is correct for the chicken to be blackened in parts. Serve with rice and Indian chutney.

Note: The authentic Indian dish is cooked in a tandoor, a special clay oven.

Murgh Tikka

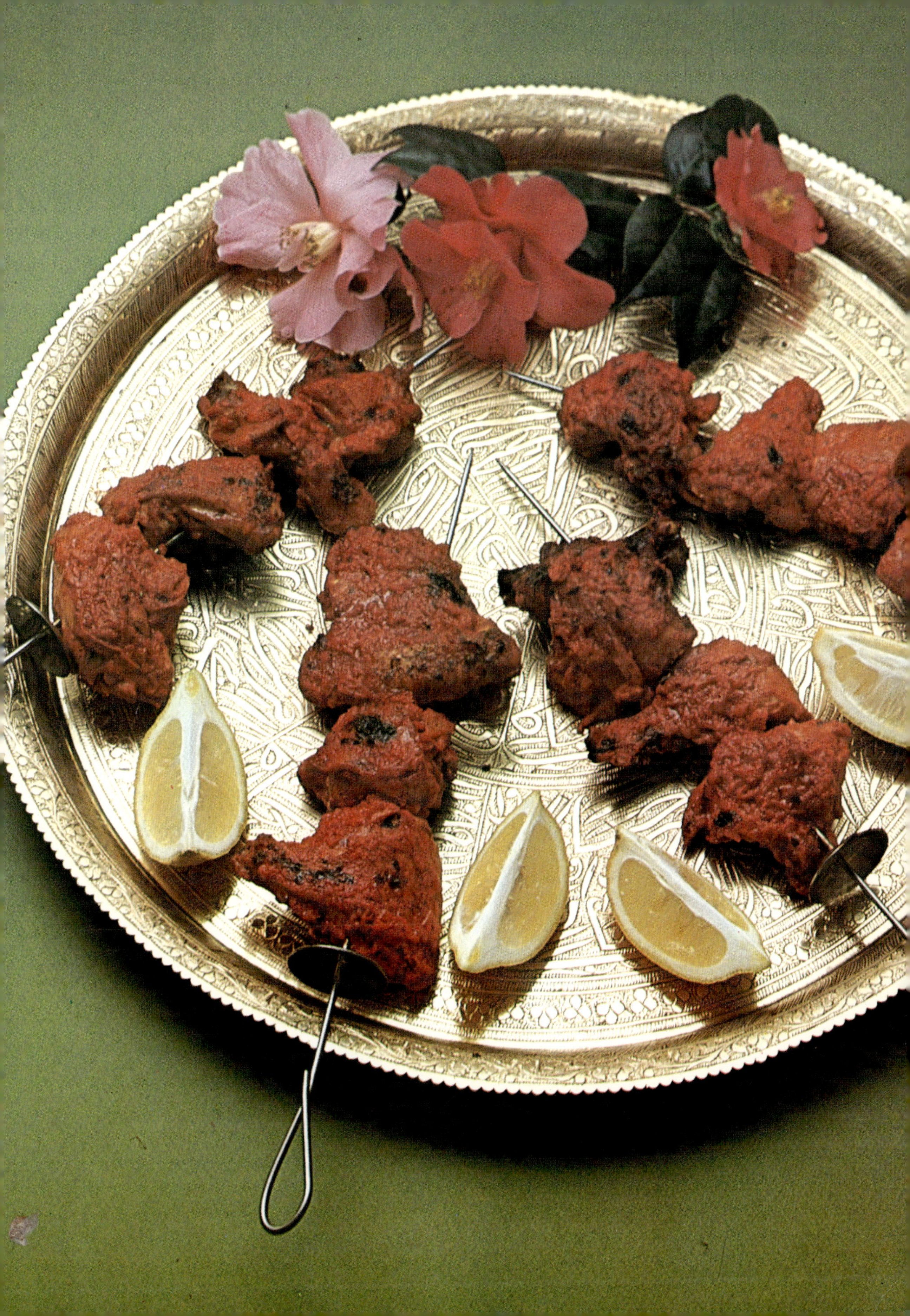

Chicken Biryani

INDIA

SERVES FOUR

1 small chicken, cut into small serving pieces
3 onions, sliced
12 almonds, shelled
2 cups medium-grain rice
3½ cups chicken stock
¼ cup yoghurt
4 tablespoons ghee
2 cloves garlic, crushed
2 cinnamon sticks
8 cloves
4 cardamom pods
½ teaspoon ground ginger
½ teaspoon ground turmeric
2 teaspoons salt

Fry the almonds in the ghee in a large pan until they are golden; then remove and drain. Put two of the onions in the pan and sauté them until they are brown. Remove, and keep them aside with the almonds. Now add to the pan the remaining onion, the garlic, ginger, cinnamon, cloves and cardamom pods. Fry for a few minutes; then reduce the heat, add the yoghurt and turmeric, and mix well. Add the chicken pieces, cover, and simmer for 30 minutes.

Meanwhile, heat the chicken stock in a separate pan. Add the rice and the salt to it and simmer for 10 minutes. Then add the partially-cooked rice and the chicken stock to the chicken pan, and continue cooking until the chicken is tender and the liquid has been absorbed by the rice (approximately 15 minutes). Put on to a serving platter and top with the almonds and onions.

Kundou Chicken

INDIA

SERVES FOUR OR SIX

1 large chicken, cut into serving pieces
2 tomatoes, chopped
4 onions, sliced
¼ cup ground almonds
¼ cup ground cashew nuts
½ cup thick cream
1½ cups buttermilk
5 tablespoons ghee
2 cloves garlic, crushed
1 teaspoon ground ginger
¼ teaspoon dried ground chilli peppers
2 teaspoons salt

Sauté the onions for 10 minutes in the ghee in a large pan. Add the garlic, ground chillis and ginger, and cook over low heat for 5 minutes, stirring occasionally. Add the tomatoes and the buttermilk and cook for a further 10 minutes. Then add the chicken pieces, the almonds, cashew nuts and salt, and continue cooking over low heat until the chicken is tender (approximately 1 hour). Add a little more buttermilk if the pan becomes dry. When the chicken is tender, add the cream and stir well; then serve.

Chicken Biryani

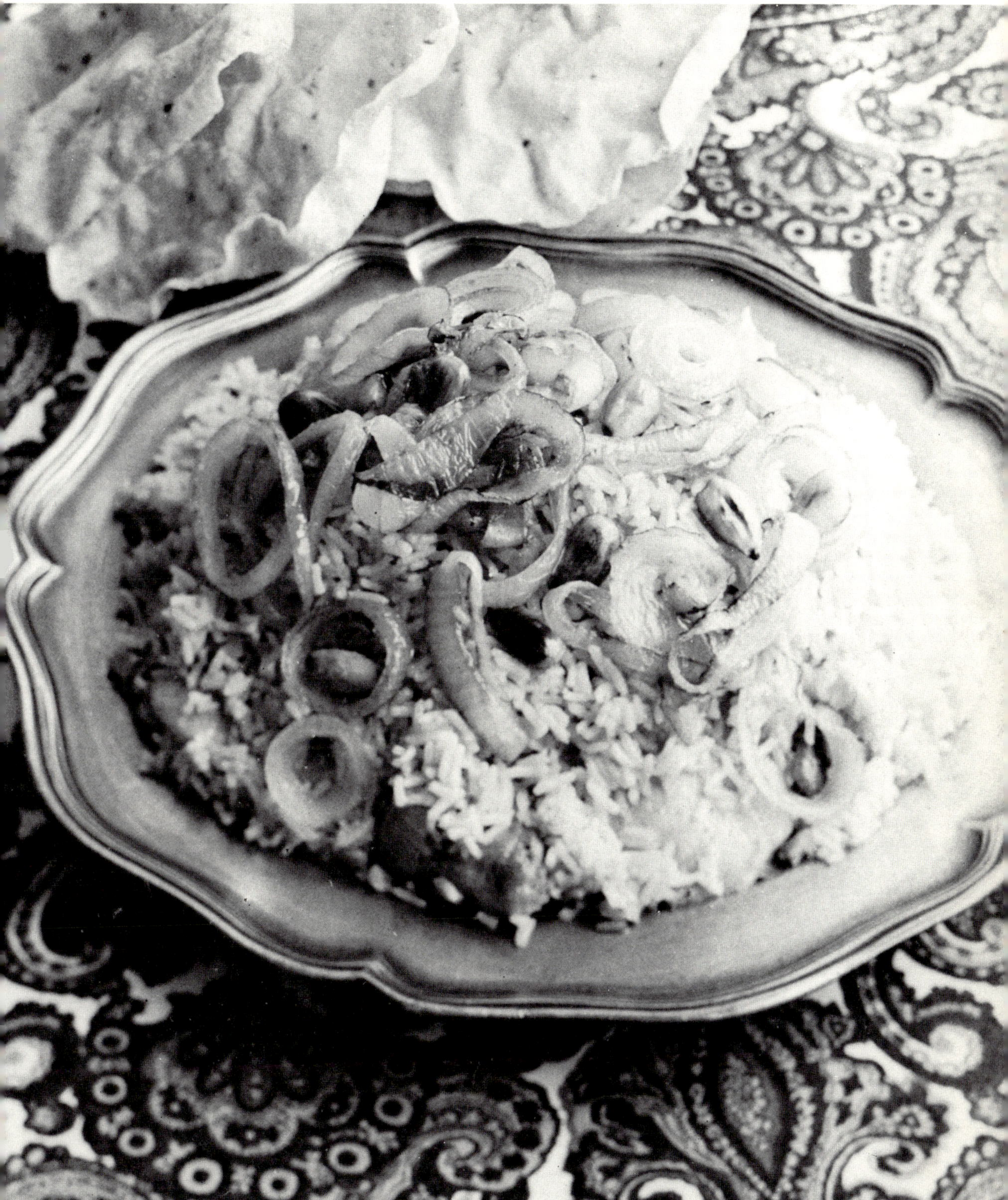

Dhansak (Chicken with Lentils) INDIA

SERVES FOUR TO SIX
1 medium chicken, cut into serving pieces
185 g/6 oz tuar dhal (lentils), soaked overnight, drained
60 g/2 oz channa dhal (lentils), soaked overnight, drained
60 g/2 oz moong dhal (lentils), soaked overnight, drained
60 g/2 oz masoor dhal (lentils), soaked overnight, drained
125 g/4 oz pumpkin, chopped
125 g/4 oz spinach, chopped
2 potatoes, peeled, chopped
1 egg-plant, chopped
1 onion, whole
3 onions, chopped
2½ cups water
1 tablespoon peanut oil
3 cloves garlic, finely chopped
3 green chilli peppers, finely chopped
2½ cm/1" root ginger, finely chopped
4 mint leaves
2 bay leaves
2 teaspoons ground coriander
1 teaspoon ground cumin
1 teaspoon ground turmeric
1 teaspoon dried ground chilli peppers
½ teaspoon ground cloves
½ teaspoon ground cinnamon
¼ teaspoon fenugreek
¼ teaspoon mustard seeds
salt

Put the chicken pieces into a large pan. Add the potatoes, egg-plant, spinach, pumpkin, mint leaves, one of the chopped onions, and the water. Cover, and cook over low heat until the chicken is tender (approximately 40 minutes). Remove the chicken pieces and keep them warm. Strain the sauce and keep aside.

Meanwhile, bake the whole onion in the oven. When it is tender, remove the skin and chop it very finely. Mix it with the finely chopped garlic, green chilli peppers and ginger. Fry the remaining two chopped onions in the oil until they are golden, then add the above mixture and fry for 2 minutes. Add the bay leaves, ground chillis, coriander, cumin, turmeric, cloves, cinnamon, fenugreek and mustard seeds. Fry for another 2 minutes. Add all the drained dhal (lentils) and the strained sauce from the cooking of the chicken. Season with salt to taste, then cook over low heat for 20 minutes. Add the chicken pieces to the pan, and cook for a further 10 minutes. Remove the bay leaves. Serve with rice and curry accompaniments.

Dhansak (Finished Dish)

Right: Dhansak (Ingredients)

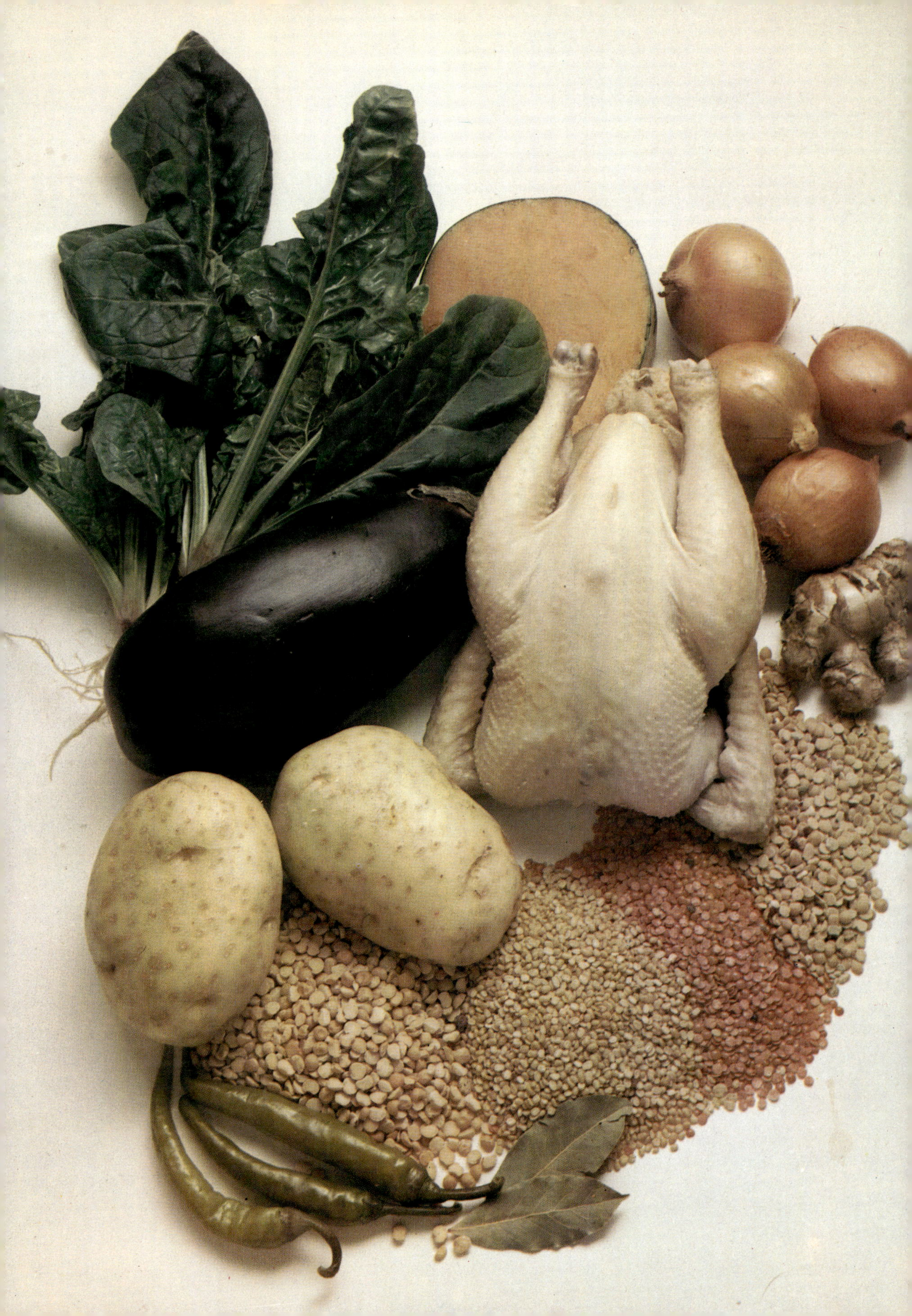

Chicken Pidee (Chicken Curry with Dumplings)   INDIA

SERVES FOUR TO SIX
1 medium chicken, cut into serving pieces
2 onions, finely sliced
60 g/2 oz medium-grain rice
125 g/4 oz rice flour
2 tablespoons coconut cream
water
3 tablespoons ghee
2 teaspoons dried ground chilli peppers
1 teaspoon ground turmeric
½ teaspoon ground cinnamon
½ teaspoon ground cloves
salt
1 teaspoon black pepper

Brown the chicken pieces in the ghee in a large pan; then remove and keep warm. Add the onions to the pan and sauté until golden. Then add the ground chillis, turmeric, cinnamon, cloves and black pepper, and fry for 5 minutes. Return the chicken pieces to the pan and coat them well with the spice mixture. Add the coconut cream, 2½ cups water, and salt to taste. Bring to the boil, then simmer for 20 minutes.

Meanwhile, mix the rice flour and the rice with water to make a stiff paste, season with salt, and shape into small dumplings. Put these dumplings into the chicken pan, and continue to simmer until the chicken is tender (approximately 20 minutes).

Pilau   INDIA

SERVES FOUR
1 medium chicken, cut into serving pieces
2 onions, sliced
500 g/1 lb medium-grain rice
10 cups chicken stock
4 tablespoons ghee
40 cardamom seeds
2 tablespoons coriander
2 tablespoons cinnamon
1 tablespoon cloves
1 tablespoon mace
1 tablespoon allspice
1 tablespoon peppercorns

Brown the chicken pieces in 3 tablespoons of the ghee in a large pan; then remove and keep warm. Wash and drain the rice, then add it to the pan and cook over low heat until the rice is slightly browned. Mix together the cardamom seeds, coriander, cloves, mace, cinnamon, allspice and peppercorns by grinding them in a mortar or blender.

Put the chicken stock into a large pan, then add the chicken pieces and the spice mixture. Bring to the boil, then simmer for 20 minutes. Add the rice and continue to simmer until the chicken is tender and the liquid has been absorbed by the rice (approximately 15 minutes). Meanwhile, sauté the onion slices until brown in the remaining 1 tablespoon ghee. Put the chicken pieces on to a serving platter, cover with the rice, and top with the fried onions.

Lahore Chicken   INDIA

SERVES FOUR TO SIX
1 large chicken
4 tomatoes, peeled, seeded, chopped
1 onion, finely chopped
juice of 1 lemon
4 tablespoons ghee, melted
2 cloves garlic, crushed
1 teaspoon ground ginger
1 teaspoon ground turmeric
1 teaspoon ground coriander
¼ teaspoon ground saffron

Mix together the tomatoes, onion, lemon juice, garlic, ginger, turmeric, coriander, saffron and 2 tablespoons of the melted ghee. Marinate the chicken in this mixture for at least 2 hours, turning occasionally.

Put a large piece of foil in a baking tin and put the chicken and its marinade into this. Pour the remaining 2 tablespoons melted ghee over the chicken and cover it with the foil. Roast in the oven (190°C/375°F) for 1½ hours. Then open the foil at the top and continue cooking until the chicken is tender (approximately 20 minutes). Place the chicken on a serving platter and pour the juices over it.

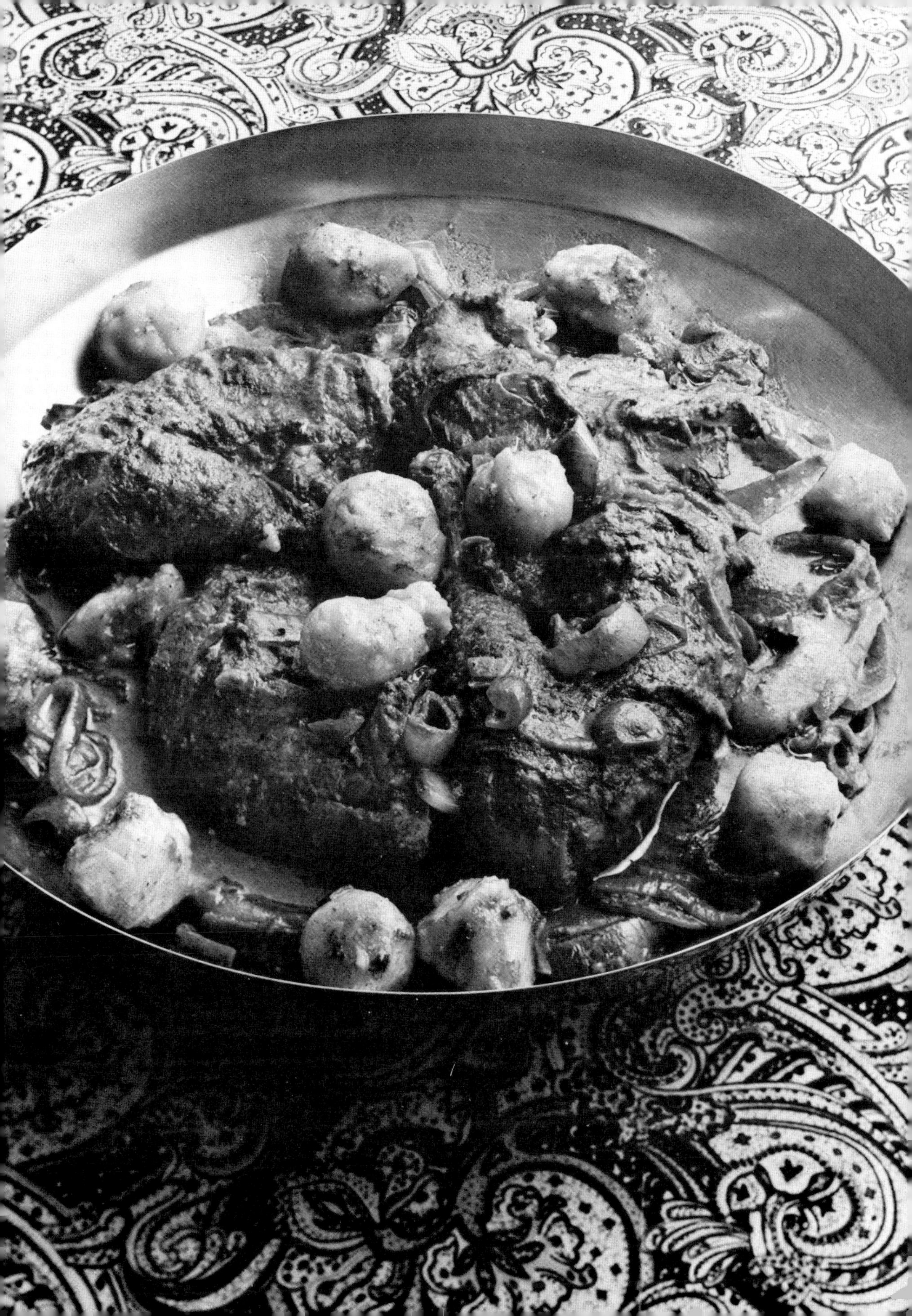

Dahi Murgh (Chicken with Yoghurt)

INDIA

SERVES FOUR
1 medium chicken, cut into serving pieces
4 onions, finely chopped
3 cups yoghurt
2 tablespoons coconut cream
juice of 1 lemon
1 tablespoon ghee
3 cloves garlic, crushed
2 green chilli peppers, finely chopped
1 tablespoon poppy seeds
½ teaspoon ground ginger
salt

Put the chicken pieces, the yoghurt and salt to taste into a large pan. Cook over low heat until the chicken is tender (approximately 30 minutes). Meanwhile, fry the onions in the ghee over low heat for 10 minutes. Add the garlic, ginger, chillis, poppy seeds and coconut cream, and cook for a further 10 minutes. Then add this mixture to the chicken pan and cook over moderate heat for 10 minutes. Stir in the lemon juice. Serve with chappatis.

Shahjehan Kaleja (Spiced Chicken Livers)

INDIA

SERVES FOUR
500 g/1 lb chicken livers, chopped
250 g/½ lb mushrooms, sliced
2 tomatoes, chopped
1 onion, finely sliced
2 tablespoons yoghurt
2 tablespoons ghee
1 clove garlic, crushed
1 teaspoon ground coriander
½ teaspoon dried ground chilli peppers
½ teaspoon ground turmeric
½ teaspoon ground cumin
½ teaspoon garam masala
salt

Sauté the onion and garlic in the ghee until the onion is transparent. Add the tomatoes, ground chillis, turmeric, cumin, coriander and garam masala, and cook over low heat for 5 minutes. Next add the mushrooms and cook for a further 5 minutes. Finally add the chicken livers, the yoghurt, and salt to taste. Simmer for 20 minutes; then serve.

Goreng Ajam Balado (Fried Chicken with Chilli) — INDONESIA

SERVES FOUR
1 medium chicken, cut into serving pieces
2 tomatoes, chopped
2 onions, chopped
juice of 1 lemon
1 tablespoon white vinegar
peanut oil
1 tablespoon dried ground chilli peppers
salt

Rub the lemon juice over the chicken pieces, then deep-fry them in peanut oil in a large pan. When they are brown, remove them and keep warm. Strain the peanut oil and return $\frac{1}{4}$ cup of it to the pan, then fry the onions in it until they are golden. Add the tomatoes, ground chillis, vinegar, any remaining lemon juice, and salt to taste. Stir well, reduce the heat and simmer for 3 minutes. Return the chicken pieces to the pan and coat them well with the sauce. Continue cooking over low heat until the chicken is tender.

Ajam Panggang Bumbu Saté (Roast Chicken with Saté) — INDONESIA

SERVES FOUR
1 medium chicken
2 onions, finely chopped
2 candle nuts (or macadamia nuts)
2 cups thick coconut milk
3 tablespoons water
3 tablespoons peanut oil
3 cloves garlic, crushed
1 tablespoon dried ground chilli peppers
1 tablespoon ground coriander
2 teaspoons tamarind juice
2 teaspoons ground ginger
$\frac{1}{2}$ teaspoon ground turmeric
$\frac{1}{2}$ teaspoon ground caraway seed
$\frac{1}{2}$ teaspoon shrimp paste
1 stalk lemon grass
salt

Put the ground chillis, ginger, coriander, caraway seed, candle nuts, shrimp paste and water into a blender. Blend until a smooth paste is formed. Sauté the onion and garlic in the peanut oil until the onion becomes transparent. Then stir in the spice paste, and add salt to taste. Cook, stirring, for 2 minutes; then remove from the heat. Cool the mixture slightly, and rub it over the chicken both inside and out. Keep some of the mixture aside and add it to the coconut milk; bring to the boil, stirring, and simmer for 10 minutes. Stir in the tamarind juice.

Put the chicken into a roasting pan and pour the coconut milk mixture over it. Roast in the oven (180°C/350°F) until the chicken is tender (approximately 1 hour). Baste occasionally.

Semur Ajam (Chicken in Soy Sauce) — INDONESIA

SERVES FOUR TO SIX
1 large chicken, cut into serving pieces
3 tomatoes, sliced
2 onions, sliced
1 teaspoon brown sugar
3 tablespoons peanut oil
2 tablespoons thick soy sauce
3 cloves garlic, finely chopped
2 teaspoons ground cinnamon
5 whole cloves
salt
1 teaspoon black pepper

Half-cook the chicken pieces in salted water in a large pan over moderate heat. Remove the chicken pieces, strain the stock and keep it aside. Brown the half-cooked chicken pieces in the peanut oil in another large pan; then remove and keep warm. Pour off all but 1 tablespoon of the peanut oil from the pan, then put in the onions, garlic, cinnamon, cloves and black pepper. Cook these over moderate heat until the onions become transparent. Return the chicken pieces to the pan, add the tomatoes, and continue cooking for 5 minutes. Dissolve the brown sugar into the soy sauce. Then add this mixture to the pan, salt to taste, and cook over high heat for 2 minutes. Add $2\frac{1}{2}$ cups of the stock from the cooking of the chicken, reduce the heat, and simmer until the chicken is tender and the sauce has thickened.

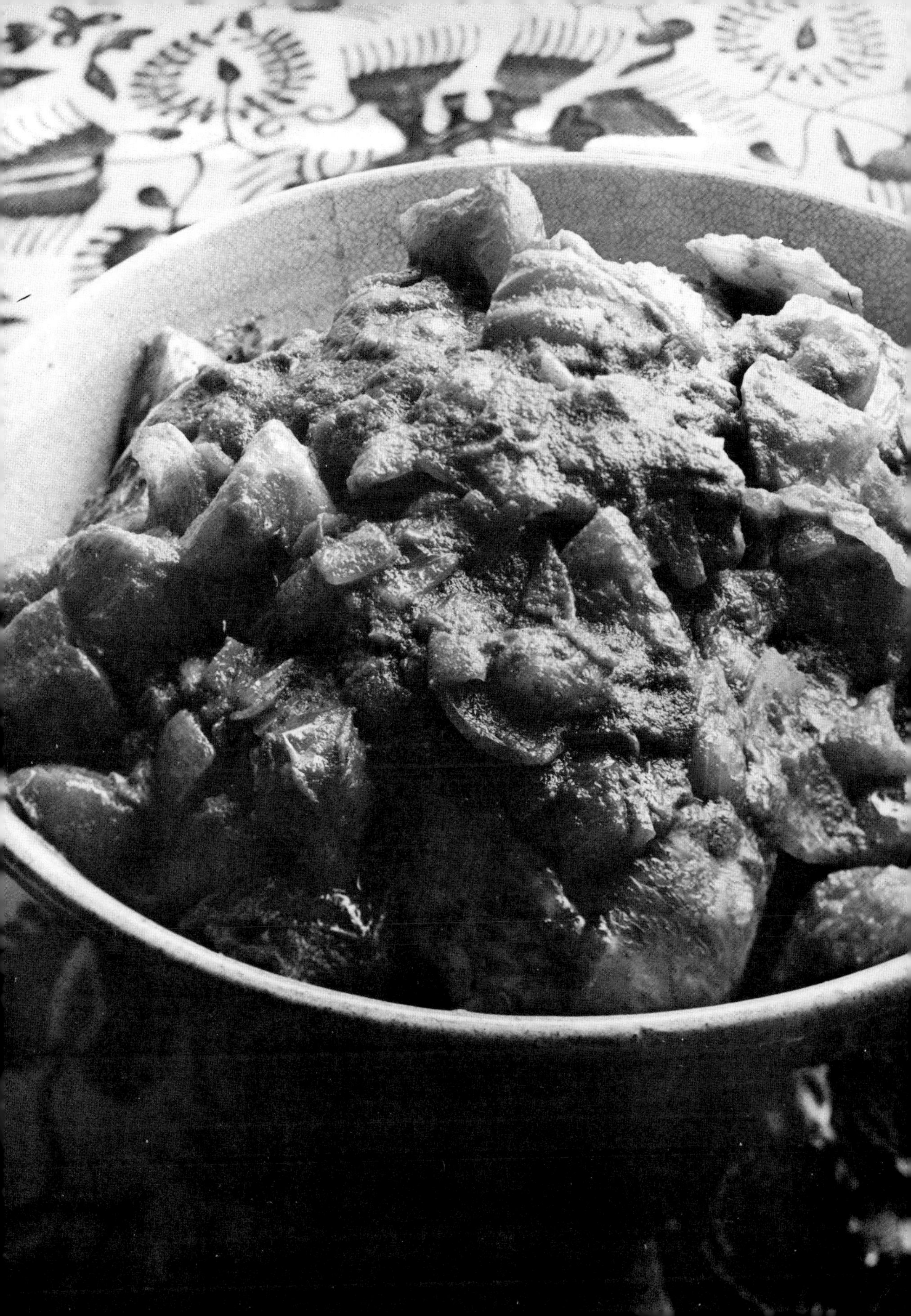

Soto Ajam (Chicken and Ginger Soup)

INDONESIA

SERVES SIX
1 large chicken
1 cup bean sprouts, drained
2 sticks celery, coarsely chopped
2 spring onions, coarsely chopped
3 onions, sliced
6 lemon slices
3 eggs, hard-boiled, sliced
12 cups water
3 tablespoons peanut oil
3 cloves garlic, finely chopped
2 teaspoons ground ginger
1 teaspoon ground nutmeg
1 teaspoon ground turmeric
¼ teaspoon ground cloves
2½ teaspoons salt

Place the chicken in a large pan with the celery, spring onions, cloves, and the water. Bring to the boil, skim, then cook over moderate heat until the chicken is tender (approximately 2½ hours). Add the salt to the pan after the first hour. Remove the chicken and cut the meat away from the bones. Then dice the chicken meat and keep warm. Strain the stock, add the ginger, and keep warm. Sauté the onions and garlic in the peanut oil in a pan for 15 minutes. Then add the bean sprouts, nutmeg and turmeric and cook over low heat for 5 minutes.

Put the chicken, onions, bean sprouts and sliced eggs on to a large serving platter. Put the ginger soup into individual serving bowls and float 1 slice of lemon on top of each bowl. Each person helps himself from the platter of chicken mixture while eating the soup.

Saté Ajam (Chicken Saté)

INDONESIA

SERVES FOUR TO SIX
1 large chicken, the meat diced
500 g/1 lb peanuts, fried, crushed
1 tablespoon lemon juice
¾ cup peanut oil
2 tablespoons thick soy sauce
salt and black pepper

Season the diced chicken with salt and black pepper. Then skewer the pieces of chicken on to saté sticks. Mix together the soy sauce, the crushed peanuts, lemon juice and peanut oil. Dip the skewers of diced chicken into this mixture, then put them under the grill and cook until the chicken meat is brown and tender. Baste frequently with the sauce mixture. Arrange the saté sticks on a large serving platter, and serve with the remaining sauce.

Ajam Santan (Chicken in Coconut Milk)　　　INDONESIA

SERVES FOUR TO SIX
1 large chicken, cut into serving pieces
1 onion, chopped
2 cups thick coconut milk
2 tablespoons peanut oil
2 cloves garlic, finely chopped
3 red chilli peppers, chopped
2 leaves daun salam
1 teaspoon lemon grass
½ teaspoon shrimp paste
½ teaspoon laos
salt

Sauté the onion, garlic, chilli peppers, shrimp paste and laos together in the oil in a large pan. When the onions become transparent, add the chicken pieces and cook over high heat for 5 minutes. Add the coconut milk, lemon grass, daun salam and salt to taste. Reduce to moderate heat and cook until the chicken is tender (approximately 30 minutes). Remove the chicken pieces from the pan and grill them for a few minutes until they are golden. Arrange the chicken on a serving platter, and pour the coconut milk sauce over it.

Nasi Goreng　　　INDONESIA

SERVES SIX
1 large chicken, cooked, the meat diced
250 g/½ lb pork, diced and fried
125 g/¼ lb ham, sliced
375 g/¾ lb crab or lobster, diced and fried
125 g/¼ lb shrimps, fried
4 tomatoes, sliced
1 cucumber, sliced
1 bunch spring onions, chopped
5 onions, chopped
4 eggs, beaten
1 kg/2 lb cooked long-grain rice
1 tablespoon brown sugar
3 tablespoons peanut oil
4 cloves garlic, finely chopped
7 red chilli peppers, chopped
2 leaves daun salam
2 teaspoons ground coriander
1 teaspoon ground cumin
¾ teaspoon shrimp paste
¼ teaspoon laos
salt and black pepper

Brown the diced chicken in 2 tablespoons of the peanut oil in a large pan. Remove and keep warm. Then add to the pan 2 of the onions, the garlic, chilli peppers, coriander, cumin, shrimp paste, laos, daun salam, brown sugar and salt to taste. Cook over low heat until the onion becomes transparent. Add the pork and the shrimps and cook for 3 minutes. Return the chicken to the pan, add the crab or lobster, and stir well. Add the rice gradually, stirring constantly until the ingredients are well mixed.

Season the beaten eggs with the salt and black pepper, and fry them into an omelette. Then cut this into thin strips. Fry the remaining 3 onions in 1 tablespoon peanut oil until they are brown. Put the chicken and rice mixture on to a serving platter and top with the omelette strips, the fried onions, the ham, tomatoes, cucumber and spring onions.

Ajam Setan (Grilled Spiced Chicken)　　　INDONESIA

SERVES FOUR TO SIX
1 large chicken, cut into serving pieces
1 onion, finely chopped
½ cup peanut oil
3 tablespoons thick soy sauce
3 cloves garlic, crushed
8 red chilli peppers, crushed
½ teaspoon ground coriander
salt and black pepper

Mix together the onions, garlic, chilli peppers, coriander, soy sauce and peanut oil. Season the chicken pieces with salt and black pepper, then marinate them in this mixture for at least 1 hour. Turn the pieces occasionally to coat them thoroughly. Now grill the chicken pieces until they are brown and tender. Baste frequently with the marinade.

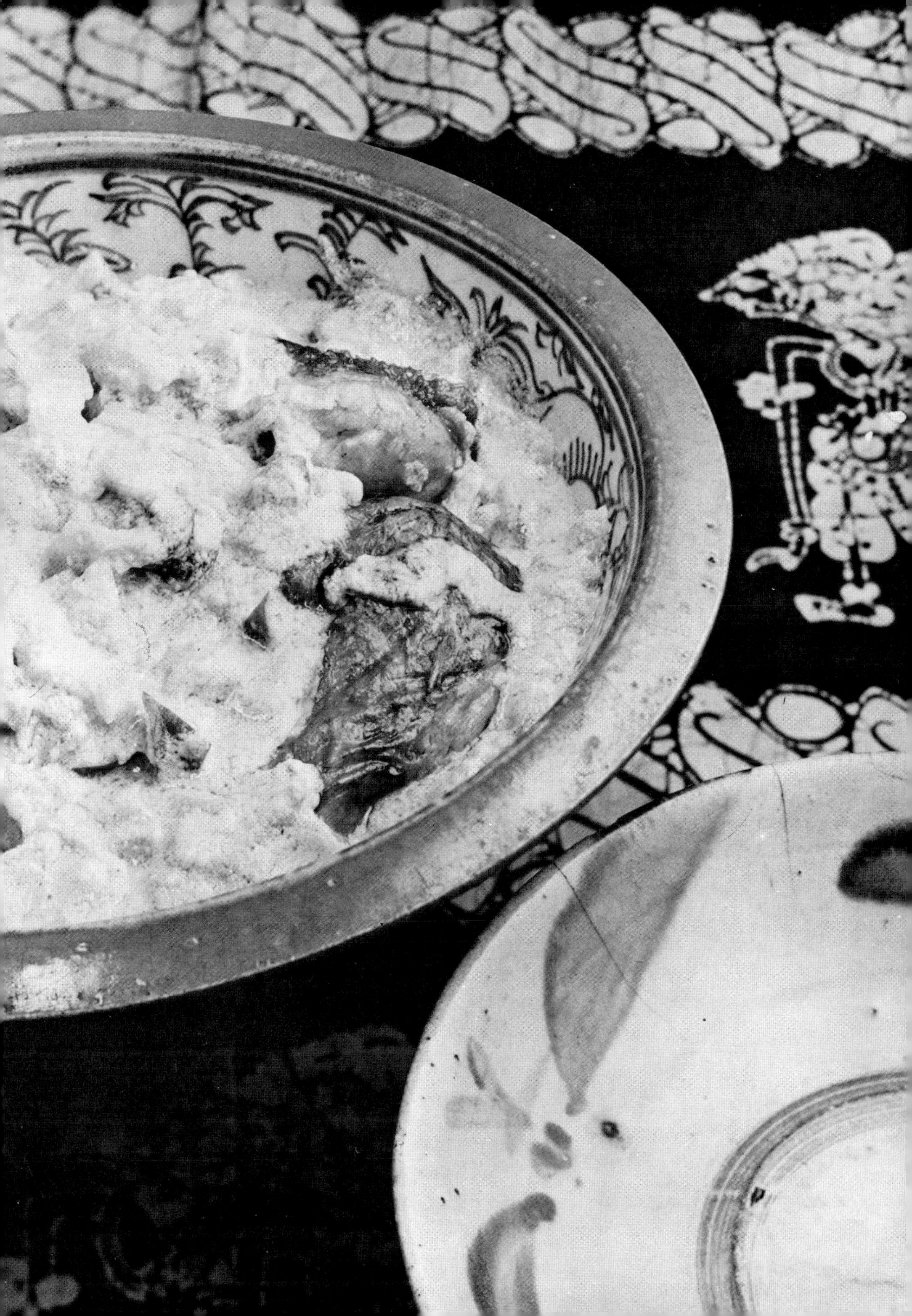

Ajam Masak Bali (Balinese Chicken)　　　　　INDONESIA

SERVES FOUR
1 medium chicken
1 onion, finely chopped
4 candle nuts (or macadamia nuts)
½ teaspoon brown sugar
1 tablespoon white vinegar
2 tablespoons peanut oil
1 tablespoon thick soy sauce
2 cloves garlic, crushed
2 teaspoons ground ginger
1 teaspoon dried ground chilli peppers

Split the chicken in half through the breast and flatten it out. Put the onion, candle nuts, garlic, ground chillis, ginger and 2 tablespoons water in a blender and blend until a smooth paste is formed. Put this mixture in the heated peanut oil in a large pan and cook over moderate heat, stirring constantly, for 30 seconds. Then put in the chicken and coat well all over with the spice paste. Add the soy sauce, vinegar, brown sugar and 1 cup water (hot). Stir well, then cover and cook, stirring occasionally, until the chicken is tender (approximately 30 minutes).

Alo-Balo Polo (Chicken and Sour Cherries)　　　　　IRAN

SERVES FOUR TO SIX
1 medium chicken
1 onion, coarsely chopped
1 large jar sour cherries
500 g/1 lb long-grain rice, soaked, drained
6 tablespoons water
3 tablespoons olive oil
3 tablespoons butter

Brown the chicken on all sides in the olive oil in a large casserole. Remove and keep warm. Sauté the onion in the casserole until brown (approximately 10 minutes). Then return the chicken and its juices, add the water and bring to the boil. Cover and cook over low heat until the chicken is tender (approximately 30 minutes). Put the rice into a pan of boiling water and boil for 5 minutes, stirring occasionally; then drain.

When the chicken is cooked, remove it from the casserole, cut it into serving pieces, and keep warm. Discard the onions and all but 1½ tablespoons of the cooking liquids. Add the butter to the casserole and mix well with the remaining cooking liquids. Add half of the rice, smooth it down and cook over moderate heat for 5 minutes. Remove from the heat, then add the chicken pieces and half of the sour cherries. Put the remaining rice over these, then top with the remaining cherries and their liquid. Cover and cook over low heat until the rice is tender (approximately 15 minutes).

Alo-Balo Polo

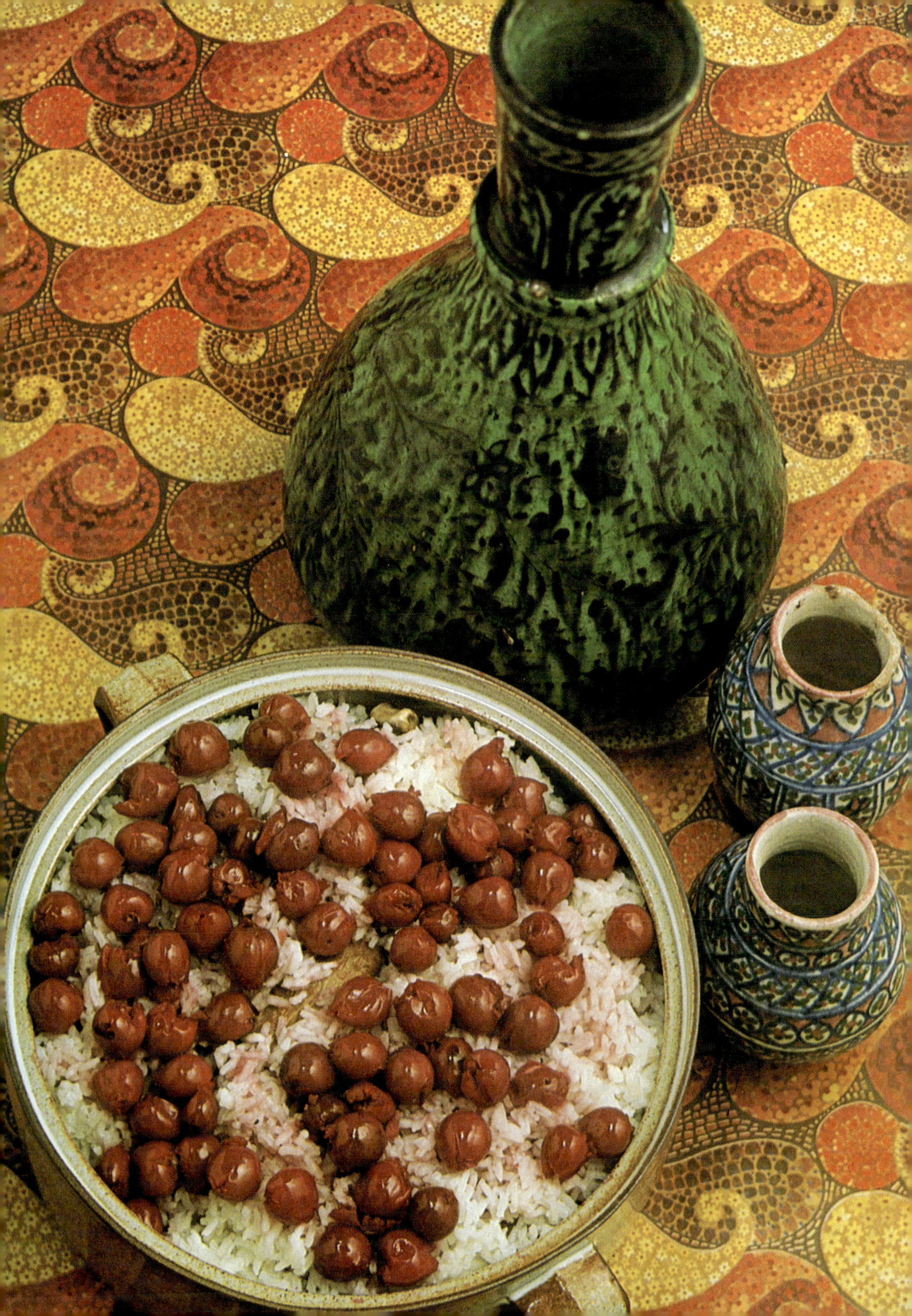

Chicken with Chick Peas

IRAN

SERVES FOUR
1 medium chicken, cut into serving pieces
1½ cups chick peas, cooked
2 onions, finely chopped
1½ cups chicken stock
2 tablespoons lemon juice
3 tablespoons olive oil
3 cloves garlic, crushed
½ teaspoon ground turmeric
salt and pepper

Brown the chicken pieces in the oil in a large pan, then remove and keep warm. Put the onions into the pan and sauté until golden; then stir in the turmeric. Return the chicken pieces to the pan and coat them well with the onion and turmeric mixture. Add the chicken stock, lemon juice, garlic, and salt and pepper to taste. Then cover and simmer for 30 minutes. Add the chick peas and continue to simmer, partially covered, until the chicken is tender (approximately 30 minutes).

Kababe Morgh (Skewered Chicken) — IRAN

SERVES FOUR
2 small chickens, each cut into 8 serving pieces
4 onions, finely chopped
6 tablespoons lemon juice
3 tablespoons butter (melted)
¼ teaspoon saffron
1½ teaspoons salt

Mix together the onions, lemon juice and salt. Marinate the chicken pieces in this mixture for at least 2 hours, turning the pieces occasionally to coat them well. Then put the chicken pieces on to 4 long skewers. Mix the melted butter and saffron into the marinade, and coat the chicken pieces well with this mixture.

Put the skewers of chicken under a very hot grill, and turn frequently until the chicken is tender (approximately 10-15 minutes). Baste the chicken frequently with the marinade mixture. Serve with rice.

Tarnegolet Bemitz Hadarim (Chicken with Kumquats) ISRAEL

SERVES FOUR

1 medium chicken, cut into serving pieces
1 jar preserved kumquats
1 cup orange juice
5 teaspoons lemon juice
3 tablespoons honey
1½ tablespoons chilli peppers, seeded, finely chopped
orange and lemon slices (for garnish)

Make one layer of the chicken pieces in a baking dish. Mix together the orange juice, lemon juice and honey and pour over the chicken. Turn the chicken pieces in the mixture until they are well coated. Then sprinkle the chopped peppers over the top. Bake, skin side down, in the oven (190°C/375°F) for 15 minutes. Turn the chicken pieces over, add the kumquats, and baste well with the liquids. Continue baking the chicken, basting occasionally, until it is tender (approximately 30 minutes). Place the chicken pieces on a serving platter, pour the kumquats and juices over them, and garnish with the orange and lemon slices.

Maafeh Awf Vematza Metubal Beshamir (Chicken, Matzoh and Dill) ISRAEL

SERVES FOUR

1 small chicken, cooked, and meat diced
1 onion, finely chopped
6 eggs, beaten
3 plain square matzohs
2 cups chicken stock
6 tablespoons olive oil
3 tablespoons chopped parsley
5 teaspoons dried dill
1½ teaspoons salt
¼ teaspoon black pepper

Mix together the beaten eggs, onion, parsley, dill, salt and black pepper. Stir the diced chicken into this mixture. Heat the oil, then pour 1 teaspoon of it into a square baking dish and spread it evenly. Keep the remaining oil aside.

Moisten the matzohs well in the chicken stock. Lay one matzoh on the bottom of the baking dish and spread half of the chicken mixture over it. Cover with a second moistened matzoh, spread the remaining chicken mixture over this, and top with the third matzoh. Pour half the remaining oil over the top and bake in the oven (200°C/400°F) for 15 minutes. Then pour over the remaining oil and bake until the top is browned (approximately 15 minutes).

Maafeh Awf Vematza Metubal Beshamir

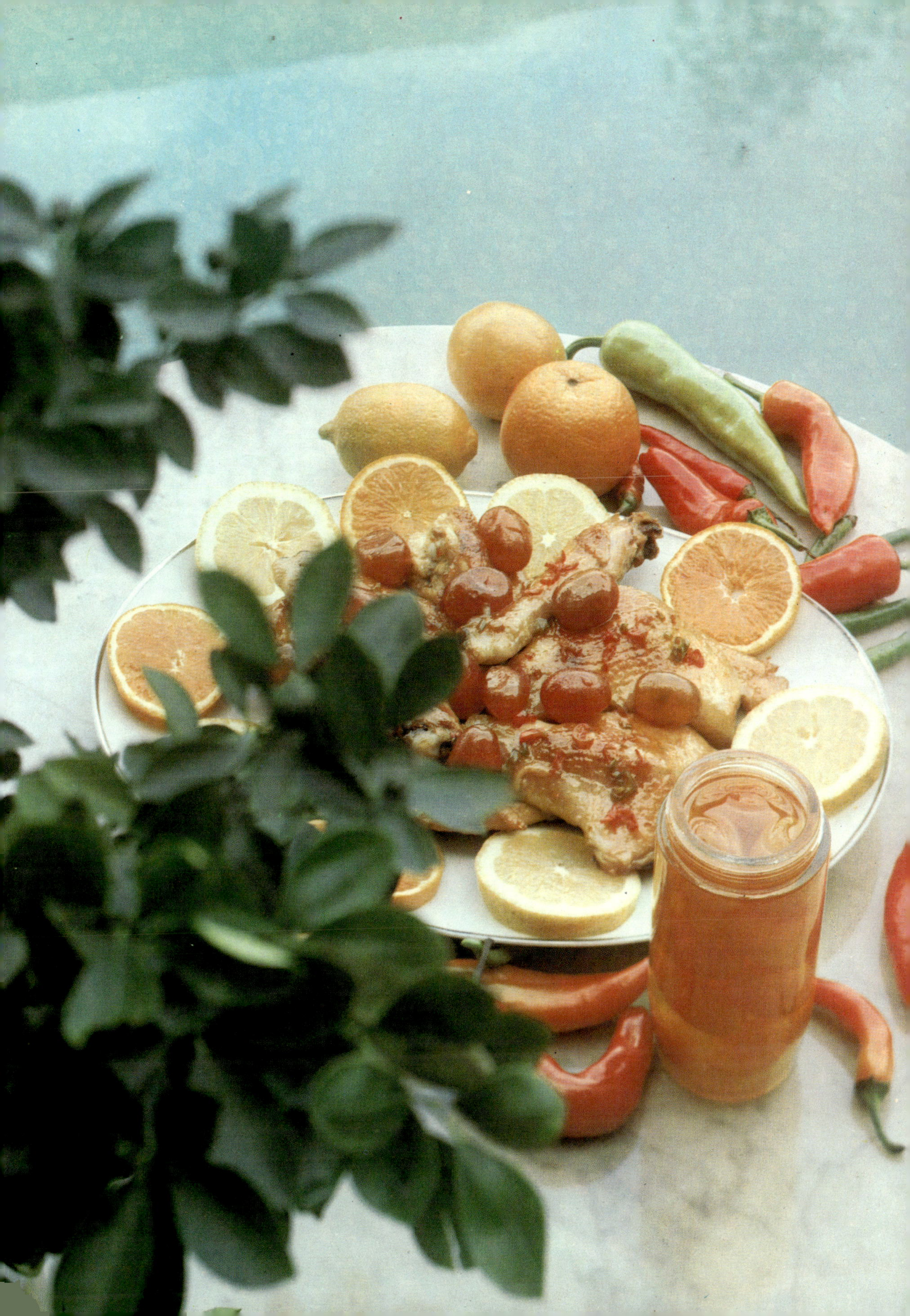

Pollo con Peperoni (Chicken with Peppers)

ITALY

SERVES FOUR
1 medium chicken, cut into serving pieces
4 tomatoes, peeled, seeded, chopped
4 green peppers, cut into strips
2 onions, finely chopped
1 cup dry white wine
3 tablespoons olive oil
2 cloves garlic, finely chopped
salt and black pepper

Brown the chicken pieces in the olive oil in a large pan. Remove and keep warm. Add the onions, garlic and white wine to the pan and cook over high heat until the wine has reduced by half. Now stir in the green pepper strips and cook over moderate heat for 2 minutes. Add the tomatoes, and salt and black pepper to taste, and cook for another 2 minutes. Then return the chicken pieces to the pan, cover, and cook over low heat, basting occasionally, until the chicken is tender (approximately 30 minutes).

Place the chicken pieces on a serving platter. Remove the vegetables from the pan and put them on top of the chicken pieces. Cook the liquids over high heat for a few minutes so that the sauce thickens; then pour it over the chicken and vegetables.

Chicken in Vermouth

ITALY

SERVES FOUR
1 medium chicken, cut into serving pieces
1 onion, finely chopped
1 teaspoon tomato paste
4 tablespoons Italian sweet vermouth
1 cup chicken stock
2 tablespoons olive oil
2 cloves garlic, crushed
1 teaspoon oregano
1 teaspoon paprika
salt and pepper

Brown the chicken pieces in the olive oil in a large pan; then remove and keep warm. Pour off all but 1 tablespoon of the oil, then add the onion and garlic to the pan and sauté until the onion is transparent. Add the tomato paste, oregano, paprika, and a little salt and pepper, and mix well. Return the chicken pieces to the pan and coat them well with the mixture. Add the vermouth and the chicken stock, bring to the boil, then simmer until the chicken is tender (approximately 1 hour). Remove the chicken pieces and place them on a serving platter. Boil the sauce over high heat to reduce and thicken, then pour it over the chicken pieces, and serve.

Pollo con Peperoni

OLIO PURO DI OLIVA
ITALIANO
BERTOLLI
LUCCA
ALIMONT S.p.A.·LUCCA·ITALIA
LUCCA

Chicken Marengo

ITALY

SERVES FOUR
1 medium chicken, cut into serving pieces
1 lobster, cooked, cut into 4 pieces
250 g/½ lb mushrooms, sliced
24 green olives, stoned
3 tomatoes, peeled, chopped
1 tablespoon tomato paste
1 cup dry white wine
4 tablespoons olive oil
1 tablespoon chopped parsley
1 clove garlic, finely chopped
salt and pepper

Brown the chicken pieces in the oil in a large pan (10 minutes). Remove and keep warm. Pour off all but 1 tablespoon of the oil from the pan, then add the tomatoes and the garlic. Cook over low heat for 10 minutes, then add the mushrooms, the wine, tomato paste, and salt and pepper to taste. Cover, and cook over low heat until the sauce has the consistency of cream. Return the chicken pieces to the pan and add the olives. Cover and cook until the chicken is tender (approximately 25 minutes). Arrange the chicken and the lobster on a serving platter, pour over the sauce, and garnish with the parsley.

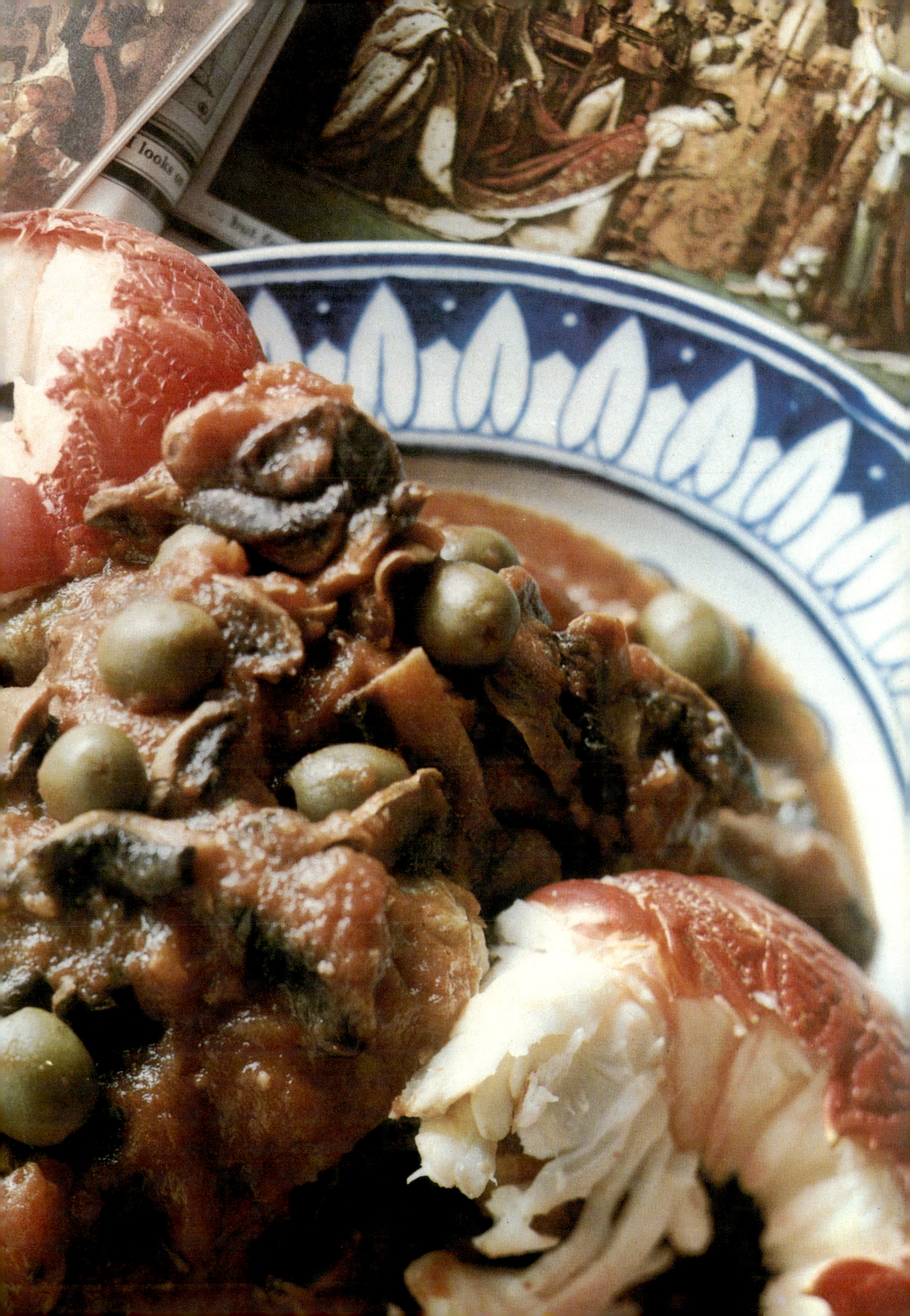

Pollo alla Crema (Chicken Baked in Cream) ITALY

SERVES FOUR
1 medium chicken, cut into serving pieces
2 tablespoons flour
1 teaspoon potato flour
3 tablespoons brandy
fresh cream
juice of 1 lemon
2 tablespoons butter
salt and pepper

Rub the chicken pieces with the lemon juice, then roll them in the flour (seasoned with salt and pepper). Brown the chicken pieces in the butter in a casserole, then pour in enough cream to cover them. Put the casserole into the oven (200°C/400°F) and bake the chicken until it is tender (approximately 45 minutes). Baste occasionally with the cream. When the chicken is cooked, remove the pieces, put them on a serving dish, and keep warm.

Mix the potato flour with a little water to form a paste, then stir this into the cream to thicken it. Add the brandy and 1 more cup of cream, and cook over low heat until the mixture is almost boiling. Pour this sauce over the chicken pieces; and serve.

Pollo alla Parmigiana (Chicken with Cheese Sauce) ITALY

SERVES FOUR
2 small chickens, halved (half-chicken per person)
3 tablespoons grated parmesan cheese
1 egg yolk, beaten
2 tablespoons cream
grated rind and juice of $\frac{1}{2}$ lemon
2 tablespoons butter
salt and pepper
Béchamel Sauce

Brown the chicken halves, skin side down, in the butter in a large pan. Turn them over, season to taste, and sprinkle the lemon juice and rind over the top. Cover and cook over low heat until the chicken is tender (approximately 20-30 minutes). Add a little water to the pan if it becomes dry during the cooking. When cooked, remove the chickens, trim away the backbones, and arrange them on a serving dish. Keep warm.

Make the Béchamel Sauce. Then add 2 tablespoons of the parmesan cheese, reheat, and season to taste. Mix the egg yolk and cream together, blend in a little of the hot sauce, then stir this mixture into the sauce in the pan. Heat through but do not boil. Spoon this sauce over the chickens. Sprinkle with the remaining parmesan cheese and put under the grill until the cheese is golden.

Béchamel Sauce
1 cup milk
1 tablespoon cream
2 tablespoons flour
2 tablespoons butter
1 slice of onion
1 bay leaf
1 blade of mace
6 peppercorns
salt and pepper

Warm the milk with the onion, bay leaf, mace and peppercorns in a covered pan over low heat for 5 minutes. Strain the milk and keep aside. Wipe out the pan, then melt the butter in it. Remove from the heat and mix in the flour until smooth. Gradually blend in the milk. Season with salt and pepper, then return to the heat and stur until boiling. Boil for 2 minutes only, then remove from the heat and stir in the cream.

Pollo Tonnato ITALY

SERVES FOUR
8 slices of chicken breast, cooked
185 g/6 oz tuna fish
185 g/6 oz mayonnaise

Put the tuna fish and half the mayonnaise into the blender and blend until a smooth paste is formed. Add the remaining mayonnaise, and continue blending until the mixture has the consistency of soft butter. Coat each slice of chicken breast thickly with the tuna paste, then chill in the refrigerator. Serve with asparagus tips.

Pollo alla Crema

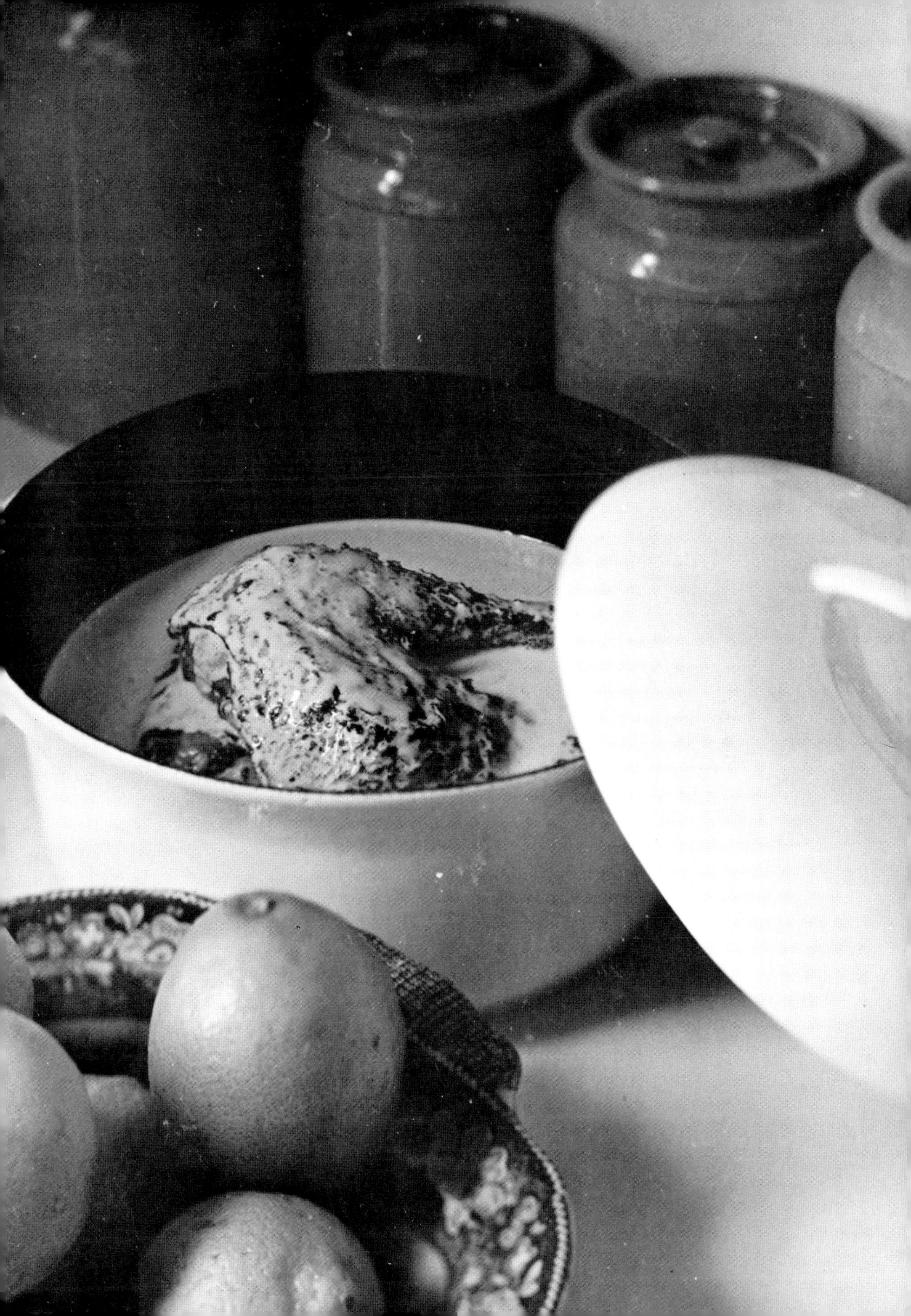

Pollo Marsala

SERVES FOUR

1 medium chicken, cut into serving pieces
2 tablespoons flour
marsala
2 tablespoons olive oil
2 cloves garlic, crushed
1 teaspoon paprika
salt and black pepper

ITALY

Coat the chicken pieces with the flour (seasoned with salt and black pepper), then brown them in the olive oil in a casserole. Pour off all but 1 tablespoon of the oil, then add the garlic, paprika, and enough marsala to cover the chicken. Cover the casserole, and simmer until the chicken is tender (approximately 40 minutes). Serve from the casserole with the sauce.

Pollo alla Cacciatora

SERVES FOUR

1 medium chicken, cut into serving pieces
4 tomatoes, peeled, chopped
1 green pepper, seeded, chopped
2 tablespoons black olives, stoned, sliced
2 onions, finely chopped
1 cup dry white wine
$\frac{1}{2}$ cup chicken stock
2 tablespoons olive oil
2 cloves garlic, finely chopped
1 bay leaf
1 teaspoon oregano
salt and black pepper

ITALY

Brown the chicken pieces in the olive oil in a large pan. Then remove and keep warm. Pour away all but 1 tablespoon of the oil from the pan. Put in the onions and garlic and cook over moderate heat until the onions are golden (approximately 8 minutes). Add the wine and cook over high heat until it has been reduced to about $\frac{1}{3}$ cup liquid. Pour in the chicken stock and boil for 2 minutes, stirring constantly. Return the chicken pieces to the pan and add the tomatoes, pepper, oregano, bay leaf, and salt and black pepper to taste. Bring to the boil, then cover and simmer, basting occasionally, until the chicken is tender (approximately 30 minutes). Discard the bay leaf.

Remove the chicken pieces and put them on to a serving platter. Boil the sauce in the pan until it thickens slightly, stir in the black olives and cook for another 2 minutes. Pour the sauce over the chicken pieces, and serve.

Pollo alla Cacciatora

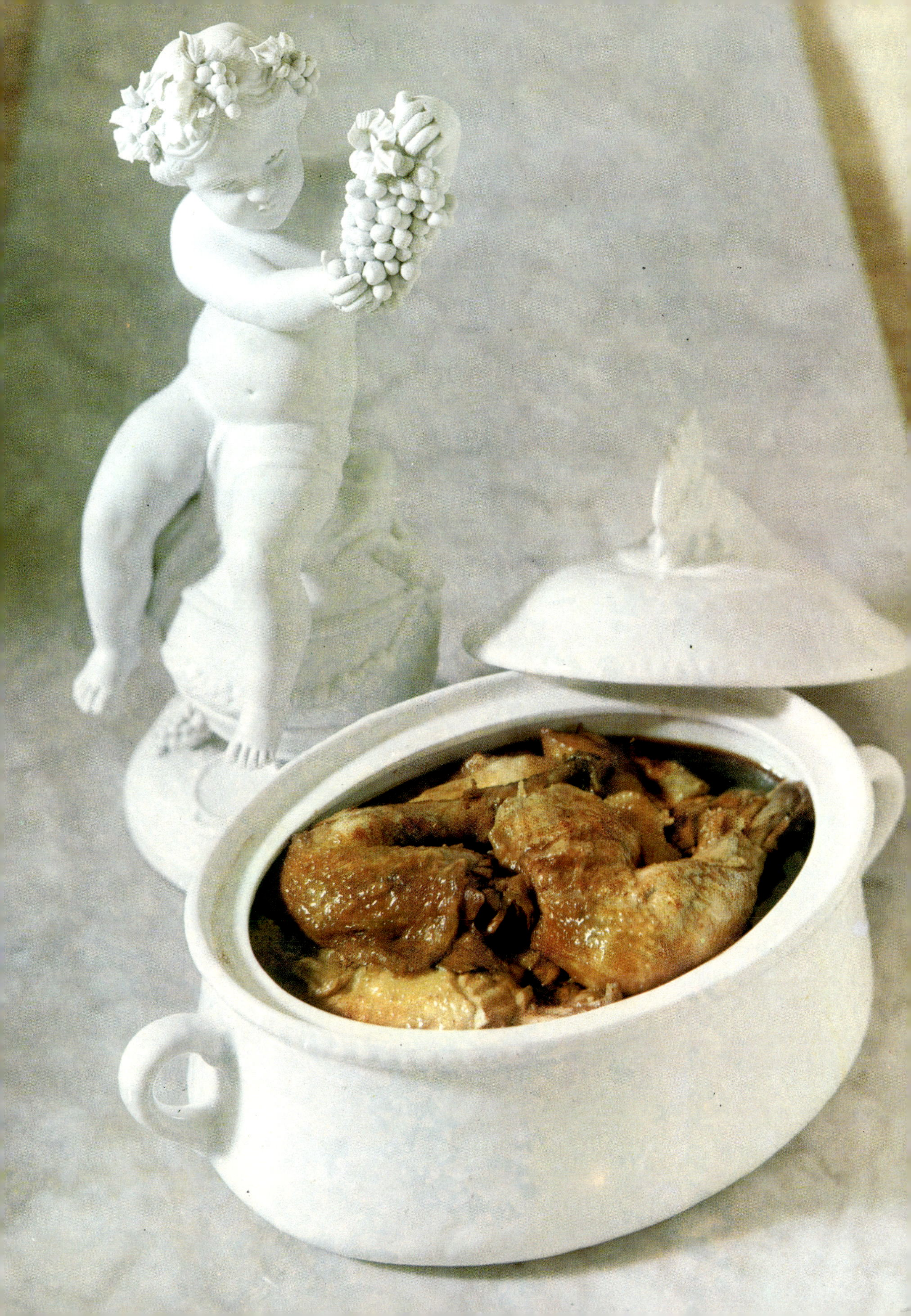

Pollo alla Napoletana

ITALY

SERVES FOUR
1 medium chicken
3 rashers of bacon, cut up
125 g/4 oz dried mushrooms, soaked in warm water for 20 minutes, sliced
2 onions, chopped
2 tablespoons tomato paste
1 cup dry white wine
3 tablespoons olive oil
3 tablespoons butter
2 cloves garlic, finely chopped
1 teaspoon rosemary
salt and pepper

Put the chicken into a large pan, cover with salted water, and cook over low heat until tender (approximately 2 hours). Remove, and cut into serving pieces.

Sauté the onions in the oil and butter in a pan. When they become transparent, add the sliced mushrooms, the bacon, garlic, rosemary, and salt and pepper to taste. Simmer for a few minutes, then add the tomato paste and 2 tablespoons of the stock from the chicken pan. Simmer for a further 10 minutes, then add the wine, stir well, and add the chicken pieces. Cook over low heat for another 10 minutes. Place the chicken pieces in a serving dish and pour the sauce over them.

Pollo all'Aretina

ITALY

SERVES FOUR TO SIX
1 medium chicken, cut into serving pieces
250 g/½ lb green peas
3 onions, chopped
125 g/¼ lb medium-grain rice
1 cup dry white wine
1¼ cups chicken stock
2 tablespoons olive oil
salt and pepper

Brown the chicken pieces in the olive oil in a large pan; then remove and keep warm. Add the onions to the pan and sauté until they are golden. Return the chicken pieces and add the wine and the chicken stock. Bring to the boil, then add the peas, the rice, and salt and pepper to taste. Simmer until the chicken is tender and the peas and rice are cooked (approximately 20 minutes).

Pollo all'Aretina

Chicken with Egg-plant

ITALY

SERVES FOUR
1 medium chicken, cut into 8 serving pieces
1 egg-plant, peeled, thinly sliced
2 onions, thinly sliced
5 tablespoons flour
⅔ cup dry white wine
⅔ cup tomato juice
⅓ cup olive oil
salt and pepper

Season the flour with salt and pepper. Coat the chicken pieces with the seasoned flour, then brown them in the olive oil in a large pan. Remove the chicken pieces and put them into a casserole; pour over the wine and the tomato juice. Cover, and cook over low heat until the chicken is tender (approximately 1 hour). Take out the chicken pieces, put them on to a serving platter, and keep warm. Cook the juices in the casserole over high heat until they are reduced by half, then pour this sauce over the chicken pieces.

Meanwhile, sauté the onions in the oil remaining in the pan until they are transparent. Keep warm. Now coat the egg-plant slices with the seasoned flour, then brown them in the oil. Garnish the chicken and sauce with the onions and egg-plant slices.

Pollo alla Fontina

SERVES FOUR

4 chicken breasts, skinned, boned
250 g/½ lb mushrooms, sliced
125 g/¼ lb fontina cheese, cut into 4 slices
½ cup sweet white wine
4 tablespoons olive oil
1 teaspoon oregano
1 teaspoon paprika

ITALY

Brown the chicken breasts gently in the oil in a large pan (approximately 10 minutes). Then remove the chicken breasts, put them into a baking dish, and keep warm. Now sauté the mushrooms in the pan until they are soft, then sprinkle these over the chicken. Pour off most of the oil, then add the white wine and the oregano to the pan and cook until the liquids have reduced by half. Pour this sauce over the chicken breasts. Top each of the chicken breasts with one slice of the fontina cheese, and put under the grill until the cheese has melted. Sprinkle the paprika over the top; and serve.

Pollo alla Diavola (Devilled Chicken)

SERVES FOUR

2 small chickens, halved
1 onion, finely chopped
1 lemon, thinly sliced
juice of 1 lemon
2 tablespoons olive oil
1 tablespoon chopped parsley
2 teaspoons ground ginger
1 teaspoon paprika
salt and pepper

ITALY

Mix together the olive oil, ginger, and a little salt and pepper. Rub the chicken halves with the lemon juice, then brush the olive oil and ginger mixture all over them. Put the chicken halves under a hot grill and cook, turning occasionally, until the chicken is tender. Baste frequently with any remaining olive oil and ginger mixture.

When the chicken is tender, turn skin side up and spread the top with a mixture of the onion and parsley. Grill for another few minutes until the mixture is slightly browned. Put the chicken halves on to a serving platter and sprinkle the paprika over the top. Garnish with the lemon slices.

Pollo alla Diavola

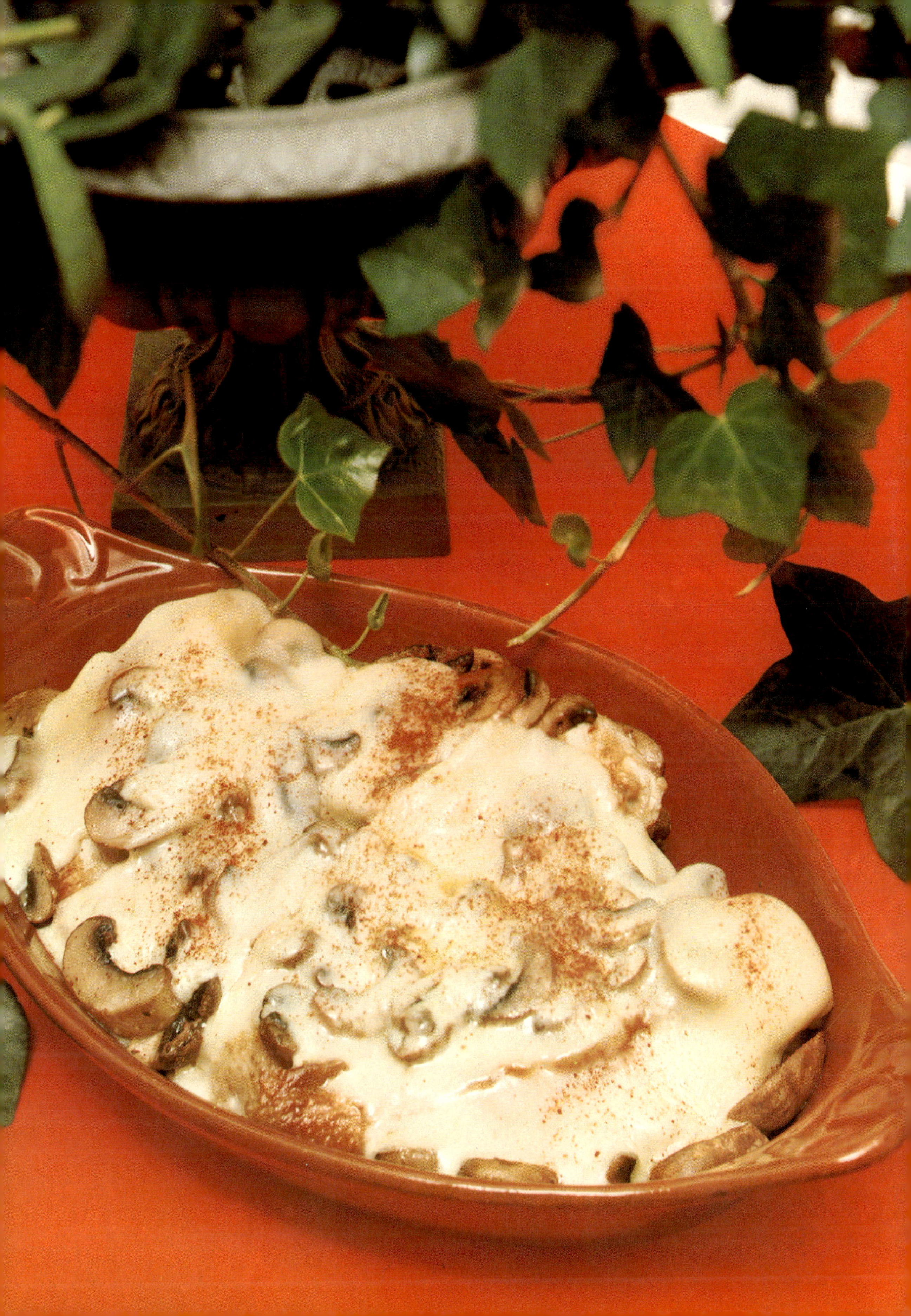

Yaki-Tori (Skewered Chicken and Chicken Livers) JAPAN

SERVES FOUR
1 small chicken, the meat diced
8 chicken livers, halved
2 green peppers, cut into skewer-size pieces
1 tablespoon sugar
3 tablespoons sake (rice wine)
3 tablespoons Japanese soy sauce

Mix together the sake, soy sauce and sugar. Halve this mixture, and marinate the diced chicken and the chicken livers separately for at least 1 hour. Thread 8 skewers with alternate pieces of the chicken and the green pepper, and thread 4 skewers with the chicken livers. Cook under a grill or over an hibachi (charcoal grill), basting twice with the marinade.

Chawan Mushi (Steamed Chicken and Egg) JAPAN

SERVES SIX
1 medium chicken, the meat cut into strips
8 dried mushrooms, soaked in cold water for 1 hour, drained, sliced
12 spinach leaves
20 chestnuts, cooked, shelled
4 onions, thinly sliced
6 thin slices of lemon
4 eggs, beaten
1 tablespoon sake (rice wine)
2 cups chicken stock
3 tablespoons peanut oil
3 tablespoons Japanese soy sauce

Heat the oil in a pan, put in the chicken strips and cook over low heat for 5 minutes, stirring frequently. Add the mushrooms, chestnuts, onions, sake, soy sauce and 4 tablespoons of the chicken stock. Bring to the boil, then cook over low heat for 2 minutes.

Put this mixture into a bowl (or into individual serving bowls). Beat together the eggs and the remaining stock, then pour this over the chicken mixture. Cover the mixture completely with the spinach leaves. Put the bowl(s) into a pan of hot water, then cover the pan and steam until the egg mixture is set (approximately 25 minutes). Serve, garnished with the lemon slices.

Chawan Mushi

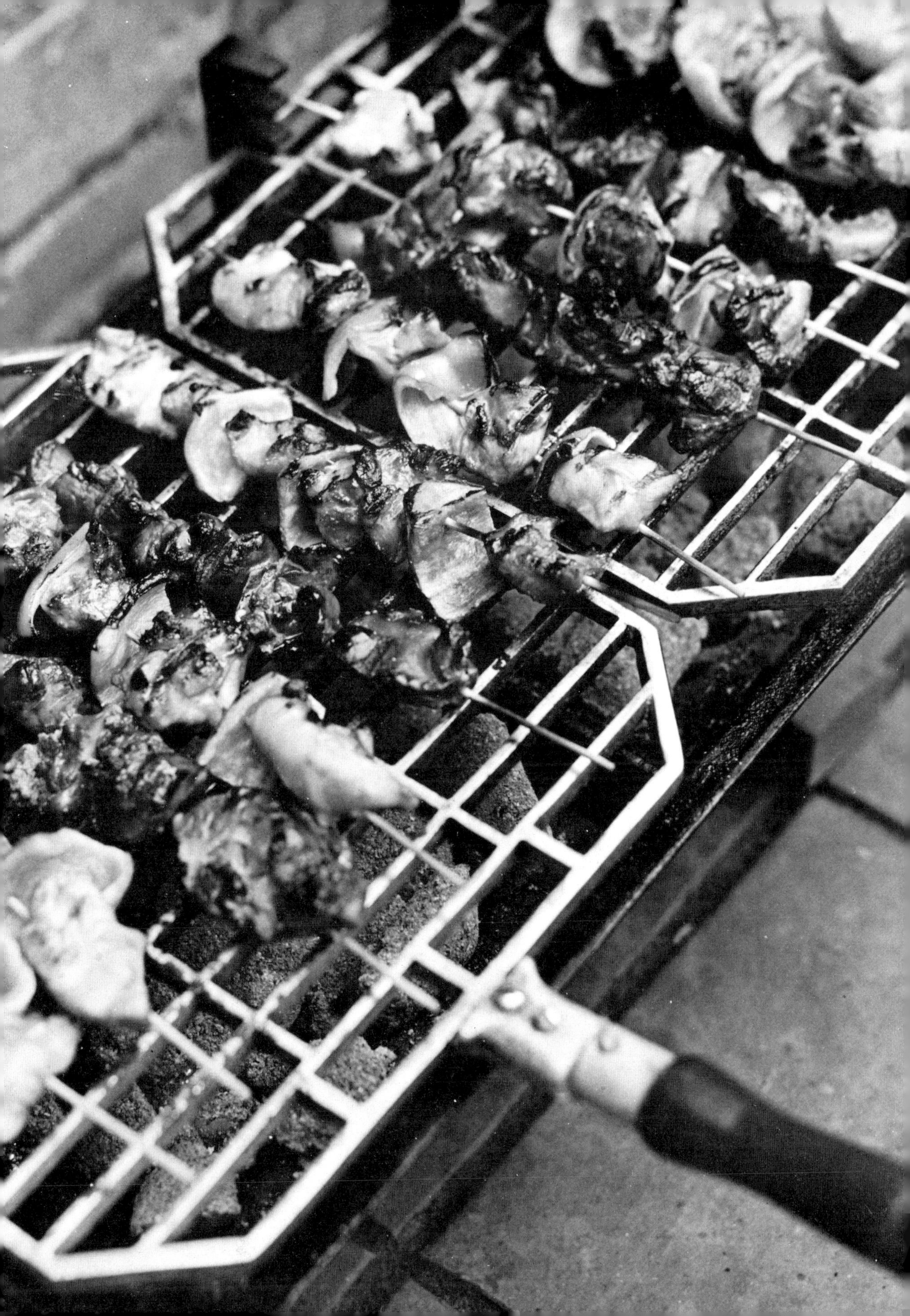

Toyaji-Kogi wa Tark-Kogi (Korean Chicken and Pork)   KOREA

SERVES SIX
1 medium chicken, cut into serving pieces
500 g/1 lb lean pork, diced
500 g/1 lb green peas
3 tomatoes, chopped
1 cup radishes, sliced
1 onion, sliced
1 tablespoon cornflour
2 cups water
2 tablespoons peanut oil
3 tablespoons soy sauce
2 cloves garlic, crushed
2 tablespoons sesame seeds
¼ teaspoon cayenne pepper
2½ teaspoons salt
¼ teaspoon pepper

Put the water and 1 teaspoon of the salt into a large pan and bring to the boil. Add the chicken pieces and the diced pork, and simmer for 15 minutes. Then remove the chicken and pork and keep aside. Also keep aside the stock.

Sauté the onion, garlic and sesame seeds in the oil in a large pan. When the onion is golden, add the chicken pieces and the pork and brown them lightly. Then add the tomatoes, radishes, soy sauce, cayenne pepper, pepper, 1½ teaspoons salt, and ¾ cup of the stock. Cover and simmer for 30 minutes. Blend the cornflour with ¼ cup of the stock, then stir it into the mixture in the pan. Add the peas and continue to cook until the chicken is tender and the peas are cooked (approximately 8 minutes).

Korean Chicken

KOREA

SERVES FOUR

1 medium chicken, cut into serving pieces
$\frac{1}{3}$ cup peanut oil
$\frac{1}{4}$ cup honey
1 cup soy sauce
1 clove garlic, crushed
$\frac{1}{4}$ cup chives
1 teaspoon ground ginger
$\frac{1}{4}$ teaspoon dry mustard

Mix together the peanut oil, honey, soy sauce, garlic, chives, ginger and mustard. Marinate the chicken pieces in this mixture for at least 3 hours, turning the pieces occasionally. Then put the chicken pieces into a casserole and pour the marinade over them. Cover, and bake in the oven (160°C/325°F) for 1$\frac{1}{2}$ hours. Take off the cover, then bake for a further 30 minutes, basting frequently.

Spiced Malaysian Chicken

MALAYSIA

SERVES FOUR
1 medium chicken, cut into serving pieces
4 onions, thinly sliced
½ cup water
4 tablespoons peanut oil
2 cloves garlic, crushed
2 red chilli peppers, seeded, sliced
1 teaspoon ground turmeric
2 teaspoons salt
½ teaspoon black pepper

Mix together the garlic, turmeric, salt and black pepper, then rub this mixture over the chicken pieces. Sauté half the onions in the oil in a large pan until they are brown; remove and keep aside.

Now put the chilli peppers and the remaining onions into the pan. When the onions are transparent, add the chicken pieces and brown them. Then add the water, cover, and simmer until the chicken is tender. Uncover, and continue to simmer until all the liquid has evaporated. Put the chicken pieces on to a serving platter, and garnish with the fried onion.

Pollo Pibil (Mexican Steamed Chicken)

MEXICO

SERVES FOUR TO SIX
1 large chicken
12 tortillas
⅔ cup orange juice
5 tablespoons lemon juice
1 teaspoon ground saffron
2 cloves garlic, finely chopped
½ teaspoon oregano
½ teaspoon ground cumin
¼ teaspoon ground cloves
¼ teaspoon ground cinnamon
1½ teaspoons salt
¼ teaspoon black pepper

Mix together the orange juice, lemon juice, saffron, garlic, oregano, cumin, cloves, cinnamon, salt and pepper. Marinate the chicken in this mixture for at least 6 hours, turning occasionally to coat well on all sides.

Place the chicken in the middle of a large piece of aluminium foil. Then bring the corners of the foil up over the chicken and pour in the marinade. Fold the edges of the foil together to seal in the chicken and the marinade. Place this 'parcel' in a large pan, preferably lifted slightly away from the bottom (e.g. on a cake-stand), then add water sufficient to come half-way up the 'parcel'. Bring to the boil, then reduce the heat, cover, and simmer until the chicken is tender (approximately 1½ hours). Add more water if the pan becomes dry.

When the chicken is cooked, remove the 'parcel' from the pan and open it. Put the chicken on a serving platter, and pour the sauce over. Serve with the tortillas.

Note: The authentic dish involves cooking the chicken in banana leaves.

Spiced Malaysian Chicken

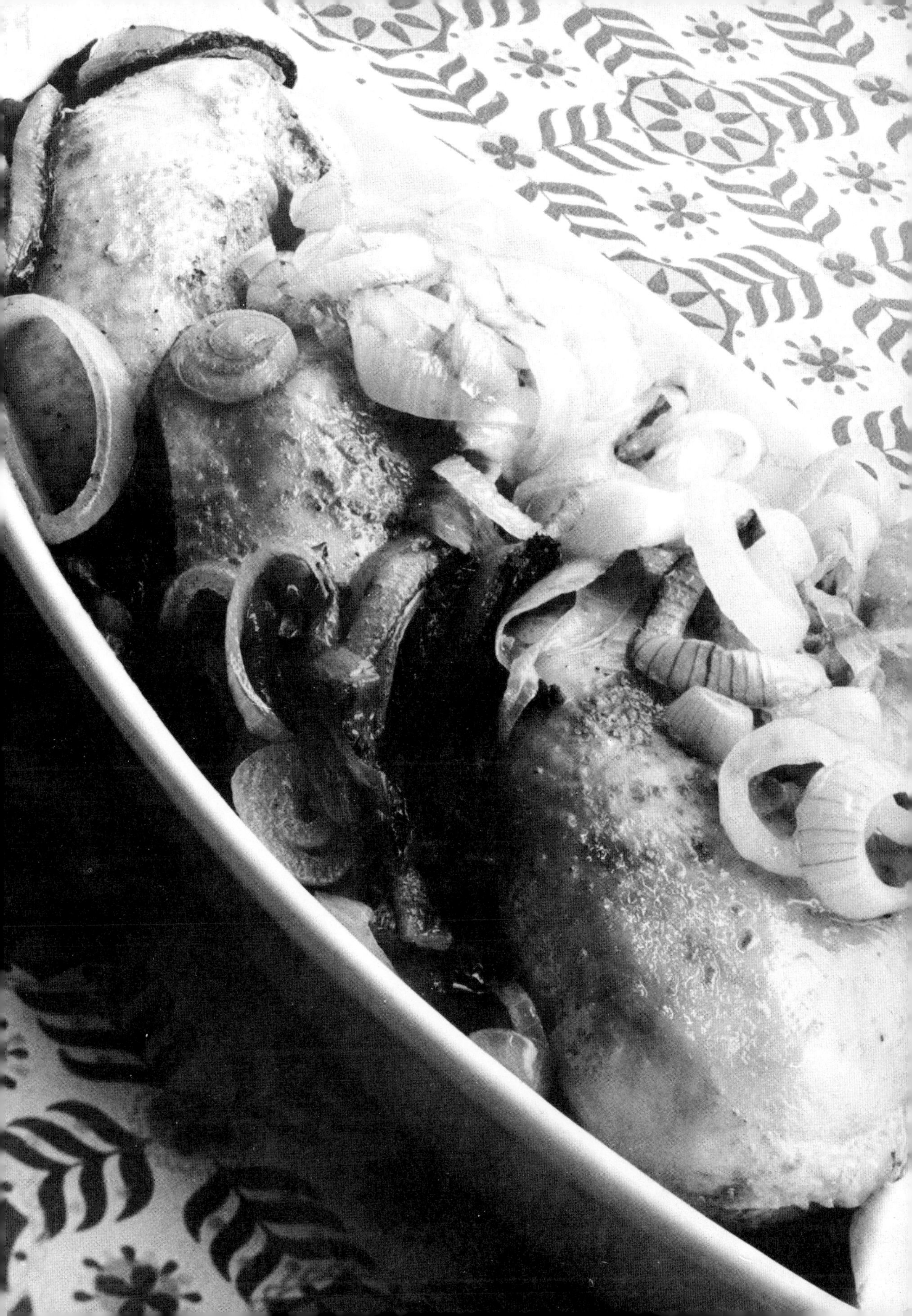

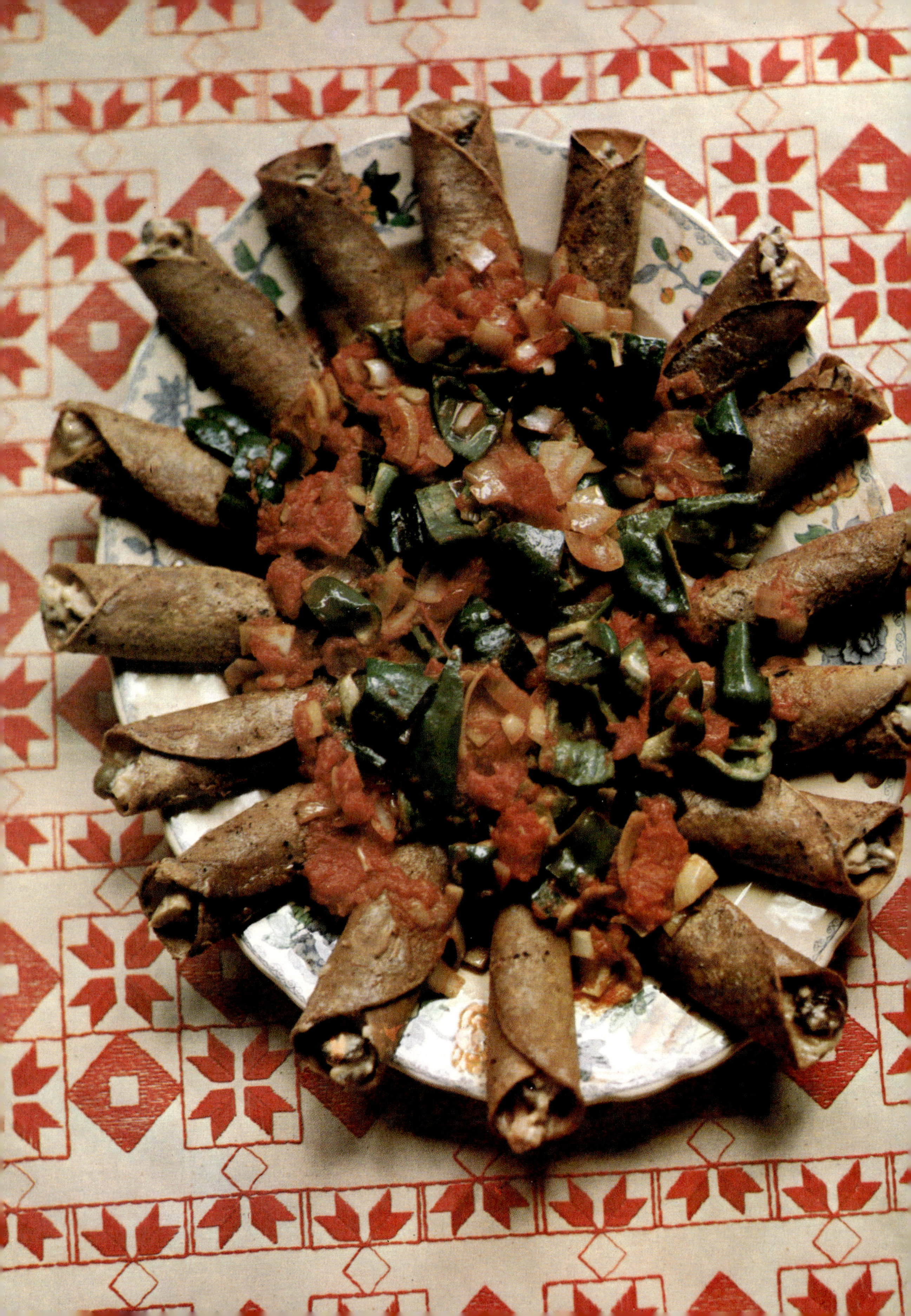

Enchiladas de Pollo (Chicken-filled Tortillas) MEXICO

SERVES SIX

1 small chicken, cooked, the meat diced
8 tomatoes, peeled, seeded, chopped
3 green peppers, seeded, chopped
2 onions, chopped
3 tablespoons green olives, stoned, chopped
2 tablespoons seedless raisins
3 cups cheddar cheese, grated
3 eggs, beaten
18 tortillas
2 cups sour cream
1 cup peanut oil
2 cloves garlic, crushed
1 tablespoon dried ground chilli peppers
salt and pepper

Mix together the diced chicken, the cheese, sour cream, raisins and olives. Keep aside. Heat 3 tablespoons of the oil in a pan, then add the tomatoes, green peppers, onions, garlic, ground chillis, and salt and pepper to taste. Cook over low heat, stirring occasionally, for 20 minutes.

Dip the tortillas in the beaten eggs. Heat the remainder of the oil to 190°C/375°F, then fry the tortillas for one minute on each side until they are limp. Remove the tortillas from the pan and place 1 tablespoon of the chicken mixture in the centre of each. Roll the tortillas around the chicken mixture and fasten each with a toothpick. Return these enchiladas to the pan and fry them for 3 minutes. Drain them, then place them on a serving platter. Pour the cooked tomato mixture over the tortillas; and serve.

Left: Enchiladas de Pollo (Finished Dish)

Below: Enchiladas de Pollo (Ingredients)

Pollo en Adobo (Chicken and Chillis) MEXICO

SERVES FOUR

1 medium chicken, cut into serving pieces
3 tomatoes, peeled, seeded, chopped
2 onions, chopped
1 teaspoon sugar
1 cup chicken stock
2½ teaspoons white vinegar
4 tablespoons peanut oil
2 cloves garlic, finely chopped
1½ tablespoons dried ground chilli peppers
½ teaspoon ground coriander
¼ teaspoon ground cinnamon
¼ teaspoon ground cloves
1 teaspoon salt
¼ teaspoon black pepper

Put the chicken stock and the ground chillis into a blender and mix at high speed for a few seconds. Then add the tomatoes, onions, sugar, vinegar, garlic, coriander, cinnamon, cloves, salt and black pepper. Blend until a thick, smooth mixture is formed (approximately 1 minute). Heat 1 tablespoon of the oil in a casserole, add this tomato and chilli mixture and cook over moderate heat, stirring occasionally, for 5 minutes. Remove the casserole from the heat.

Brown the chicken pieces in the remaining 3 tablespoons of the oil in a large pan. Then put the chicken pieces into the casserole with the tomato and chilli mixture, and turn the pieces until they are well coated with the sauce. Cover the casserole, and bake in the oven (180°C/350°F) for 45 minutes. Remove the cover and bake for a further 15 minutes, basting occasionally. Serve from the casserole.

Pollo en Nogado (Chicken in Nut Sauce) MEXICO

SERVES FOUR

1 medium chicken, cut into serving pieces
1 tomato, peeled, seeded, chopped
1 onion, chopped
½ cup pecan nuts
3 tablespoons blanched almonds
1 slice white bread, cut up
6 tablespoons chicken stock
2 cups water
4 tablespoons peanut oil
1 clove garlic, finely chopped
1 tablespoon dried ground chilli peppers
½ teaspoon oregano
¼ teaspoon ground cinnamon
¼ teaspoon ground cloves

Brown the chicken pieces in 3 tablespoons of the oil in a large pan. Remove to another large pan, and add the water. Bring to the boil, then cover and simmer until the chicken is tender (approximately 30 minutes).

Meanwhile, put the pecans and almonds into the blender, and blend at high speed until they are finely ground. Then add the tomato, onions, bread, ground chillis, cinnamon, cloves, oregano, garlic and chicken stock. Blend until smooth. Put the blended mixture into the remaining 1 tablespoon oil in a pan over moderate heat, and cook, stirring occasionally, for 5 minutes. Remove the pan from the heat.

When the chicken is cooked, put the pieces into the pan with the nuts and chilli mixture, and turn the pieces until they are coated with this sauce. Cook, uncovered, over low heat for 10 minutes. Baste occasionally.

Pollo en Nogado

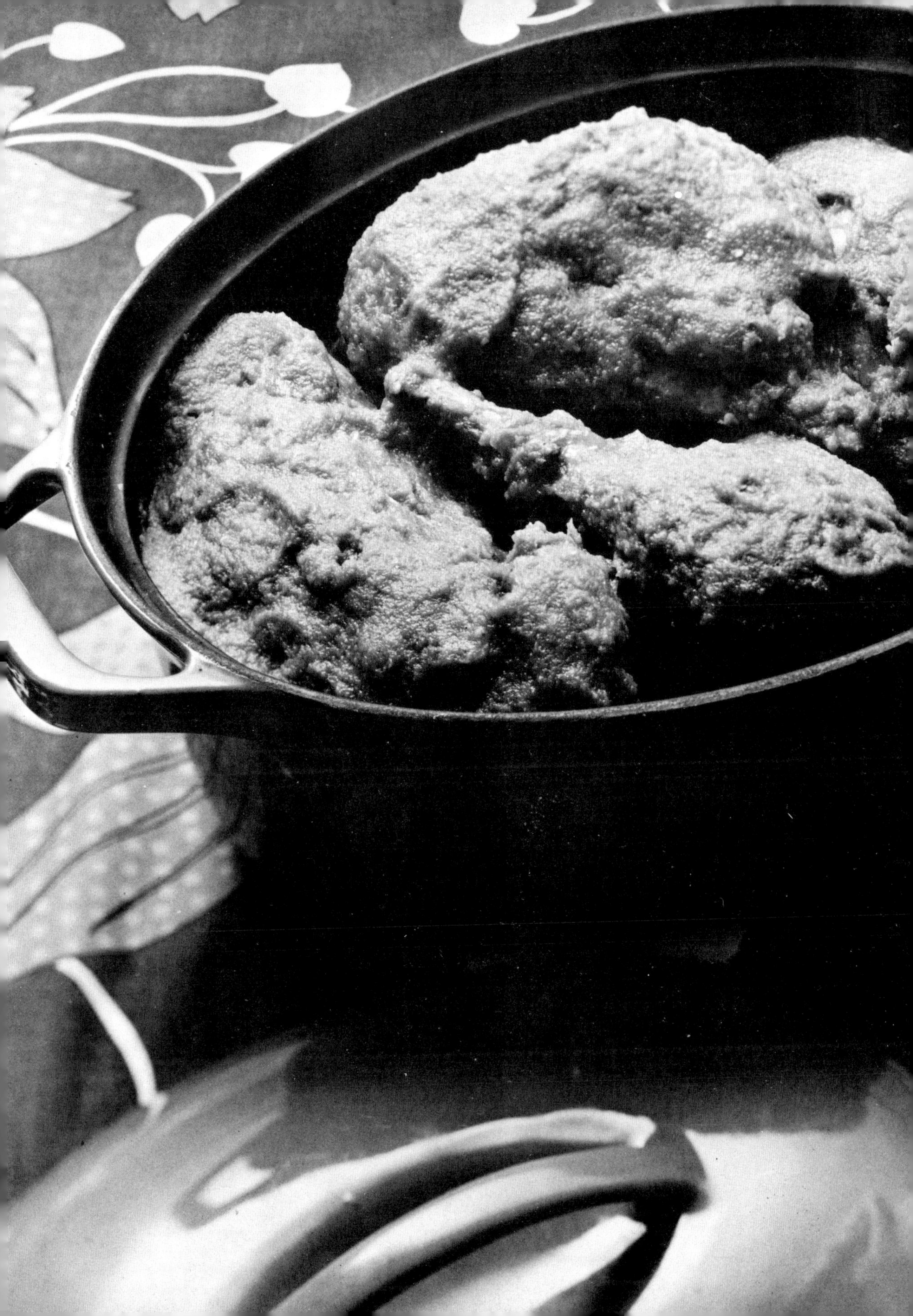

Mexican Chicken and Rice

MEXICO

SERVES FOUR TO SIX
1 large chicken
4 tomatoes, chopped
2 green peppers, seeded, chopped
2 onions, chopped
1 cup long-grain rice
1 tablespoon olive oil
2 chilli peppers, seeded, chopped
2 teaspoons dried ground chilli peppers
1 teaspoon ground cumin
salt

Put the chicken into a large pan and cover with salted water. Bring to the boil, then simmer until the chicken is very tender (approximately $1\frac{1}{4}$ hours). Remove from the pan; then take the chicken meat from the bones, and keep aside. Strain the stock, and return 7 cups of it to the pan. Add the chicken meat, the tomatoes, green peppers, onion, chilli peppers, ground chillis, cumin and salt to taste. Bring to the boil, then simmer for 20 minutes. Meanwhile, brown the rice in the oil, then add this to the chicken pan and continue cooking until the rice is tender (approximately 25 minutes).

Chicken Mole

MEXICO

SERVES FOUR TO SIX
1 medium chicken, cut into serving pieces
4 tomatoes, peeled, seeded, chopped
3 onions, chopped
1 cup sliced almonds
2 tortillas, fried brown
30 g/1 oz bitter chocolate, grated
2 tablespoons lime juice
2 cups chicken stock
5 tablespoons peanut oil
3 cloves garlic, crushed
$\frac{1}{4}$ cup sesame seeds
$\frac{1}{3}$ cup pepitas (pumpkin seeds)
1 tablespoon dried ground chilli peppers
1 teaspoon ground cinnamon

Put the almonds, sesame seeds and pepitas (pumpkin seeds) into a dry pan and heat, stirring constantly, until they become brown. Then put them in a blender and blend until smooth. Cut the tortillas into small pieces and add to the mixture in the blender. Blend until they are reduced to a powder and are well mixed with the other ingredients. Sauté the onions and garlic in 2 tablespoons oil until the onions become transparent, then add these to the blender. Also add the tomatoes, chocolate, lime juice, chicken stock, ground chillis and cinnamon. Blend until a smooth mixture is formed.

Brown the chicken pieces in 3 tablespoons of the oil in a large pan. Then put the pieces in a single layer in a large casserole and pour the above mixture over them. Cover, and bake in the oven (190°C/375°F) until the chicken is tender (approximately 1 hour). Remove the chicken pieces and place them on a serving platter. Then stir the sauce well, pour it over the chicken; and serve.

Mexican Chicken and Rice

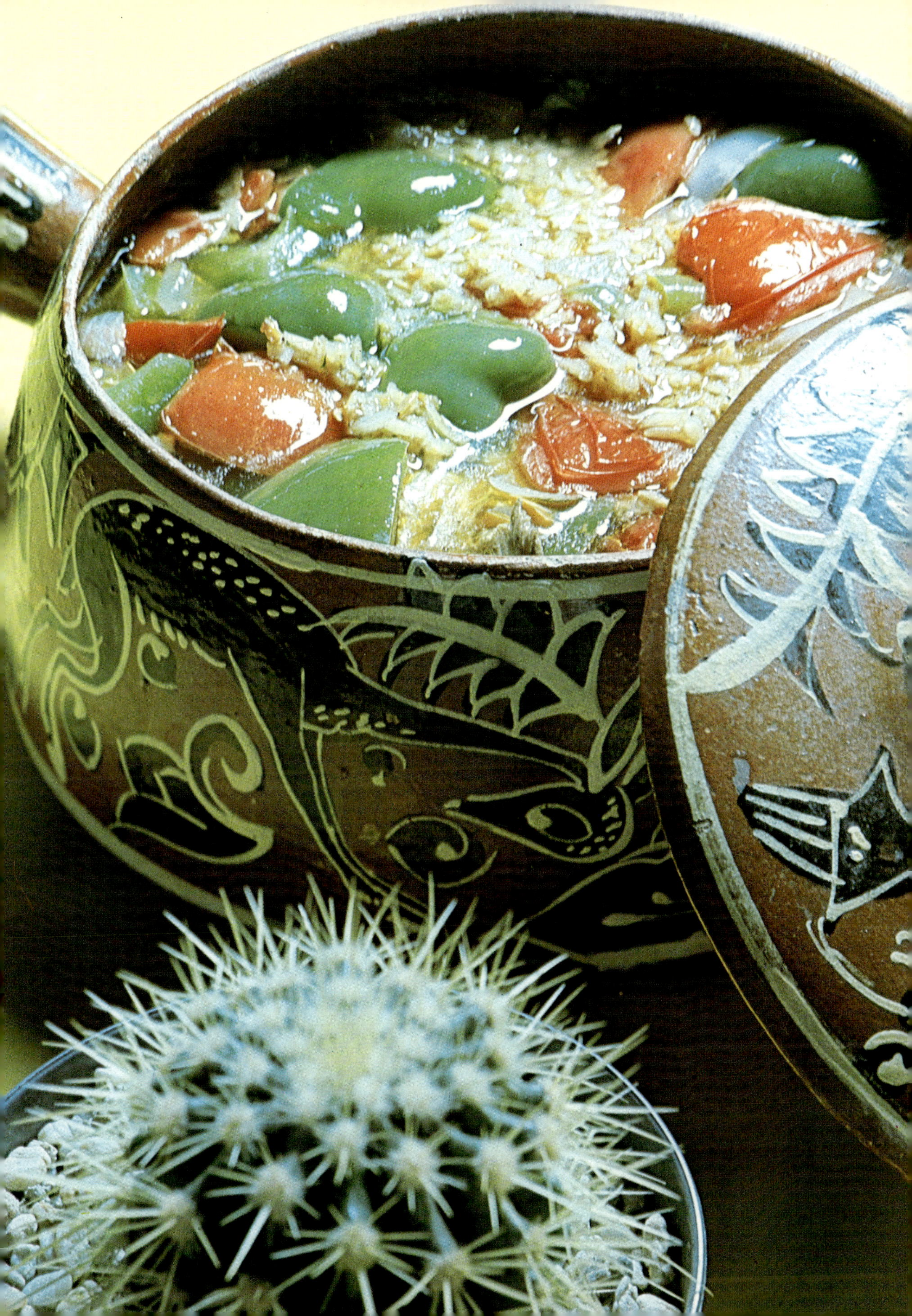

Djeja M'Qalia (Chicken with Coriander and Mint)   MOROCCO

SERVES FOUR
1 medium chicken
3 onions, coarsely chopped
1 cup water
½-1 tablespoon olive oil
2 cloves garlic, finely chopped
3 tablespoons finely chopped mint
2 tablespoons ground coriander
2½ teaspoons paprika
½ teaspoon ground cumin
¼ teaspoon ground saffron

Mix together the garlic, coriander, mint, paprika, saffron, cumin, and enough of the oil to form a paste. Coat the outside of the chicken completely with this mixture. Put the chicken into a casserole, and surround it with the onions. Then pour the water into the casserole (but pour it down the sides so that it does not touch the chicken). Cover, and bring to the boil over high heat. Place the casserole in the oven (190°C/375°F) and cook until the chicken is tender (approximately 1 hour). Remove the chicken and keep the casserole juices warm. Now grill the chicken, turning frequently, until it is browned on all sides (approximately 8 minutes). Serve the chicken, passing the juices from the pan separately.

Shoua (Moroccan Stuffed Chicken)   MOROCCO

SERVES SIX
1 large chicken
½ cup seedless raisins, soaked in hot water, drained
¼ cup chopped walnuts
¼ cup chopped blanched almonds
1½ cups cooked couscous (semolina) or cooked medium-grain rice
2½ teaspoons honey
1¼ cups water
5 tablespoons butter
¾ teaspoon ground ginger
¾ teaspoon ground cinnamon
½ teaspoon ground saffron
2¼ teaspoons salt
¾ teaspoon pepper

Mix together the couscous (or rice), the raisins, walnuts, almonds, honey, 1 tablespoon butter (melted), and ¼ teaspoon each of the ginger, cinnamon, saffron and pepper. Stuff the chicken with this mixture and close the opening with thread or skewers.

Brown the stuffed chicken on all sides in the remaining 4 tablespoons butter in a large pan. Then mix together ½ teaspoon each of the ginger, cinnamon and pepper, ¼ teaspoon saffron, the salt and the water. Pour this mixture over the chicken, then cover and simmer until the chicken is tender (approximately 1½ hours). Put the chicken on a serving platter and pour some of the sauce from the pan over it. Serve the remaining sauce separately.

Chicken Ginger Stew   NEW HEBRIDES

SERVES FOUR
1 medium chicken, cut into serving pieces
125 g/¼ lb mushrooms
1 tablespoon cornflour
1 tablespoon brown sugar
3 tablespoons olive oil
¾ cup thick soy sauce
1 clove garlic, finely chopped
2 teaspoons ground ginger

Mix together the soy sauce and the sugar. Marinate the chicken pieces in this mixture for at least 30 minutes, turning the pieces occasionally. Heat the oil in a large pan and put in the ginger and the garlic. When they are slightly browned, add the pieces of chicken and brown them, stirring well to coat with the spices. Then pour in the marinade and add enough water to just cover the chicken. Cover, and cook over low heat, stirring occasionally, until the chicken is tender (approximately 1 hour). Add the mushrooms and the cornflour to the pan 10 minutes before the end of cooking time.

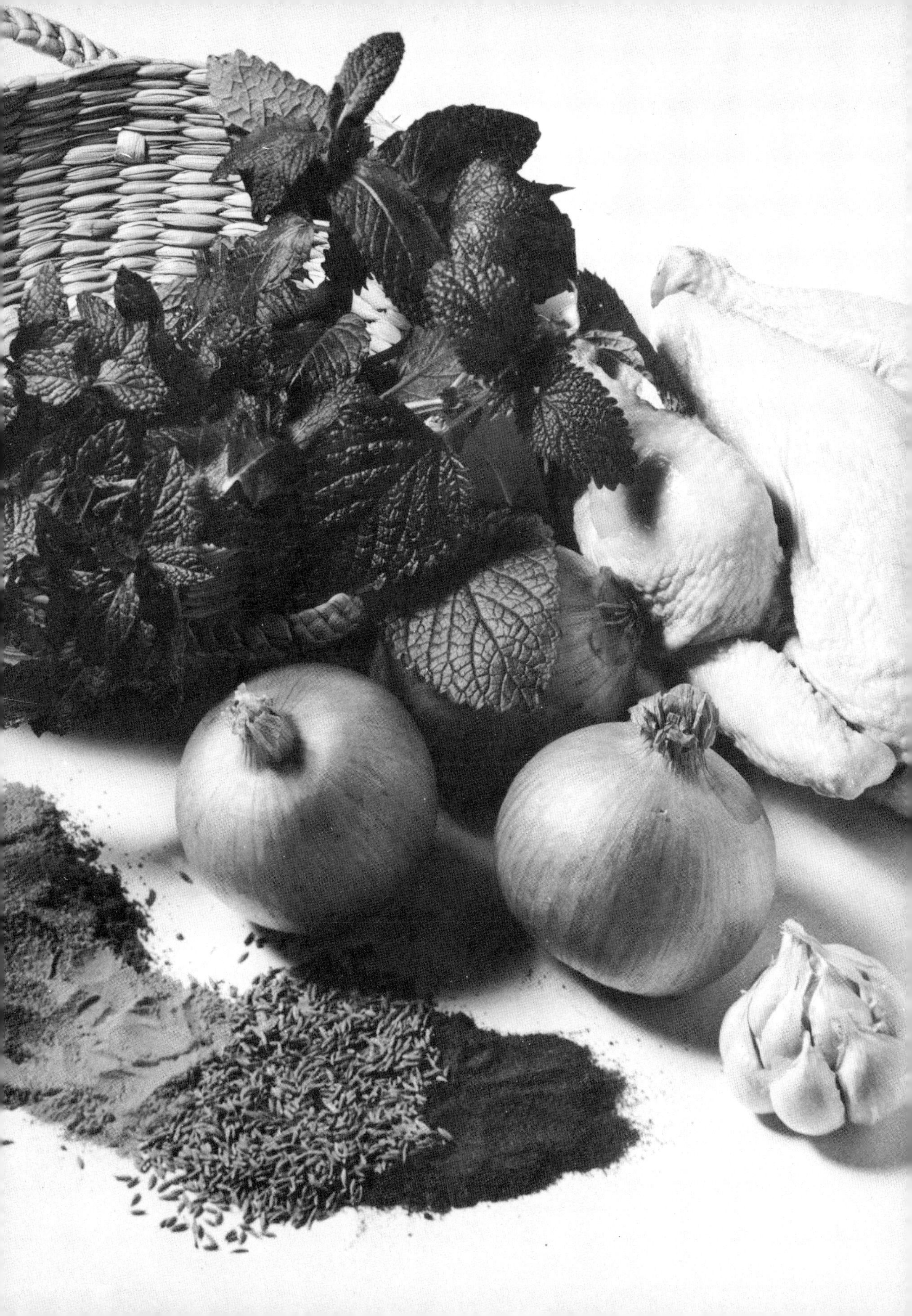

Chicken Casserole with Coconut Cream

NEW HEBRIDES

SERVES FOUR
1 medium chicken, the meat diced
1 onion, finely chopped
1 tablespoon medium-grain rice flour
2½ cups coconut cream
3 tablespoons butter
½ teaspoon dried ground chilli peppers

Roll the diced chicken in flour, then brown it in the butter in a casserole. Add the onion, rice, ground chillis and coconut cream, and put the casserole in the oven (180°C/350°F). Cook until the chicken is tender (approximately 1 hour).

Murgh-I-Musallam (Spicy Baked Chicken)

PAKISTAN

SERVES FOUR TO SIX
1 large chicken
2 onions, finely chopped
½ cup ground almonds
2 tablespoons water
4 tablespoons ghee (melted)
6 cloves garlic, crushed
½ teaspoon dried ground chilli peppers
½ teaspoon ground ginger
½ teaspoon ground cloves
2 cardamom seeds, ground
1½ teaspoons salt
1 teaspoon black pepper

Remove the skin from the chicken; then prick the chicken all over with a fork. Mix together into a paste (preferably in a blender) the onions, almonds, garlic, ground chillis, ginger, cloves, cardamom seeds, salt, pepper, ghee and water. Spread this mixture well all over the outside of the chicken and rub the remainder over the inside. Put the chicken into a greased baking tin and roast in the oven (180°C/350°F) until the chicken is tender (approximately 1½ hours). Add water to the pan if it becomes too dry. Carve the chicken; and serve.

Ají de Gallina (Chicken in Nut Sauce)   PERU

SERVES FOUR

1 medium chicken, cooked, and meat cut into strips
1 kg/2 lb potatoes, peeled, thickly sliced
12 black olives
2 onions, finely chopped
1 cup ground walnuts
3 tablespoons grated parmesan cheese
3 eggs, hard-boiled, cut into wedges
8 slices white bread, crusts removed
2 cups milk
$\frac{2}{3}$ cup olive oil
1 clove garlic, finely chopped
2 red chilli peppers, cut into strips
3 tablespoons dried ground chilli peppers
$\frac{1}{2}$ teaspoon ground saffron
$1\frac{1}{2}$ teaspoons salt
$\frac{1}{4}$ teaspoon black pepper

Cut up the slices of bread and soak them in half the milk for 5 minutes. Then mix the bread and milk to form a paste. Put the potatoes in boiling, salted water and simmer until cooked. Meanwhile, sauté the onions and garlic in the oil in a large pan over moderate heat. When the onions are transparent, add the walnuts, ground chillis, salt and black pepper. Cook over low heat for 5 minutes, then add the annatto, 1 tablespoon oil, the bread and milk mixture, and the remaining milk. Continue cooking, stirring constantly, until the sauce thickens. Add the diced chicken and the cheese and simmer, stirring occasionally, until the cheese melts.

Put the boiled potato slices into the bottom of a serving dish. Then put the chicken mixture over them. Garnish with the olives, hard-boiled egg wedges and chilli pepper strips.

Adobo (Chicken and Pork Casserole)   THE PHILIPPINES

SERVES SIX

1 medium chicken
1 kg/2 lb pork, diced
$\frac{1}{2}$ cup chicken stock
1 cup thick coconut milk
$\frac{1}{2}$ cup wine vinegar
$\frac{1}{4}$ cup olive oil
6 cloves garlic, crushed
2 bay leaves
1 tablespoon salt
4 peppercorns
1 teaspoon pepper

Chop the chicken (including the bones) into bite-size pieces. Brown the chicken and pork pieces in the oil in a casserole. Then add the chicken stock, vinegar, garlic, bay leaves, peppercorns, salt and pepper. Cover, and cook over low heat, stirring frequently, until the chicken and pork are tender (approximately 1 hour). Add the coconut milk and cook for a further 10 minutes.

Adobo

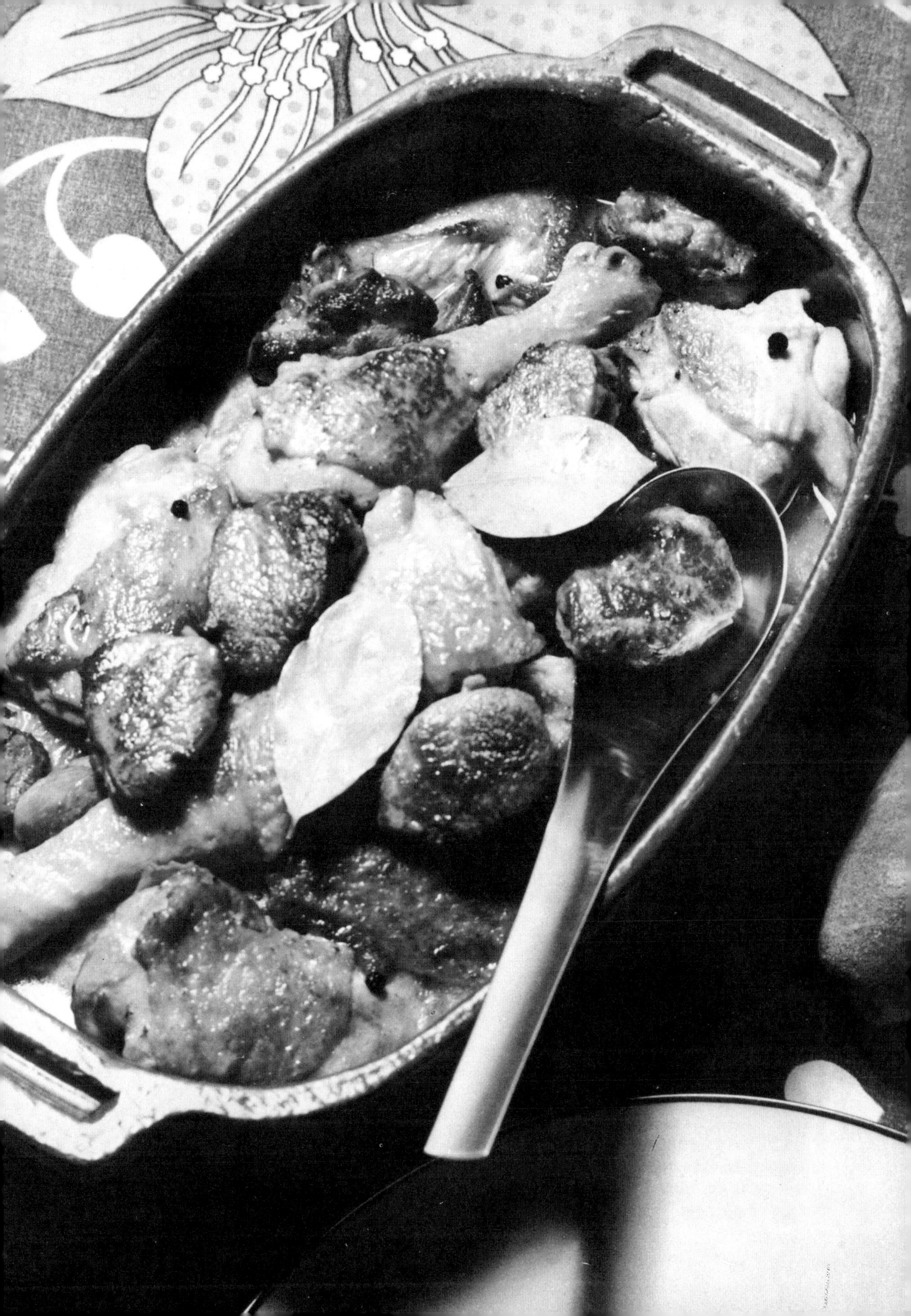

Mango Chicken

POLYNESIA

SERVES FOUR

1 medium chicken, cut into serving pieces
2 onions, finely sliced
1 mango, sliced
2 tablespoons flour
1 cup jellied chicken stock
⅔ cup thick cream
2 tablespoons butter
salt and pepper

Season the flour with salt and pepper, then roll the chicken pieces in it. Brown the pieces in the butter in a large pan; then remove and keep warm. Add the onions to the pan and cook over low heat until they are transparent. Then add the sliced mango and continue cooking until the onions are brown. Return the chicken pieces to the pan, pour over the chicken stock, and season with salt and pepper. Cover, and simmer until the chicken is tender (approximately 35 minutes). Stir in the cream; and serve.

Frango na Pucara (Chicken in the Pot)

PORTUGAL

SERVES FOUR
1 small chicken
90 g/3 oz ham, chopped
2 potatoes, peeled, chopped
6 onions, chopped
½ cup port
½ cup brandy
½ cup dry white wine
2 tablespoons butter
2 cloves garlic, crushed
1 tablespoon mustard
salt and pepper

Put all the ingredients into a casserole. Cover, and cook in the oven (160°C/325°F) until the chicken is tender (approximately 1 hour). Remove the cover and continue to cook until the top of the chicken is golden.

Portuguese Chicken Casserole

PORTUGAL

SERVES FOUR
1 medium chicken, cut into serving pieces
60 g/2 oz Spanish sausage
1 onion, chopped
250 g/8 oz almonds, crushed (not ground)
2 cups dry white wine
4 tablespoons lard
2 cloves garlic, crushed
2 bay leaves
1 teaspoon dried ground chilli peppers
1 teaspoon cayenne pepper
salt and pepper

Mix together the almonds, garlic and wine, and leave to stand for at least 1 hour so that the wine is soaked up by the almonds and garlic. Sauté the onion in the lard in a casserole. When the onion is golden, add the cayenne pepper, ground chillis and the Spanish sausage (make a slit in the sausage before cooking). Cover, and cook over low heat until the sausage is tender (approximately 4 minutes). Add the chicken pieces to the casserole and continue cooking over low heat until the chicken is tender (approximately 45 minutes). Add the wine and almond mixture, and season with salt and pepper. Remove the lid and leave until the sauce thickens (approximately 30 minutes). Add the bay leaves, then leave to cool. Reheat the dish when ready to serve.

Galuiha Rechiada (Stuffed Chicken)

PORTUGAL

SERVES SIX
1 large chicken (and gizzard and liver)
1½ cups green olives, stoned, sliced
4 onions, chopped
6 eggs, hard-boiled, chopped
2 cups breadcrumbs
3 cups dry white wine
½ cup milk (hot)
1 teaspoon vinegar
4 tablespoons olive oil
1 teaspoon ground cinnamon
½ teaspoon ground nutmeg
salt and pepper

Rub the chicken inside and out with salt and pepper. Then put the chicken into the wine in a bowl and leave it to marinate overnight. Boil the chicken gizzard in water for 30 minutes, then add the chicken liver and cook for a further 10 minutes. Drain; then chop the gizzard and the liver. Sauté the onions in the butter in a pan for 10 minutes. Then mix them with the chopped chicken gizzard and liver, the breadcrumbs, olives, eggs, vinegar, hot milk, and salt and pepper to taste.

Remove the chicken from the wine marinade, and drain. Keep the marinade aside. Stuff the chicken with the above mixture and fasten the opening with thread or skewers. Then roast the chicken in the oven (180°C/350°F) until tender (approximately 2 hours). Add 1 cup of the marinade after 30 minutes of the cooking time, and add more later if necessary. Baste frequently.

Portuguese Chicken Casserole

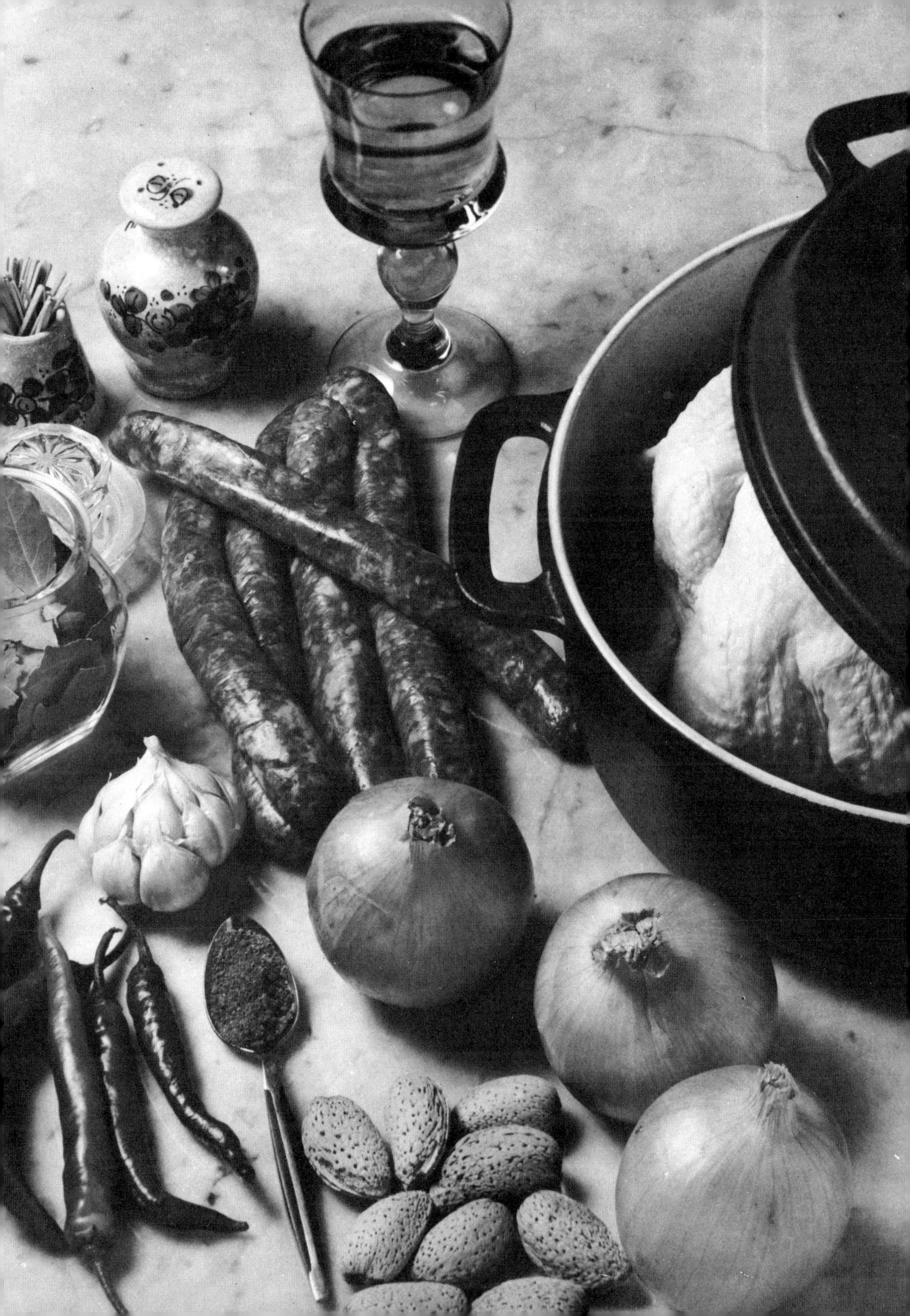

Pui cu Gutui (Chicken with Quinces)

RUMANIA

SERVES FOUR TO SIX

1 large chicken, cut into small serving pieces
1 onion, chopped
4 large quinces, unpeeled, cut into strips
1 tablespoon flour
1 cup chicken stock
¼ cup olive oil
salt

Sauté the onion in the oil in a large pan. Then add the chicken pieces, cover, and cook over low heat until tender (approximately 40 minutes). Add the quinces, the chicken stock and salt to taste, and continue cooking until the quinces are soft (approximately 30 minutes). Remove the chicken pieces and put them into a serving dish. Thicken the sauce by stirring in the flour, then pour it over the chicken and serve.

Wedding Soup

RUMANIA

SERVES SIX TO EIGHT

1 large chicken, cut into small serving pieces
3 carrots, finely chopped
4 leeks, finely chopped
½ celery root, finely chopped
½ bunch parsley
8 onions, finely chopped
⅔ cup sultanas
1 egg, beaten
½ cup long-grain rice
½ cup sour cream
7½ cups water
salt

Boil all the vegetables in the water (to which salt has been added) in a large pan for 1 hour. Add the chicken to the pan and continue cooking until it is tender (approximately 30 minutes). Remove the chicken pieces and keep warm. Strain the soup and discard the vegetables. Return the soup to the pan, add the rice, and boil until cooked (approximately 20 minutes). Stir in the beaten egg and the sour cream, and add the sultanas. Put the chicken pieces into individual serving bowls and pour the soup over them.

Wedding Soup

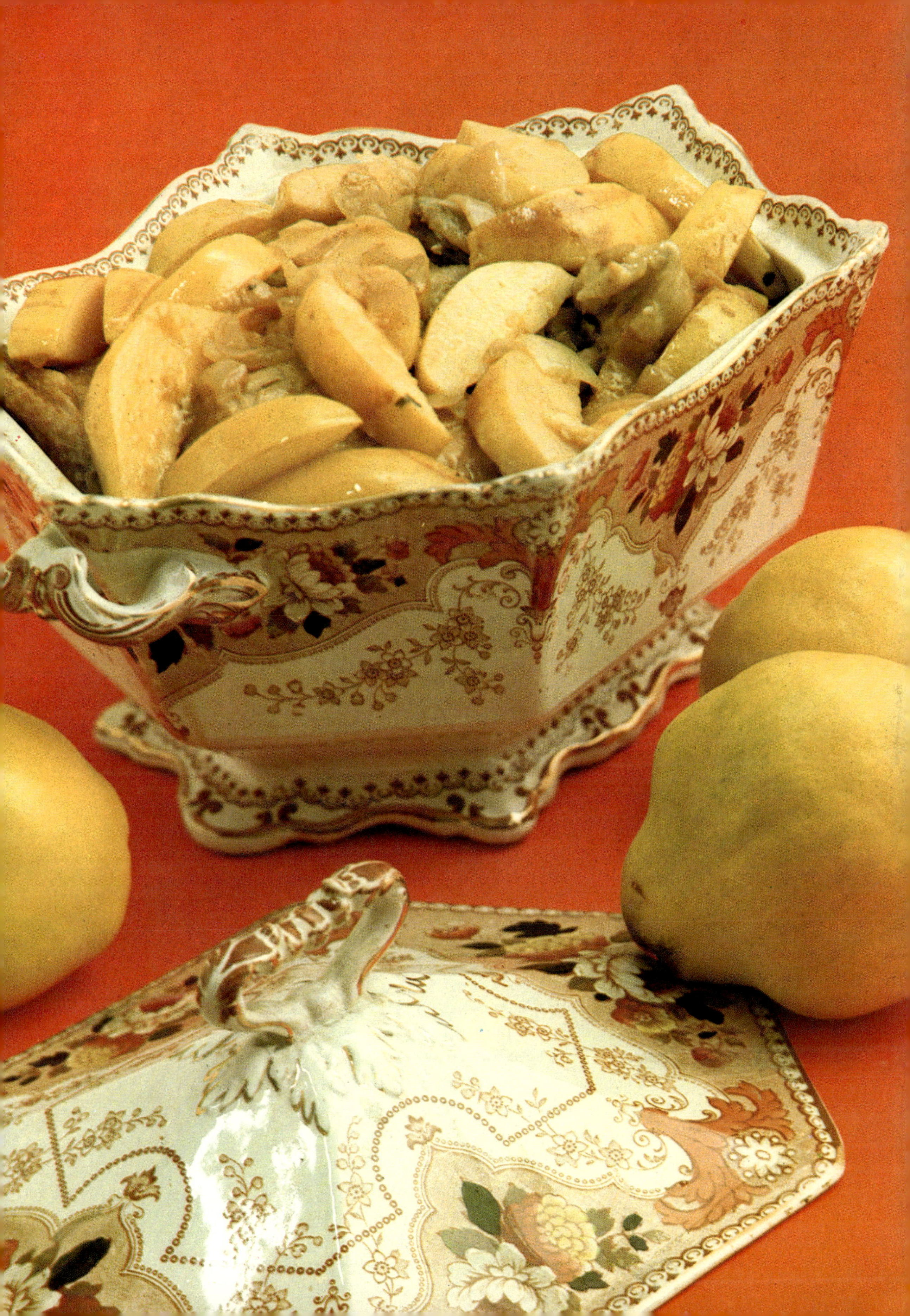

Kotlety Po-Kyivskomu (Chicken Kiev)   RUSSIA

SERVES FOUR
4 chicken suprêmes (half the breast with wing bone attached)
2 eggs, beaten
2 tablespoons flour
breadcrumbs
1 teaspoon lemon juice
olive oil (for deep-frying)
5 tablespoons unsalted butter
2½ teaspoons chopped parsley
1 teaspoon chives
pinch of nutmeg
salt and black pepper

Mix the butter with the lemon juice, parsley, chives, nutmeg, 1 teaspoon salt and a little black pepper. Chill this butter mixture in the refrigerator until hard. Then cut it into 4 finger-length pieces.

Cover the chicken suprêmes with greaseproof paper and flatten them out by pounding with a heavy knife or cutlet bat. Then wrap each suprême around 1 piece of the butter. Roll the cutlets in the flour (seasoned with salt and black pepper) then shape each of them into a long cylinder, tapering slightly at each end, and with the wing bone standing up. Dip them into the beaten eggs, and coat them well with breadcrumbs. Refrigerate for at least 1 hour before cooking.

Heat the oil to 190°C/375°F and deep-fry the chicken cutlets in this until golden-brown (approximately 5 minutes). Remove and drain. Put a cutlet frill around each wing bone; then serve.

Tabaka (Pressed Fried Chicken)   RUSSIA

SERVES FOUR
4 very small chickens (one chicken per person)
3 tablespoons sour cream
4 tablespoons clarified butter
salt
Tkemali Sauce

Remove the backbones of the chickens and flatten them. Sprinkle the chickens all over with salt, then spread half the sour cream over the skin sides. You will probably be able to fit only 2 of the chickens into the pan at the one time, therefore cook them as follows. Heat half the clarified butter in a large pan. Put 2 chickens (skin side down) into the pan, then put a heavy weight on top of them (e.g. heavy fry-pan). Cook over moderate heat for 10 minutes. Then turn the chickens over, spread over them half of the remaining sour cream, and fry under the weight until they are golden-brown and tender (approximately 10 minutes). Remove the chickens and put them skin side up on a serving platter. Keep them warm while the process is repeated with the remaining 2 chickens (using the remaining clarified butter and sour cream). Serve the chickens, and pass the Tkemali Sauce separately.

Tkemali Sauce
250 g/½ lb prunes
1½ tablespoons lemon juice
2 cups water
1 clove garlic
2½ tablespoons coriander
¼ teaspoon cayenne pepper
¼ teaspoon salt

Bring the water to the boil in a saucepan, then put in the prunes, remove from the heat and leave to stand for 10 minutes. Return to the heat, bring to the boil, and cook until the prunes are tender (approximately 10 minutes). Strain the prunes and keep aside the liquids. Stone the prunes, then put them into a blender with the garlic, coriander and 3 tablespoons of the prune liquid. Blend, gradually adding all the prune liquid. Put this mixture into the saucepan, add the cayenne pepper and the salt, and bring to the boil. Remove from the heat and stir in the lemon juice. Leave to cool.

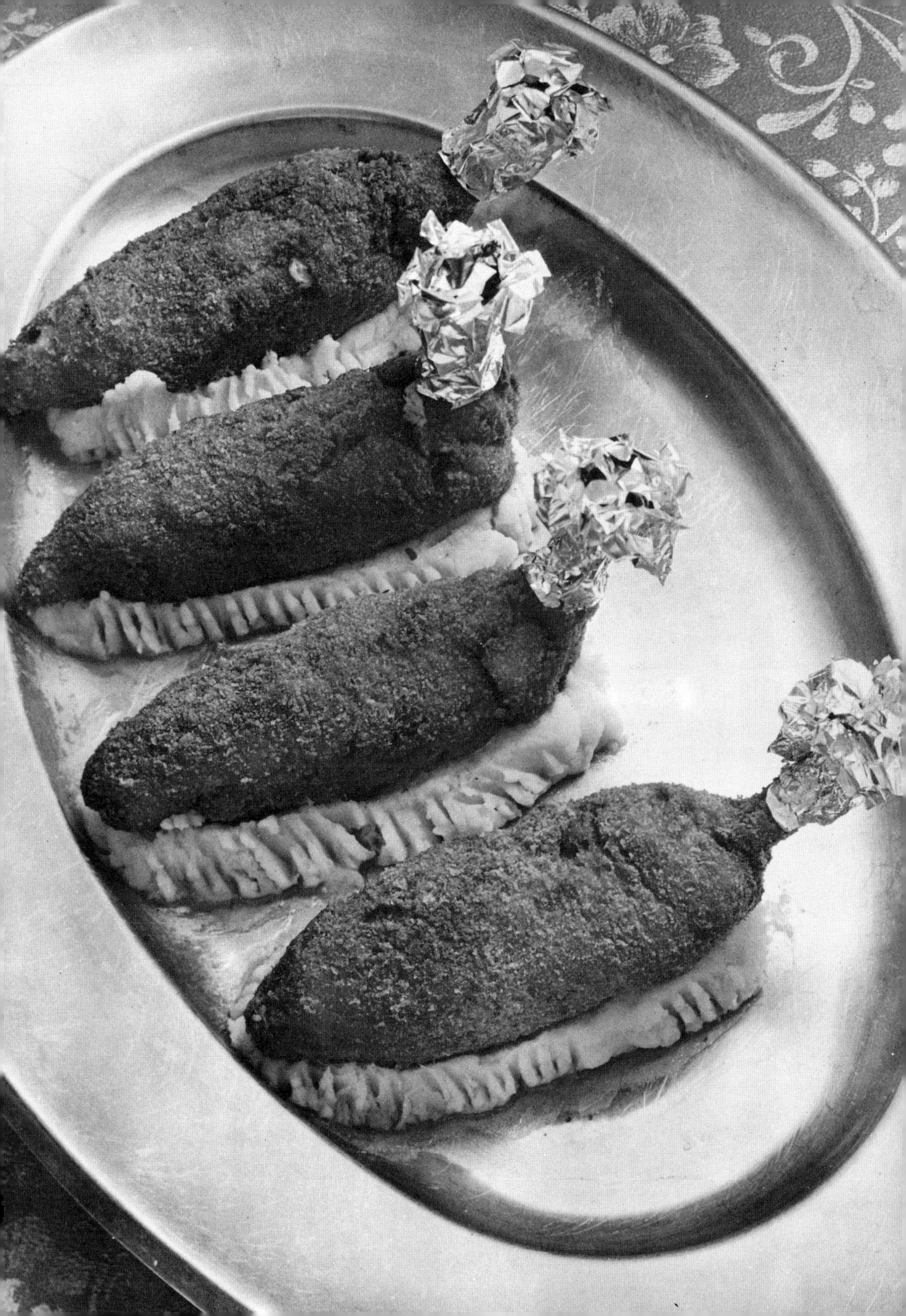

Salat Olivier (Russian Chicken Salad) RUSSIA

SERVES FOUR TO SIX
2 chicken breasts
4 potatoes, peeled, boiled, thinly sliced
1 tomato, cut into wedges
1 lettuce
6 green olives
1½ tablespoons capers
60 g/2 oz sour dill pickles, chopped
1 onion, quartered
3 eggs, hard-boiled, sliced
⅔ cup sour cream
⅔ cup mayonnaise
4 cups water
1 teaspoon dried dill
1½ teaspoons salt
¼ teaspoon pepper

Put the chicken breasts, the onion, and 1 teaspoon of the salt into a large pan. Cover with the water, bring to the boil, then skim. Cover the pan and cook over low heat until the chicken is tender (approximately 20 minutes). Remove the chicken breasts, then skin them and cut the meat away from the bones. Cut the chicken meat into strips and mix it with the potatoes, the eggs, dill pickles, pepper and remaining salt. Beat together the mayonnaise and sour cream, then mix half of this mixture with the chicken mixture.

Heap the salad on to a serving platter. Completely cover it with the remainder of the mayonnaise and sour cream mixture, then sprinkle it with the capers and dried dill. Decorate with the tomatoes, olives and lettuce.

Pechene Kuryata (Baked Chicken) RUSSIA

SERVES FOUR TO SIX
1 large chicken, cut into serving pieces
2 eggs, beaten
¾ cup flour
1½ cups breadcrumbs
3 cups sour cream
2 teaspoons olive oil
3 tablespoons butter
salt and pepper

Coat the chicken pieces with the flour, seasoned with salt and pepper. Then beat together the eggs and the oil, dip the chicken pieces into this mixture, and roll them in the breadcrumbs. Brown the chicken pieces in the butter in a large pan; then remove them and put them into a baking dish. Sprinkle with salt and pepper and bake in the oven (190°C/375°F) for 25 minutes. Pour half the sour cream over the chicken, then bake for another 20 minutes. Now add the remaining sour cream and continue baking until the chicken is tender (approximately 30 minutes).

Salat Olivier

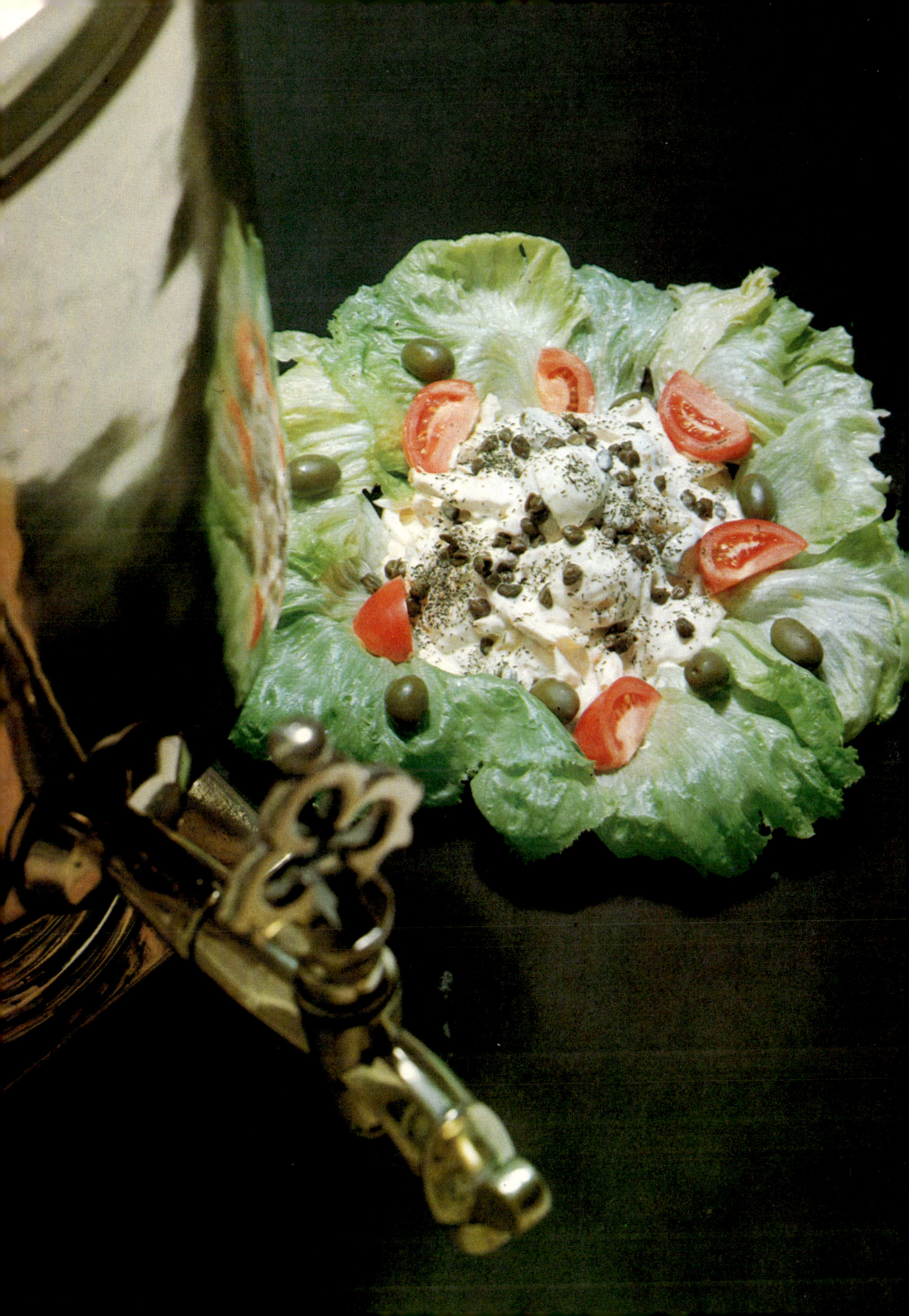

Tushenaia Kuritsa pod Sousom iz Chernosliv (Chicken with Prunes) RUSSIA

SERVES FOUR
1 medium chicken, quartered
1 carrot, coarsely sliced
1 stick celery, coarsely chopped
2 onions, finely chopped
250 g/½ lb prunes, stoned
1 tablespoon flour
2½ teaspoons sugar
6 tablespoons chicken stock
2½ teaspoons lemon juice
1½ cups water
1½ tablespoons olive oil
2½ tablespoons butter
1 sprig of parsley
1 bay leaf
salt and black pepper

Brown the chicken pieces in a mixture of the oil and 1½ tablespoons of the butter; then remove and keep warm. Add the carrot, celery and onions to the pan and cook over moderate heat, stirring occasionally, until the vegetables are soft (approximately 5 minutes). Return the chicken to the pan, and add the parsley, bay leaf, chicken stock, and salt and pepper to taste. Bring to the boil, cover, then reduce the heat and simmer, basting occasionally, until the chicken is tender (approximately 30 minutes). Remove the chicken pieces, place them on a serving platter and keep warm. Strain the juices from the pan and discard the vegetables; keep the juices aside.

Meanwhile, put the water, prunes, lemon juice and sugar into a pan. Bring to the boil, then reduce the heat and simmer until the prunes are tender (approximately 15 minutes). Arrange the cooked prunes on the serving platter with the chicken, and keep aside the cooking juices.

Melt the remaining 1 tablespoon butter in a saucepan, and blend in the flour until smooth. Cook, stirring, until the flour turns brown (2-3 minutes). Then pour in 6 tablespoons of the juices from the prunes and 6 tablespoons of the juices from the chicken. Bring to the boil, stirring constantly. Continue boiling until the sauce is smooth and has thickened. Pour this sauce over the chicken and prunes; and serve.

Chicken with Mustard and Dill Sauce SCANDINAVIA-SWEDEN

SERVES FOUR
1 medium chicken, cut into serving pieces
2 tablespoons flour
1 cup chicken stock
2 tablespoons butter
1 tablespoon mustard
2 teaspoons dill
salt and pepper

Coat the chicken pieces with the flour (seasoned with salt and pepper) and brown them in the butter in a large pan. Add half the chicken stock to the pan, then stir in the mustard and the dill. Cover, and simmer for 20 minutes. Turn the chicken pieces over and add the remaining chicken stock, and salt and pepper to taste. Continue cooking until the chicken is tender, then remove the chicken pieces and place them on a serving dish. Boil the sauce until it is thick; pour this over the chicken pieces, and serve.

Tushenaia Kuritsa pod Sousom iz Chernosliv

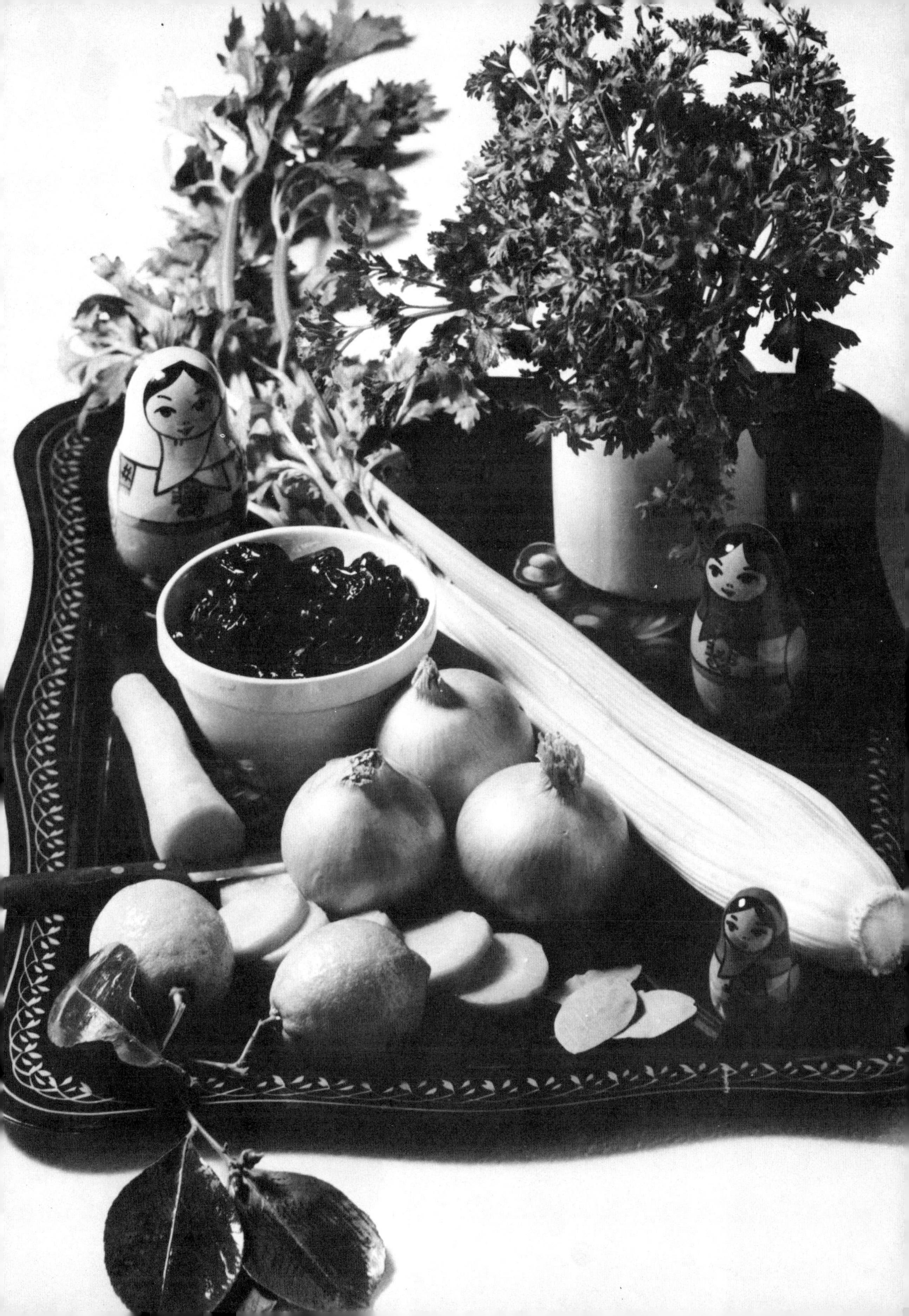

Danish Parsley Chicken

Danish Parsley Chicken

SCANDINAVIA-DENMARK

SERVES FOUR

2 small chickens (half-chicken per person)
8 rashers of bacon
2 tablespoons cornflour
2½ cups chicken stock
⅔ cup cream
1 cup butter
2 tablespoons parsley leaves (not chopped)
salt and pepper

Mix together the parsley leaves and half of the butter. Spread half of this mixture inside each of the chickens. Then brown the chickens on all sides in the remaining butter in a large pan. Add the chicken stock, and cook over low heat until the chickens are tender (approximately 1 hour). Stir in the cream 10 minutes before the end of the cooking time. Meanwhile, fry the bacon rashers, then form each of them into a roll.

Remove the chickens from the pan when they are tender, and put them on to a serving platter. Mix the cornflour with a little of the sauce, then stir the mixture into the sauce in the pan to thicken. Season with salt and pepper, then pour the sauce over the chickens. Garnish with the fried bacon rolls.

SCANDINAVIA-FINLAND

Kananmaksaa Omenien Kanssa (Chicken Livers with Apples and Onions)

SERVES FOUR TO SIX

750 g/1½ lb chicken livers
1 onion, thinly sliced
6 apples, peeled, cored, thickly sliced
flour
1½ tablespoons cornflour
4 tablespoons sugar
¼ cup chicken stock
1 cup apple juice
1 tablespoon lemon juice
2 tablespoons red currant jelly
1 cup butter
1½ teaspoons salt
1½ teaspoons pepper

Melt half the butter in a pan, then put in the apples and sprinkle them with the sugar. Cook over low heat, turning frequently, until the apples are soft (approximately 10 minutes). Meanwhile, in another large pan, sauté the onions in the remaining butter until golden. Remove and keep warm. Dust the chicken livers with flour, then sauté them in the pan for 5 minutes. Sprinkle with the salt and pepper, then add the chicken stock and cook over moderate heat for 5 minutes.

Blend the cornflour and 2 tablespoons of the apple juice together until smooth. Then gradually add the red currant jelly, the lemon juice and the remaining apple juice. Put this mixture into a saucepan and cook over low heat, stirring constantly, until it thickens.

Place the apples on a serving platter and arrange the chicken livers and the onions over them. Serve the sauce separately.

Kananmaksaa Omenien Kanssa

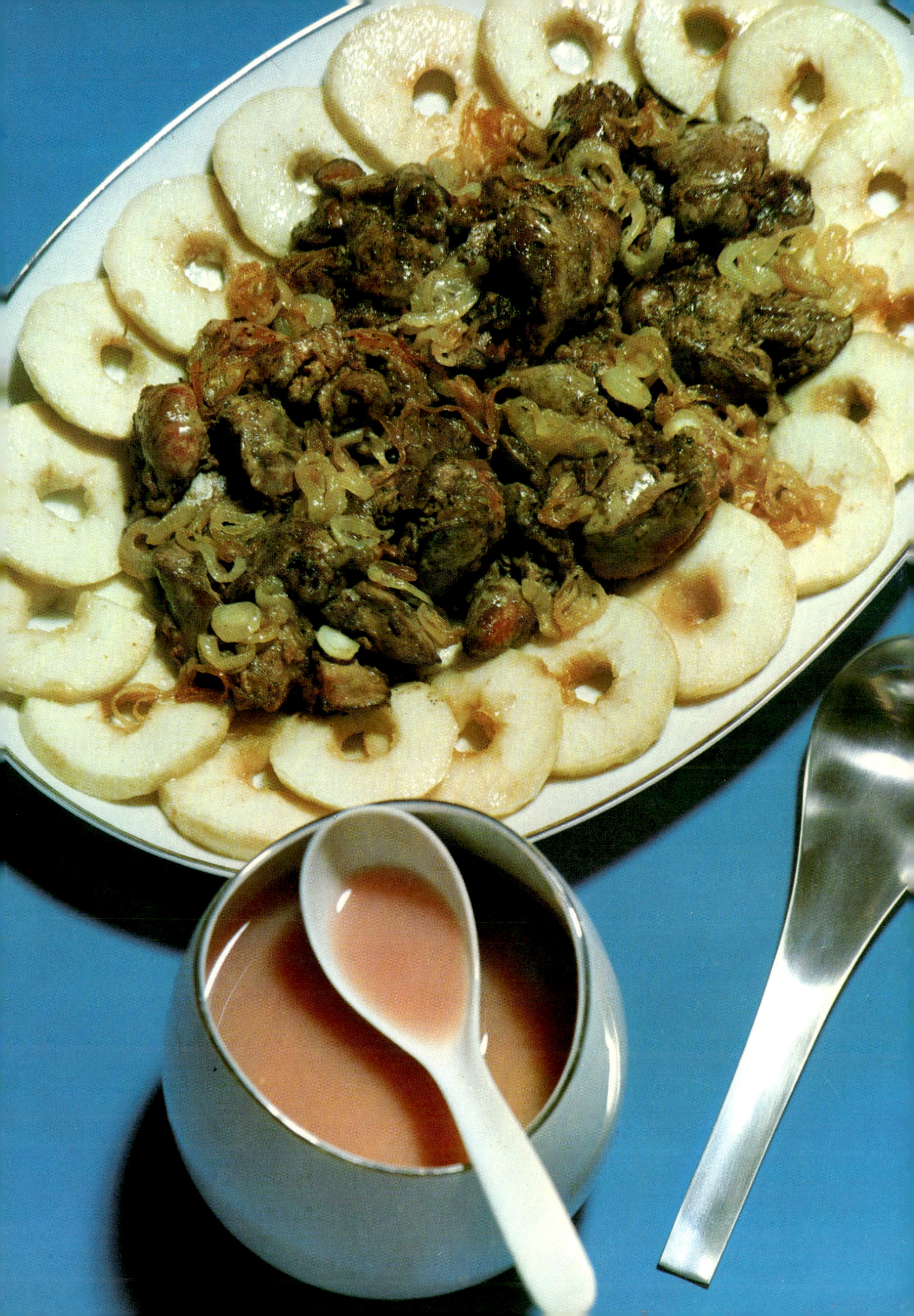

Chicken with Horseradish Sauce
SCANDINAVIA-DENMARK

SERVES FOUR TO SIX
1 medium chicken
1 onion
3 tablespoons flour
2 tablespoons sugar
1½ cups cream
1 tablespoon vinegar
water
3 tablespoons butter
4 tablespoons horseradish
salt and pepper

Put the chicken, onion, and salt and pepper into a large pan. Cover with water, bring to the boil, then simmer until the chicken is tender (approximately 1 hour). Remove the chicken and cut it into serving pieces. Put the pieces into a serving dish and keep warm.

Melt the butter in a saucepan, then remove from the heat and blend in the flour. Gradually stir the cream into this mixture, then return the pan to the heat and cook gently for 2 minutes. Blend in the horseradish, sugar and vinegar, and slowly bring to the boil, stirring constantly. Pour this sauce over the chicken pieces; and serve.

Norwegian Parsley Chicken
SCANDINAVIA-NORWAY

SERVES FOUR
2 small chickens (half-chicken per person)
¼ cup water (hot)
1 cup butter
2 tablespoons parsley leaves (not chopped)
salt and pepper

Mix together the parsley leaves and half the butter and spread half of this mixture inside each of the chickens. Brown the chickens on all sides in the remaining butter in a large pan. Reduce the heat, cover, and cook until the chickens are tender (approximately 1 hour). Remove the chickens and place them on to a serving platter. Add the water to the pan juices, stir, and scrape any drippings of chicken from the bottom of the pan. Season with salt and pepper, and cook until a thick, clear sauce is formed. Then pour the sauce over the chickens.

Paella
SPAIN

SERVES SIX
1 medium chicken, cut into serving pieces
250 g/½ lb pork, diced
125 g/¼ lb Spanish sausage, chopped
500 g/1 lb prawns, shelled
500 g/1 lb scallops
125 g/¼ lb string beans
125 g/¼ lb green peas
4 tomatoes, peeled, chopped
1 green pepper, sliced
1 red pepper, sliced
2 onions, chopped
1½ cups medium-grain rice
½ cup dry white wine
6 cups chicken stock
1 cup olive oil
2 cloves garlic, finely chopped
1 tablespoon chopped parsley
2 teaspoons paprika
1 teaspoon dried oregano
½ teaspoon saffron
salt and black pepper

Heat half the oil in a large fry-pan, then add the chicken, pork and sausage, and brown on all sides. Remove from the pan and put into a casserole. Add the onions and garlic to the fry-pan and sauté until the onion is golden. Remove and add them to the casserole, together with the tomatoes, green pepper, red pepper, parsley, paprika, oregano, saffron, chicken stock, and salt and black pepper to taste. Cover, and cook over low heat for 20 minutes.

Meanwhile, brown the rice in the remaining ½ cup olive oil, stirring frequently. Then add this to the casserole. Also add the wine, the beans and the peas. Cover, and bake in the oven (180°C/350°F) for 1 hour. (Add water if the casserole becomes too dry). Add the prawns and scallops, and cook for a further 5 minutes.

Paella

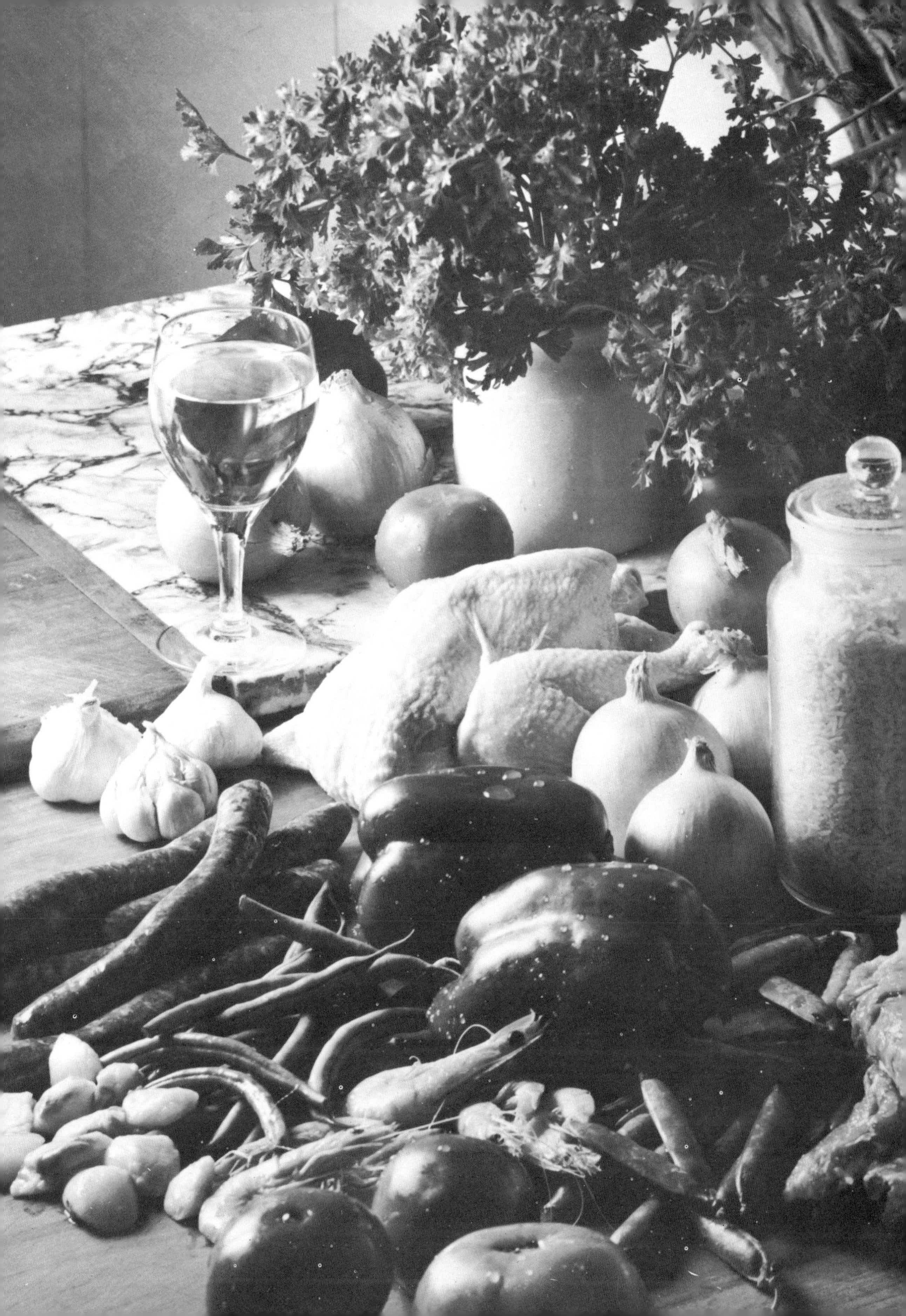

Chicken Majorca

SPAIN

SERVES FOUR

1 medium chicken, cut into serving pieces
1 red pepper, seeded, cut into strips
4 green olives, stoned, shredded
1 onion, thinly sliced
1 orange, peeled, sliced into rounds
2 strips of orange peel
2 teaspoons flour
½ cup dry white wine
½ cup chicken stock
3 tablespoons olive oil
1 tablespoon chopped parsley
bouquet garni
salt and pepper

Brown the chicken pieces in the olive oil in a large pan; then remove and keep warm. Add the onion to the pan, and sauté until golden. Blend in the flour, then add the wine, the chicken stock, and salt and pepper to taste, then bring to the boil. Return the chicken pieces to the pan, and add the bouquet garni and the strips of orange peel. Cover, and simmer until the chicken is tender (approximately 25 minutes).

When cooked, remove the chicken pieces from the pan, put them into a serving dish, and keep warm. Add the red pepper, olives, orange and parsley to the sauce in the pan and cook for a few minutes to heat through. Discard the bouquet garni. Pour the sauce over the chicken pieces; and serve.

Arroz con Pollo (Chicken with Rice)

SPAIN

SERVES FOUR TO SIX
1 medium chicken, cut into serving pieces
3 tomatoes, chopped
2 green peppers, chopped
3 pimientos, chopped
⅓ cup green peas
2 onions, chopped
1 cup medium-grain rice
5 cups water
3 tablespoons olive oil
2 cloves garlic, finely chopped
1 bay leaf
1 teaspoon saffron
¼ teaspoon dried ground chilli peppers
1 tablespoon salt

Brown the chicken pieces in the oil in a casserole, then remove and keep warm. Add the onions and garlic to the casserole and sauté until the onions are golden. Then return the chicken pieces and add the tomatoes and the water. Bring to the boil, then cook for 5 minutes. Add the green peppers, the rice, bay leaf, ground chillis, saffron and salt, and stir thoroughly. Cook in the oven (220°C/425°F) for 15 minutes. Stir in the pimientos and the peas, and continue cooking until the chicken is tender (approximately 10 minutes).

Swiss Chicken

SWITZERLAND

SERVES FOUR

1 medium chicken
4 rashers of bacon
2 carrots, thinly sliced
1 stick celery, thinly sliced
1 onion, thinly sliced
2 tablespoons grated parmesan cheese
250 g/½ lb noodles
⅓ cup chicken stock
2 tablespoons butter
bouquet garni
pepper
Cheese Sauce

Put the rashers of bacon on to the bottom of a large pan, then put the carrot, celery and onion over the top of them. Truss the chicken and place it on top of the vegetables. Cover the pan, and cook over low heat for 15 minutes. Add the chicken stock and the bouquet garni, and continue cooking over low heat until the chicken is tender (approximately 1 hour).

Meanwhile, cook the noodles in boiling, salted water; then drain. Heat them in the butter, sprinkle with pepper, then put them in a serving dish and keep warm. When the chicken is tender, remove, carve into serving pieces, and put these pieces on top of the noodles on the serving dish. Keep warm. Boil the stock in the pan to reduce it, then strain and skim. Mix this stock with the Cheese Sauce, then pour the mixture over the chicken. Top with the parmesan cheese and put under the grill until golden-brown.

Cheese Sauce

½ cup grated gruyère cheese
3 tablespoons thick cream
2 cups milk
2 tablespoons butter
2 tablespoons flour
1 slice of onion
1 bay leaf
1 blade of mace
6 peppercorns
salt and pepper

Warm the milk with the onion, bay leaf, mace and peppercorns in a covered pan over low heat for 5 minutes. Strain the milk and keep aside. Wipe out the pan, then melt the butter in it. Remove from the heat and mix in the flour until smooth. Gradually blend in the milk, season with salt and pepper, return to the heat and stir until boiling. Boil for 2 minutes only, then remove from the heat. Gradually beat in the grated gruyère cheese, then stir in the cream. Keep warm.

Bamiyeh (Chicken and Okra Stew)

SYRIA

SERVES FOUR TO SIX

1 medium chicken, cut into serving pieces
1 kg/2 lb okra, stems removed
2 cups tomato juice
2 cups water
5 tablespoons butter
2 cloves garlic, crushed
½ teaspoon coriander
1 teaspoon salt
½ teaspoon pepper

Brown the chicken pieces in 3 tablespoons of the butter in a large pan. Then add the garlic and the coriander. Cover, and cook over low heat for 30 minutes. Meanwhile, fry the okra for 5 minutes in the remaining 2 tablespoons butter in another pan. Then add the okra to the chicken pan. Also add the tomato juice, the water, salt and pepper. Stir well, then cover and simmer over low heat for 45 minutes.

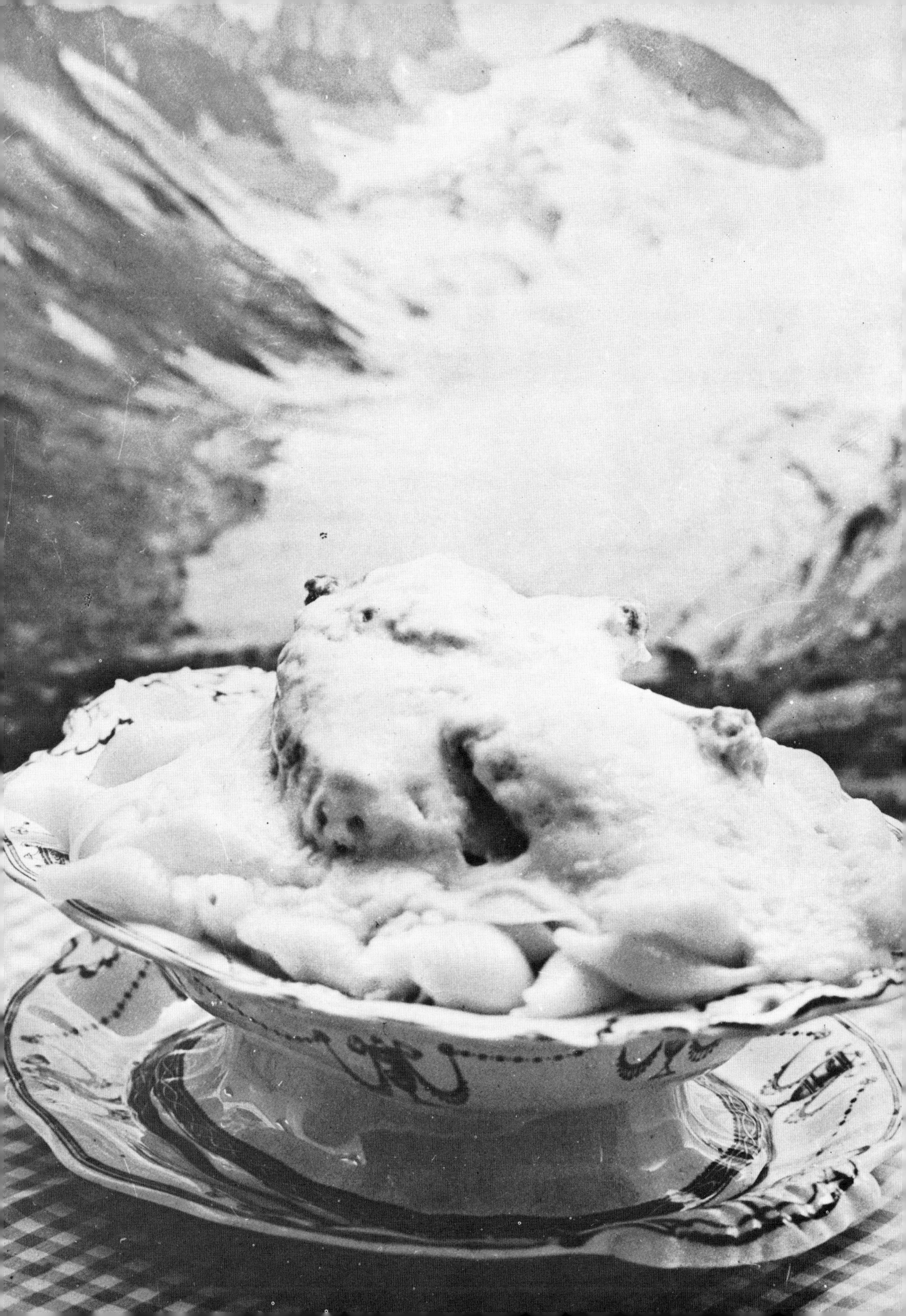

Sambousiks (Curried Pastries)

SYRIA

SERVES FOUR TO SIX
1 small chicken, cooked, the meat diced
1¼ cups flour
¾ cup milk (hot)
7 tablespoons butter
1 tablespoon curry powder
1 teaspoon salt

Keep aside 1 tablespoon flour, then sift the rest into a bowl with ½ teaspoon salt. Rub in half of the butter, then add half the milk gradually, forming a ball of dough. Knead until smooth, then chill for 15 minutes. Roll the dough out on to a lightly-floured surface. Flatten 2½ tablespoons of the butter and place it in the centre of the dough. Fold the dough in half, then in quarters, wrap it in greaseproof paper, and chill for 1 hour.

Melt the remaining 1 tablespoon butter in a saucepan. Remove from the heat and mix in the remaining 1 tablespoon flour until smooth. Gradually blend in the remaining hot milk. Return the pan to the heat and bring to the boil, stirring constantly. Add the curry powder and the remaining salt and cook, stirring, over low heat for 5 minutes. Mix in the diced chicken.

Roll out the dough on a lightly-floured surface, then cut it into circles with a pastry cutter. Place 1 tablespoon of the chicken mixture in the centre of each pastry round, then fold the pastry over, sealing the edges well. Place on a baking sheet and bake in the oven (190°C/375°F) until brown (approximately 15 minutes).

Garlic Chicken

THAILAND

SERVES FOUR TO SIX
1 large chicken, cut into serving pieces
2 tablespoons lemon juice
6 cloves garlic, crushed
1 tablespoon ground coriander
2 teaspoons salt
1 tablespoon peppercorns, crushed

Mix together the lemon juice, crushed garlic, peppercorns, coriander and salt. Rub this mixture into the chicken pieces, then leave them to stand for at least 1 hour. Put the chicken pieces under a hot grill and cook, turning frequently, until the chicken is tender and the skin is crisp and golden.

Garlic Chicken

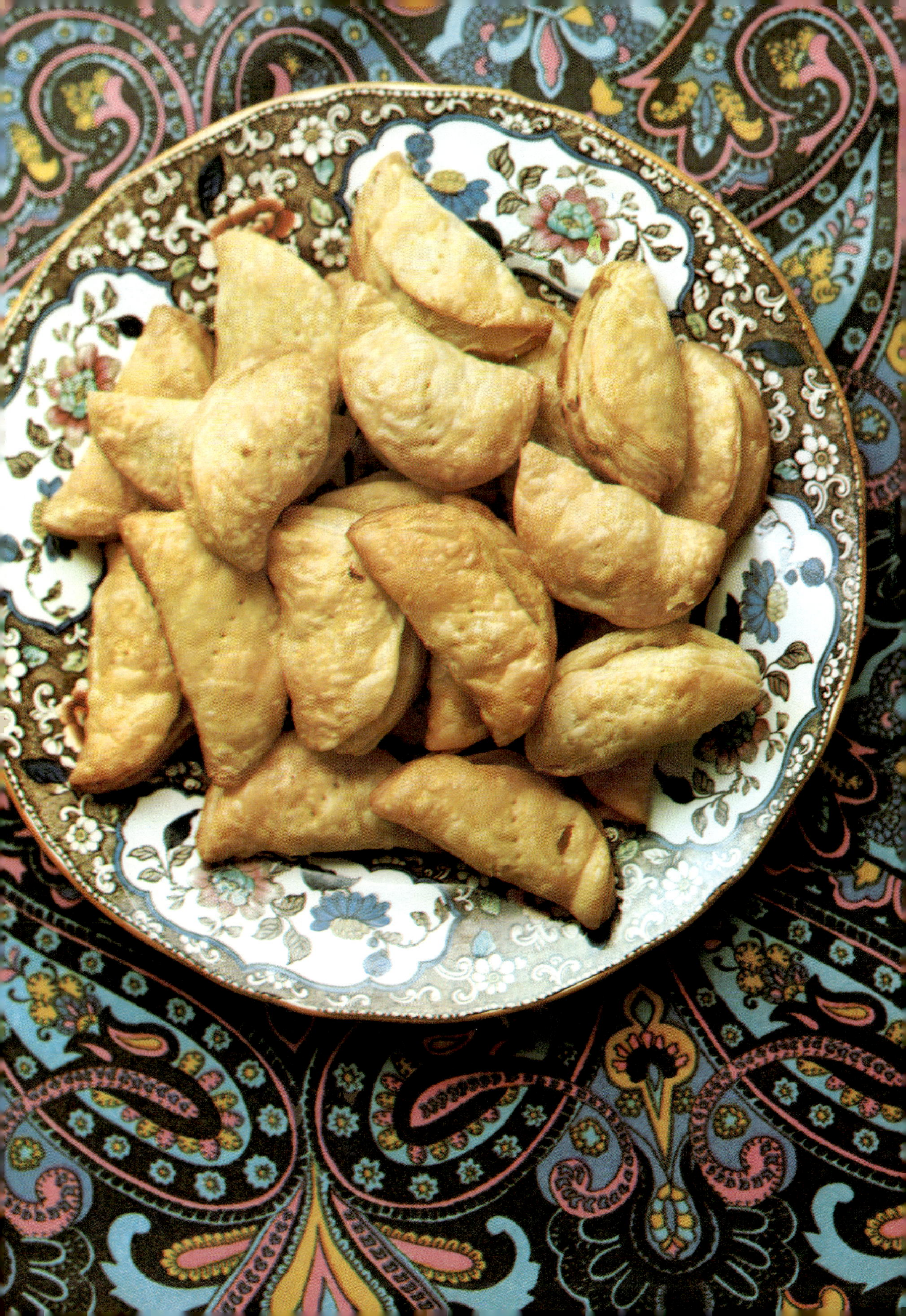

Gaeng Phed Gai Gub Makhua-tes (Chicken, Tomatoes and Chilli) THAILAND

SERVES FOUR TO SIX
1 medium chicken, cut into serving pieces
12 medium tomatoes, chopped
3 spring onions, coarsely chopped
1 teaspoon sugar
2 cups coconut cream
2 cups coconut milk
1 tablespoon water
2 cloves garlic
5 teaspoons laos
1 tablespoon ground coriander
3 teaspoons dried ground chilli peppers
1 teaspoon shrimp paste
1 teaspoon nampla (fish sauce)
1 teaspoon ground cumin
1-teaspoon lemon grass
7 peppercorns

Put into a blender the spring onions, garlic, ground chillis, coriander, laos, shrimp paste, cumin, lemon grass, peppercorns, and the water. Blend until a smooth paste is formed.

Put the coconut cream into a pan and cook over moderate heat until it comes to the boil. Then stir in the spice paste. Add the chicken pieces, pour in the coconut milk, cover, and simmer for 30 minutes. Then add the tomatoes, sugar and nampla, and continue cooking until the chicken is tender (approximately 10 minutes).

Gai P'Anaeng (Coconut Chicken) THAILAND

SERVES SIX
6 chicken breasts
2 spring onions, finely chopped
1 tablespoon grated lemon rind
3 tablespoons ground peanuts
1 teaspoon sugar
2 cups coconut cream
1 tablespoon thick soy sauce
3 cloves garlic, crushed
6 coriander seeds
1 teaspoon shrimp paste
½ teaspoon dried ground chilli peppers

Put the chicken breasts and the coconut cream into a pan. Cover, and cook over moderate heat for 30 minutes. Add the spring onions, the ground peanuts, chillis, garlic, lemon rind, sugar, coriander seeds, shrimp paste and soy sauce. Stir well, then continue cooking until the chicken is tender (approximately 15 minutes). Turn the chicken frequently, to coat well with the sauce.

Gaeng Phed Gai Gub Makhua-tes

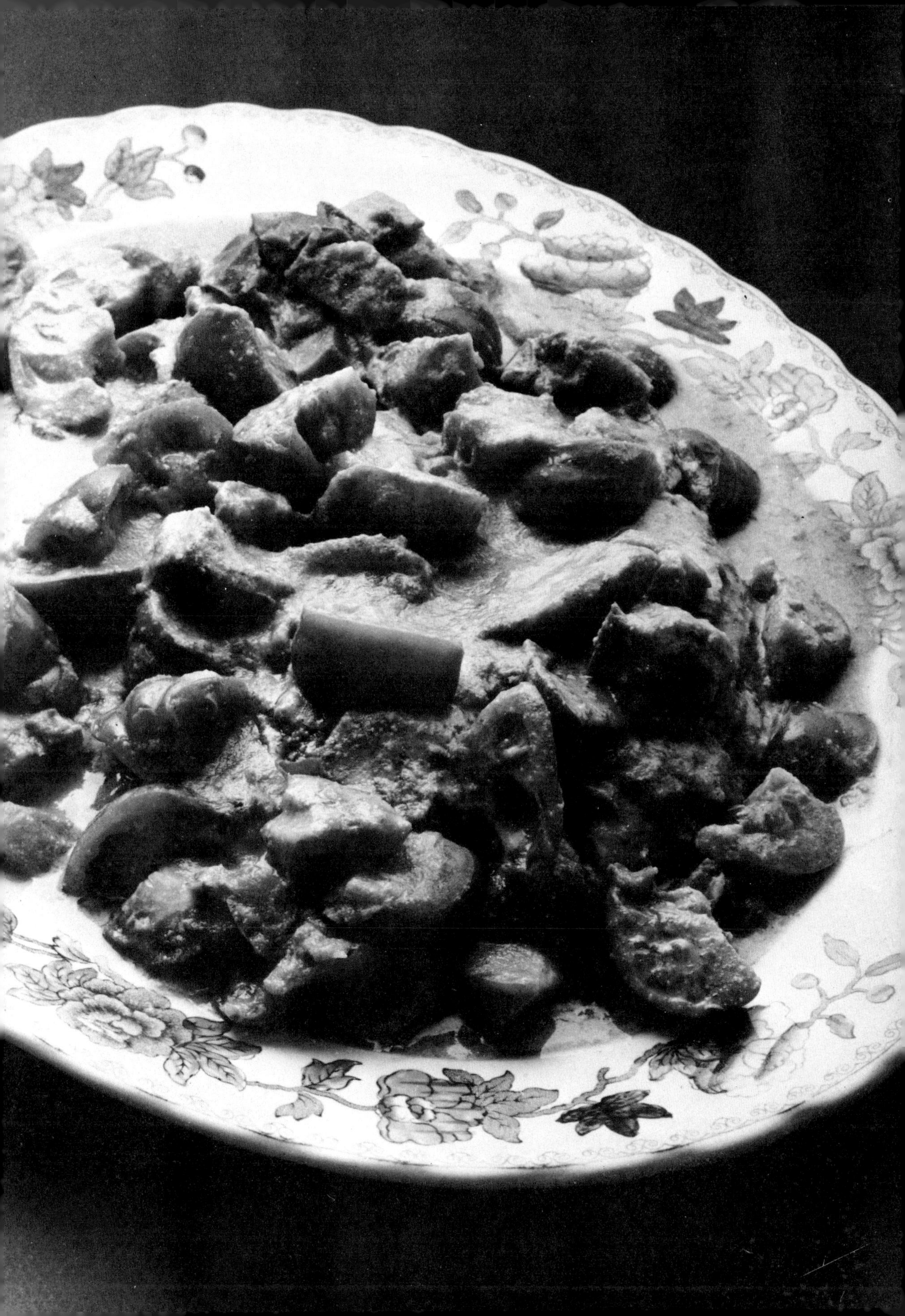

Cerkes Tavuğu (Cold Chicken with Walnut Sauce) TURKEY

SERVES SIX

1 medium chicken, cut into pieces
1 onion, finely chopped
1½ cups walnuts, shelled
3 slices white bread, cut up
3 cups water
1 teaspoon paprika
1¼ teaspoons salt
black pepper

Put the chicken pieces into a large pan, add the water and ¼ teaspoon salt. Bring to the boil, then reduce the heat to low and simmer until the chicken is tender (approximately 30 minutes). Take the chicken pieces out of the pan, remove the skin and take the meat from the bones. Cut the chicken meat into strips, and keep aside. Meanwhile, boil the stock in the pan to reduce it to 1½ cups. Put this stock, with the onions and walnuts, into an electric blender. Blend at high speed for 15 seconds, then add the bread, ½ teaspoon of the paprika, the remaining 1 teaspoon salt, and black pepper to taste. Blend until a smooth mixture is formed.

Mix together the chicken strips and 1½ cups of the walnut sauce. Put this chicken mixture on to a serving platter and cover with the remaining walnut sauce. Sprinkle with the remaining paprika, and serve cold.

Turkish Chicken TURKEY

SERVES SIX

1 medium chicken, cut into serving pieces
3 tomatoes, peeled, chopped
1 green pepper, peeled, cut into strips
3 onions, chopped
125 g/4 oz black olives, stoned
125 g/4 oz sultanas
1½ cups long-grain rice
2 cups chicken stock
3 tablespoons olive oil
1 bay leaf
10 coriander seeds
¼ teaspoon saffron
¼ teaspoon cayenne pepper
salt and pepper

Brown the chicken pieces in 2 tablespoons of the oil in a large pan over moderate heat. Then add 1 more tablespoon of oil, the onions and the bay leaf. Sauté until the onion is golden, then add the rice and cook over high heat for 5 minutes. Reduce the heat, and add the tomatoes, green pepper, sultanas, coriander seeds, saffron, chicken stock, and salt and pepper to taste. Cover and cook over low heat until the rice has absorbed all the liquid (approximately 25 minutes). Add the olives, stir, and cook gently for another 10 minutes. Sprinkle the cayenne pepper over the dish; and serve.

Chicken Kentucky Style UNITED STATES OF AMERICA

SERVES FOUR

1 medium chicken, cut into 4 serving pieces
4 carrots, diced
4 sticks celery, diced
6 onions, diced
3 tablespoons flour
¼ cup sherry
5 cups chicken stock
3 tablespoons butter
2 tablespoons paprika
¼ teaspoon cayenne pepper
salt and black pepper

Coat the chicken pieces with the flour (seasoned with salt and black pepper). Melt the butter in a casserole, then put in the chicken pieces (skin side up). Add the carrots, celery and onion, and sprinkle with the paprika. Cook over low heat until the vegetables are browned slightly. Then add the chicken stock, sherry and cayenne pepper. Bake, uncovered, in the oven (180°C/350°F) until the chicken is tender (approximately 1 hour).

Cerkes Tavuğu

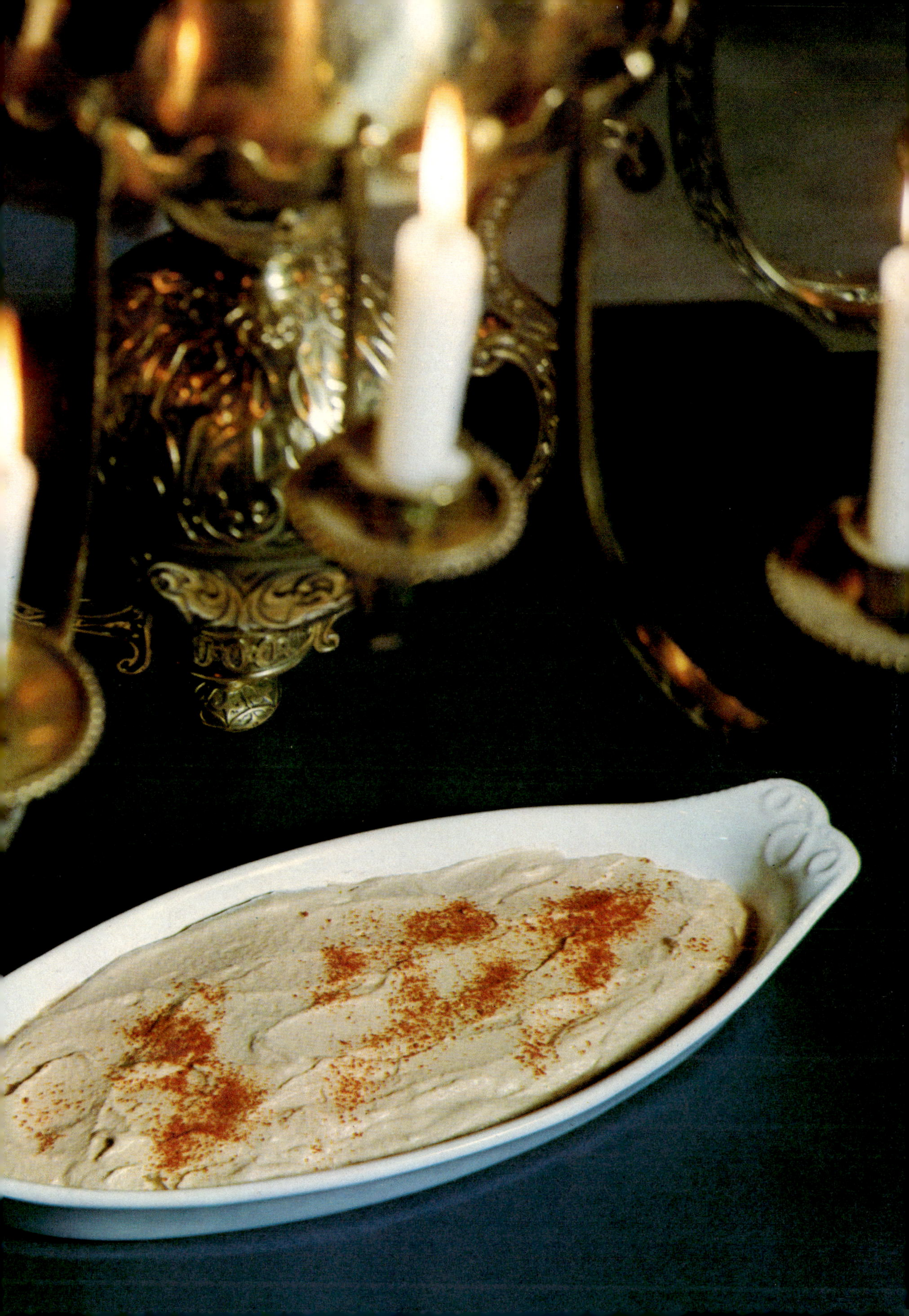

Barbecued Chicken

UNITED STATES OF AMERICA

SERVES FOUR TO SIX
1 large chicken, cut into serving pieces
3 onions, thinly sliced
1 teaspoon sugar
1½ cups tomato juice
¾ cup vinegar
3 tablespoons butter
4½ teaspoons Worcestershire sauce
3 cloves garlic, crushed
1 bay leaf
¼ teaspoon dry mustard
¼ teaspoon cayenne pepper
2 teaspoons salt
¼ teaspoon pepper

In a saucepan, mix together the sugar, tomato juice, vinegar, butter, Worcestershire sauce, garlic, bay leaf, mustard, cayenne pepper, salt and pepper. Simmer for 10 minutes, then remove from the heat and cool. Marinate the chicken pieces in this mixture for at least 30 minutes.

Put the chicken pieces (skin side down) in a single layer in a baking tin. Arrange the onion slices over the chicken, and pour the marinade over the top. Bake in the oven (220°C/425°F) for 30 minutes, basting occasionally. Turn the chicken pieces over and continue baking and basting until the chicken is tender (approximately 45 minutes).

Scandia Chicken

UNITED STATES OF AMERICA

SERVES FOUR
2 small chickens, halved (rib cages and thigh bones removed)
the chicken livers, chopped
1½ cups chopped mushrooms
1 green pepper, chopped
2 onions, chopped
½ cup medium-grain rice
1 cup water
3 tablespoons butter
2 tablespoons chopped parsley
salt and pepper
Cream Sauce

Sauté the chicken livers, mushrooms, green pepper and onion in the butter over low heat for 10 minutes. Then add the rice, water, parsley, and salt and pepper to taste. Mix well, bring to the boil, then reduce heat to low, cover, and simmer for 20 minutes. Remove from the heat and leave to cool.

Sprinkle salt on the insides of the halved chickens, then put one quarter of the above stuffing mixture on to each chicken half. Now fold the breast section over the thigh section and hook the wing over the thigh. Put each of these stuffed chicken halves on to a sheet of aluminium foil. Fold the foil up around the chicken but do not cover the top entirely. Put the chicken halves into a baking tin and bake in the oven (190°C/375°F) until they are tender (approximately 40 minutes). When cooked, remove the chicken halves from the foil and place them on a serving platter. Pour the Cream Sauce over them, and serve.

Cream Sauce
the chicken necks, hearts, gizzards
1½ tablespoons flour
1½ tablespoons butter
¾ cup cream
2 cups water
½ teaspoon salt

Put the necks, hearts and gizzards into a saucepan with the water and the salt. Bring to the boil, cover, and simmer for 35 minutes. Then remove the meat from the necks and chop this meat together with the hearts and gizzards. Melt the butter in a saucepan, then remove from the heat and blend in the flour. Gradually stir in ¾ cup of the stock, the cream, and the chopped chicken giblets. Return to the heat and cook, stirring constantly, until the mixture comes to the boil.

Chicken à la King

UNITED STATES OF AMERICA

SERVES FOUR

1 medium chicken, cooked, and meat diced
500 g/1 lb mushrooms, sliced
1 green pepper, finely sliced
1 red pepper, finely sliced
2 tablespoons flour
1½ cups chicken stock
1 cup milk
juice of ½ lemon
6 tablespoons butter
½ teaspoon paprika
salt and pepper

Sauté the green and red peppers in half the butter for a few minutes. Then stir in the flour, paprika, and salt to taste. Cook for a few minutes, then gradually blend in the chicken stock and the milk. Bring to the boil, stirring, then put in the diced chicken and simmer gently. Sauté the mushrooms in the remaining butter and the lemon juice in a separate pan. Add the mushrooms to the chicken mixture and mix well. Serve on rice.

Chicken à la King

Fried Chicken

UNITED STATES OF AMERICA

SERVES FOUR
1 medium chicken, cut into serving pieces
2 bananas, halved lengthways
4 pineapple slices
2 eggs, beaten
4 tablespoons flour
breadcrumbs
3 tablespoons olive oil
7 tablespoons butter
1 teaspoon thyme
1 teaspoon oregano
1 teaspoon salt
½ teaspoon black pepper
Horseradish Sauce

Season the flour with the thyme, oregano, salt and black pepper. Coat the chicken pieces with the flour, then shake off any surplus. Beat together the eggs and 1 tablespoon oil and dip the floured chicken pieces into this mixture. Then coat the pieces liberally with breadcrumbs. Heat 5 tablespoons butter and the remaining oil over high heat in a large pan until very hot; then add the chicken pieces. After 30 seconds, turn the chicken pieces over and reduce the heat to moderate. Cover, and cook until the chicken is tender and the breadcrumbs are golden-brown (approximately 15 minutes). Turn the chicken pieces over twice during the cooking.

Meanwhile, coat the bananas and pineapple with breadcrumbs and fry them over moderate heat in the remaining 2 tablespoons butter in a separate pan until golden-brown (approximately 5 minutes).

Put the chicken pieces, the bananas and the pineapple on to a serving dish; and serve the Horseradish Sauce separately.

Horseradish Sauce
2 tablespoons horseradish
5 tablespoons thick cream
¾ cup chicken stock
1 tablespoon butter
1 tablespoon flour

Melt the butter in a saucepan, then remove from the heat and mix in the flour until smooth. Gradually blend in the chicken stock, then return to the heat and stir until boiling. Boil for 2 minutes only, then remove from the heat. Add the horseradish and mix thoroughly; then stir in the cream. Keep warm.

Chicken Gumbo

UNITED STATES OF AMERICA

SERVES SIX
1 large chicken, cut into serving pieces
2 dozen oysters
750 g/1½ lb okra
3 tomatoes, chopped
6 onions, finely chopped
15 cups water
3 tablespoons bacon fat
1 clove garlic, finely chopped
½ teaspoon thyme
½ teaspoon rosemary
¼ teaspoon dried ground chilli peppers
2½ teaspoons salt
1 teaspoon pepper

Sprinkle the chicken pieces with the garlic, salt and pepper, then brown the pieces in the bacon fat in a large pan. Remove and keep warm. Add the onions to the pan and sauté until golden. Return the chicken pieces to the pan and add the tomatoes, thyme, rosemary, ground chillis and water. Cover, and cook over low heat for 1½ hours. Add the okra and continue cooking for 1 hour. Then add the oysters, bring to the boil, and cook for 3 minutes. Serve with rice.

Pollo Guiso con Vegetales (Chicken and Vegetable Stew) URUGUAY

SERVES FOUR TO SIX
1 medium chicken, cut into serving pieces
250 g/½ lb mushrooms, sliced
2 carrots, diced
3 onions, sliced
1 tablespoon flour
1½ cups dry white wine
3 tablespoons olive oil
2 tablespoons chives
¼ teaspoon ground mace
1 teaspoon salt
¼ teaspoon pepper

Brown the chicken pieces in the oil in a large pan; then remove and keep warm. Add the onions, carrots and mushrooms to the pan and sauté until the onions are golden (approximately 10 minutes). Then stir in the flour, salt and pepper. Return the chicken pieces to the pan, and add the wine, the chives and mace. Cover, and simmer until the chicken is tender (approximately 45 minutes); then serve.

Cacerola de Gallina Rellena (Stuffed Chicken Casserole) VENEZUELA

SERVES SIX
1 large chicken
125 g/¼ lb pork, finely chopped
3 potatoes, peeled, diced
6 carrots, halved
4 tomatoes, quartered
2 tomatoes, peeled, finely chopped
2 onions, finely chopped
2 onions, sliced
1 tablespoon capers, chopped
¼ cup mustard pickles, chopped
2 eggs, beaten
½ cup breadcrumbs
¼ cup sherry
3 tablespoons olive oil
1 bay leaf
1 teaspoon salt
½ teaspoon pepper

Mix together the pork, the finely chopped tomatoes and onions, the breadcrumbs, eggs, pickles, capers, salt and pepper. Stuff the chicken with this mixture, and close the opening with thread or skewers.

Brown the stuffed chicken in the oil in a large pan. Add the sliced onions and cook over high heat for 5 minutes. Then add the remaining 4 tomatoes and the bay leaf. Cover, and cook over low heat, basting occasionally, for 2½ hours. Add the potatoes and carrots and continue cooking until the potatoes are soft (approximately 20 minutes). Remove the chicken and potatoes and arrange them on a serving dish. Strain the cooking juices, mix them with the sherry, put into a saucepan and bring to the boil. Serve this sauce separately.

Cacerola de Gallina Rellena

Hallacas (Chicken and Corn Meal Pastries)

VENEZUELA

SERVES FOUR TO EIGHT

1 small chicken, cooked, the meat diced
500 g/1 lb pork, cooked, diced
2 tomatoes, chopped
1 green pepper, seeded, chopped
2 onions, chopped
¼ cup stuffed olives, chopped
1 tablespoon capers, chopped
¼ cup seedless raisins
1 egg, beaten
2 cups corn meal
1 tablespoon vinegar
2 tablespoons olive oil
½ cup butter
¼ cup chopped parsley
2 cloves garlic, crushed
½ teaspoon dried ground chilli peppers
2 teaspoons salt
8 25 cm/10" squares of aluminium foil

Put 3 cups water with 1 teaspoon salt into a saucepan, and bring to the boil. Gradually stir in the corn meal and cook over low heat for a few minutes. Stir the butter into the corn meal while it is cooking. Remove from the heat and blend in the beaten egg.

Sauté the onions and garlic in the olive oil in a pan until the onions are golden. Then add the tomatoes, green pepper, parsley and vinegar, and cook over low heat for 10 minutes. Add the diced chicken and pork, the olives, raisins, capers, ground chillis and 1 teaspoon salt, and mix well.

Put about ½ cup corn meal mixture into the centre of each of the foil squares. Flatten this mixture out into a 15 cm/6" square of dough. Then spread about ½ cup of the chicken mixture over one half of each dough square. Fold the other half of the dough over the top of the mixture, forming a hallaca. Wrap the foil securely around the hallacas. Put these little 'parcels' into a large pan of boiling, salted water, and simmer for 1½ hours. Remove the 'parcels' from the pan, unwrap them, and serve the hallacas.

Pile u Kaimaku (Chicken in Cream Cheese)

YUGOSLAVIA

SERVES FOUR
1 medium chicken
2 cups cream cheese
1 cup milk
4 cloves garlic, finely chopped
salt

Put the chicken into a large pan, cover with water and add a little salt. Bring to the boil, cover, and cook for 20 minutes. Meanwhile, heat the cream cheese with the milk in another large pan over low heat until the cheese has melted. Then add the garlic.

Remove the chicken from the water and place it in the pan with the cream cheese mixture. Coat the chicken on all sides with the mixture, then cover the pan and simmer until the chicken is tender. Put the chicken on a serving platter and pour the cream cheese sauce over it.

Kokośja Supa (Chicken Soup with Red Peppers)

YUGOSLAVIA

SERVES FOUR TO SIX
1 small chicken, cut into serving pieces
500 g/1 lb potatoes, peeled, quartered
500 g/1 lb cauliflower flowerets
4 tomatoes, peeled, seeded, chopped
2 red peppers, seeded, chopped
2 onions, chopped
5 cups chicken stock
2 tablespoons olive oil
1 teaspoon paprika

Sauté the onions in the oil until golden; then sprinkle with the paprika. Add the chicken stock, bring to the boil, then add the chicken pieces and cook for 10 minutes. Now add the tomatoes, red peppers and cauliflower and cook for a further 10 minutes. Add the potatoes, and continue cooking until the chicken is tender and the potatoes are cooked (approximately 20-25 minutes).

Kokośja Supa

Pećena Kokoś sa Rakom Filana (Chicken with Lobster Stuffing) YUGOSLAVIA

SERVES FOUR

1 medium chicken
1 small lobster, cooked
250 g/½ lb shelled green peas
1 egg, beaten
2 slices white bread, cut up, soaked in the milk
1 tablespoon breadcrumbs
3 tablespoons sour cream
3 tablespoons milk
2 tablespoons butter

Cook the peas in the butter over low heat until they are tender. Take the flesh from the lobster and chop it. Mix together the lobster flesh, the breadcrumbs, bread soaked in milk, beaten egg and sour cream. Now mix in the peas. Stuff the chicken with this mixture and close the opening with thread or skewers. Roast the chicken in the oven (190°C/375°F) until tender (approximately 1 hour).